BASEBALL BOYS

Rediscovering 1950s Little League Baseball in Mount Vernon, NY

Bruce Fabricant

Copyright © 2012 by **Bruce Fabricant**

All rights reserved by the author. No part of this publication may be reproduced, stored in a retrieval system or transmitted in any form or by any means electronic, mechanical, photocopying, recording or otherwise, without the prior written permission of the author.

ISBN:1481044877

Cover Photo:
Don Cook awaits throw at home plate.

For all information, contact:
Bruce Fabricant
Telephone: (914) 276-3397 or (914) 772-2434
E-Mail: bfabric459@aol.com

Acknowledgments

The first decade (1950-59) of Little League baseball in Mount Vernon, NY is the subject of this work. Without the generosity and cooperation of former players who talked to me, exchanged emails, sent me weathered newspaper game summary clippings and photographs, this book could not have been written. I am particularly indebted to Jane Borelli and Fred O'Connor.

Parts of this book rely on the memories, anecdotes, and impressions of 29 men and women, many now in their seventies, who played or were involved with Little League baseball more than six decades ago and now good naturedly share their memories. Meeting and talking with Steve Acunto, the last of the league's founding fathers, was most helpful in illuminating the league's early years. Also, grateful acknowledgment is made to Doris Hackett at the Mount Vernon Public Library for her assistance.

My wife, Bobbi, provided her own brand of support. Most important, her love and understanding made the experience of writing this book so special.

Above all, I wish to express my heartfelt thanks to a high school teammate and friend, Eddie Martin, for his steady counsel throughout the entire process even before the first page was ever written.

Contents

Acknowledgments iii

Introduction 7

1. Williamsport to Mount Vernon 10
2. Founding Fathers 16
3. Andy Karl "Mr. Little League" 22
4. Men in the Dugout 27
5. Diamonds of Our Youth 30
6. Little League Championship Game Scores 34
7. 1950 – The First Season 36
8. 1951 – Expansion 49
9. 1952 – Year of the Pitcher 59
10. 1953 – Orioles Take It All 80
11. 1954 – Pirates Win 2nd World Series 103
12. 1955 – City Leagues Consolidate 121
13. 1956 – Sponsors Support Program 137
14. 1957 – Local 338 Wins Title 149
15. 1958 – The Lions Roar 159
16. 1959 – Ken Singleton Played Here 171
17. Conversation with Ken Singleton 184
18. Conversation with Ralph Branca 188
19. Conversation with Rick Wolff 193
20. Best of the Decade 198
21. Alumni Remembrances 205

Introduction

We kids who grew up in Mount Vernon in the '50s never knew at the time just how lucky we were. I am quite sure it was the same way in other towns and cities in the metropolitan New York area. We benefited from the prosperity of the post-war years and the calm of the period. Go to school, play, and stay out of trouble was our job.

That's what these three boys were up to in the spring of 1953. That's Bill Dunsay, 11, on the left, Peter Dunsay, 11, in the middle, and Mike Hirsch, 10, on the right, standing in front of the Dunsay home at 426 Homestead Avenue in Mount Vernon. Look at those happy faces, baggy baseball pants, and Peter's pants nearly buckled up to his chest. There is even the ubiquitous Brownie camera and in the background neighbors chatting on the steps.

Life was so uncomplicated then. It surely was a secure time of our lives. There weren't any video games, soccer fields, shopping malls or car pools. For pre-teen boys the city's streets and playgrounds was our world. We got cuts and bruises and tore our jeans. We were just a bunch of kids playing baseball for the sake of playing. That was our common bond.

But up until 1950 something was missing. Our baseball games weren't organized. It was just kids getting together, choosing up sides, and playing ball. Then Little League baseball found a home in Mount Vernon and everything changed. We had uniforms. We were part of a team. We learned how to play the game. We learned how to win. We learned how to lose. And Little League gave us all a lifetime full of memories. So true, so true, memories are baseball's lifeblood and for many of us the best part of baseball is its past.

So here is a book that has nothing to do about today. It tells the story of yesterday, kid baseball, specifically Little League baseball in Mount Vernon, 60 years ago. I am sure all fellows, when they get together with old friends, find their conversations return to some ball field, school yard and maybe Little League. Stories may be embellished but rarely do they change. Even 60 years later they still matter to us.

A. Bartlett Giamatti was baseball's Renaissance man and its seventh commissioner. In a speech he argued that baseball is much more than an American "pastime." "For what is baseball but looking for home."

In recent years, I've been captivated about the city of my youth, Mount Vernon. I haven't lived there for nearly five decades. Yet, I have made the journey back there a number of times through baseball, at least in my mind. Three years ago I wrote a book, *That Perfect Spring,* about our high school baseball team 50 years after we won a Westchester County championship.

Now with *Baseball Boys*, baseball is again linked with childhood. If you were a youngster growing up in Mount Vernon in the '50s and wanted to play baseball, here it is, Little League. It was exciting and fun. It gave each of us so much, independence and camaraderie. It was a game that filled our late summer days.

Baseball Boys is a history of the first decade of Little League baseball in the city we called home. It covers the years between 1950 and 1959 and every youngster who ever played in the league can find his name in the book that blends game summaries from every season, nostalgia, and more than a good anecdote or two.

Baseball Boys takes you back to 1949 when a group of men after worked stopped by Mike O'Connell's bar and grille on Third Street in Mount Vernon for some not too serious drinking and eating. What they had in common was a love for baseball. They also wanted to help kids. This is in all likelihood where the idea for the city's Little League program was launched.

Now you will learn how Andy Karl, a former big league player and the league's architect, guiding light and first commissioner, made sure that teams were composed of kids from different city neighborhoods and not just of boys who played together at school or in the same neighborhood.

You will meet the managers who taught us how to play, soothed our egos, and built our self confidence; men like Bill Real, Steve Acunto, Joe Tripodi, Joe O'Connor, and Jeff Borelli, among others. You will revisit our baseball diamonds, Longfellow, Baker and Hutchinson Fields, that were not much too look at but were where youthful reputations were made.

Ken Singleton, who went from the city's Little League to the Major Leagues, explains how he used to ride his bike several miles to Baker Field for Little League games. Then Big Leaguer Ralph Branca tells how as a six-year-old he remembers pitching to his older brother Julius in the driveway at his home at 522 South Ninth Avenue. Nationally recognized expert in the field of sports psychology and sports parenting Rick Wolff explains the reasons behind parent over involvement today in their kid's sports participation.

So what is it about baseball where statistics and memories are two of its most endearing attractions. Newspapers capture statistics and game summaries forever. Memories fade to some degree. This book has plenty of both.

I looked through numerous scrapbooks that documented diamond exploits that were recorded in newspapers like *The Mount Vernon Daily Argus*, to be remembered for all time, just as they happened. I visited the city's library. Now, many of these games are summarized here with a chapter devoted to each year of the decade. Team photos capture and hold forever Little League friends. Pictures preserve their swings and their slides, their frowns and their smiles.

Memory meanwhile plays strange tricks when it comes to sports, particularly baseball. So what did our obsession with baseball back then leave us with. Maybe it was a shoebox full of baseball cards that our mothers eventually threw out. For sure, we all ended up with a collection of

Mount Vernon Little League moments and memories. So listen to more than two dozen alumni from the '50s reminisce about this baseball fabric of their early lives.

And finally, who were the best Mount Vernon Little Leaguers during the '50? Who should be on that all-time all-star team? There is enough controversy here to stir any fan's heart and brain. I have crossed the foul line and am on the ball field offering up my best. So let Red Barber's rhubarb begin.

Bruce Fabricant
Somers, New York
2013

1

Williamsport to Mount Vernon

A lot was happening in 1939. On the world scene, Germany was crushing Poland, starting World War II. In baseball, it was the year Lou Gehrig told a packed Yankee Stadium crowd that he considered himself "the luckiest man on the face of the earth." With summer approaching in Mount Vernon and in towns across the country, baseball was the summer game.

On June 12, baseball celebrated the centennial of its founding by dedicating the National Baseball Hall of Fame in Cooperstown, New York. Six days earlier in a sleepy city named Williamsport in Pennsylvania, not very far from Cooperstown, little did Williamsport citizens realize that the river town of about 29,500 today would occupy a big page in baseball history. June 6, 1939 was the day two teams played, for the first time, in a Little League game. Lundy Lumber walloped Lycoming Dairy, 23-8, on a ball field west of Williamsport.

So how did Little League begin? How did it eventually find its way ten years after its founding to Mount Vernon, New York, long regarded as one of the cradles of Westchester baseball? Occupying a total area of only 4.4 square miles, today Mount Vernon is the eighth most populous city in the state of New York with a suburban presence with tree lined streets and close knit homes side by side on its North side while south side Mount Vernon has a very city-like feel, nearly mirroring its border with The Bronx, a New York City borough.

Through the years it has been home to quite a number of successful people. They include the writers E.B. White, author of Charlotte's Web, and Linda Fairstein; the actors Art Carney, Denzel Washington, Ossie Davis, Ruby Dee and Sidney Poitier; the musicians Sean "P. Diddy" Combs and Heavy D; and basketball stars like Gus Williams and Ben Gordon. Major leaguers Ralph Branca, Andy Karl, Roy Smith and Ken Singleton learned their baseball skills on the city's streets and sandlots.

Baseball's roots in Mount Vernon run deep, according to Bob Mayer, a Mount Vernon native and Hudson Valley baseball historian. Mayer played Little League baseball in the city during the 1950's. According to Mayer, the first reported team in Mount Vernon was called the Una Club. Several members of a prominent family were on the team. William Hathaway Van Cott, a local judge, D. Van Cott, and T.S. Van Cott appear on the team roster in 1866. The club was a member of the National Association of Base Ball Players that year and won three games while losing six in contests with other NABBP teams. Included was a loss to the Unions of Morrisania. In 1867 the Una Club won 6 and lost 4 games. William Van Cott had previously played with the Gotham Club and had been the first president of the NABBP in 1858.

Fire companies fielded baseball teams in 1900 like Chemical Engine Co. #1

In early 1900, there were several teams in Mount Vernon. Most of the fire companies like Chemical Engine Co. #1 had teams and there may have been a local league among them.

The Mount Vernon Scarlets, sometimes known as the Red Caps, were a well-known semi-Pro team playing at Memorial Field for about 25 years (late 20's thru early 50's). Major League pitchers, Andy Karl and Emerson Dickman both played with the Scarlets as did John Branca, Ralph's brother. For several years the Scarlets were in the Metropolitan Baseball Association. The MBA was a loose affiliation of semi-pro teams.

These teams played independent clubs, minor league all-star teams, Negro League teams, barnstorming clubs like the House of David, and teams led by major leaguers. The Bushwicks of Brooklyn were the league powerhouse winning the league in 1938 and 1939 while the Scarlets played less than .500 ball. However, in 1940 Mount Vernon won the league with a won-loss percentage of .679.

For Branca, Singleton and all who loved baseball, our playgrounds and ball fields were some of the most important places in our young lives. Long before Little League, we all played the game the way our fathers brothers and even mothers taught us. Fathers and sons, baseball and summer afternoons on the south side, north side, east side and west side of Mount Vernon was what the game was about. My father, Morris, opened my heart to the game soon after we moved from the Bronx to a house on Claremont Avenue. It was on our tiny front lawn where he first tossed me a baseball. He taught me to keep my eye on it, to keep my glove low to the ground, and to watch the ball right into my mitt. I felt I achieved something when I heard him say, "Good play." That said a lot.

It was the same for kids everywhere in Mount Vernon. Take a youngster who grew up on Valois Place in the city's Chester Heights section. In his backyard there was a huge foundation because the house was close to the water and needed to be elevated. That wall made a perfect place to throw a ball against. He would throw against it all day long and play little games with himself, like figuring out which brick to hit.

For nearly 30 years, from the 1920's through the early 1950's, the Mount Vernon Scarlets were a popular semi-pro team in the New York metropolitan area.

In another section of the city on Union Avenue located about three houses down from the U.S. Post Office there was a big wall near the post office. That's where a youngster learned to play stickball. And still another boy turned to his mother who had a catcher's mitt. They would throw to each other in their driveway on North Tenth Avenue. She helped him become a pitcher. A lucky eight-year-old who lived on North High Street in a four-family house had the pick of three ball fields where he could hone his skills.

In another part of town, a fledgling ballplayer lived on South First Avenue. He had a garage in his backyard and would play stickball against the garage. On South 12th Avenue a boy used to take a tennis ball or a Spaldeen when he was bored on a Saturday with nothing to do. He would bounce the ball off his concrete stoop. The ball would come off each step differently. He would just keep throwing it and throwing it, always trying to follow the ball back to his glove. On South Seventh Avenue a youngster played stickball next to his house, which was right next door to a Baptist church. He remembers breaking more than one church window with a batted ball. Sometimes his folks had to pay to fix those windows.

But for all of us there was something missing. We didn't have Little League baseball yet. We didn't know who Carl Stotz was either. But we soon found out. You see, Little League owes it all to its founder Carl Stotz. He grew up in Williamsport, Pennsylvania. Like many kids everywhere, he often wasn't picked to play in baseball games with older boys. By the time he was 29, he had two nephews, six-year-old Jimmy and eight-year-old Harold "Major" Gehron. They ran into the same problem that Stotz endured as a youngster. They weren't picked to play in organized games.

Little League baseball founder Carl Stotz, left, was the guest of honor at the 1955 Mount Vernon Minor-Little-Pony League annual dinner. Here he talks to dinner chairwoman Mrs. Raymond Schilke and the city's Pony League Commissioner Fred Nelson.

Carl, as a grownup, never got baseball, or his youth, out of his system. He came up with an idea to get the boys into organized baseball. He even credited a thorny scratch caused by a lilac bush with being the impetus for his Little League idea. One August day in 1938, Jimmy and Major wanted to have a catch with their uncle. One of Major's tosses was off target. It was headed toward Carl's neighbors backyard. Carl took off to catch the ball. He scraped his ankle when he stepped on the sharp stems of a lilac bush. Reaching the neighbor's porch he sat down.

Carl recounted countless times years later what then happened. He sat there and a flashback came over him. The story goes that he said to the boys, "How would you like to play on a regular team with uniforms, a new ball for every game and bats you could really swing?" And they said, "Who would we play? Will people come to watch us?"

Carl then told his nephews that he had an idea for a league. At his first training session 11 Williamsport boys showed up. Carl quickly figured out what would be a close play at first base with a throw from third base or shortstop. That's where the sixty-foot distance between bases was determined. It turned out the distance between bases was exactly two-thirds the distance on a standard field. He set the pitching distance from the mound to home plate at 38 feet. It was later lengthened to 44 feet and eventually 46 feet. He also focused his attention on boys between ages of nine and twelve. But he didn't turn away eight-year-olds.

He also realized that certain rules were not right for younger boys. A batter trying to reach first base on a dropped third strike wasn't a good idea. Taking a lead off base was also a problem. A rule was created permitting runners to leave a base only when the ball had passed the plate.

When spring 1939 arrived Lycoming Dairy became the very first sponsor of a Little League baseball team. Carl immediately bought bats, a catcher's mitt, a pair of catcher's shin guards, and baseballs. He bought ten uniforms from Kresge's. His group still didn't have a name. He first thought of calling it Junior League. But that didn't work because a woman's organization already had that name. He wanted it to be just like the big leagues, but for little kids. So he thought "Little League". That night "Little League" appeared for the first time in a newspaper, *The Williamsport Sun*.

Three teams played in the first Little League in 1939, Lycoming Dairy Farm, Jumbo Pretzel Company, and Lundy Lumber. Thirty boys in all played 24 games on makeshift cut-down fields and playgrounds. Stotz had plenty of adult supervision. Rejection from older boys was eliminated for these eight to twelve year olds.

With war heating up in Europe in 1940, material for baseball uniforms became hard to find. These shortages impacted Little League expanding dramatically during the first seven year of its existence. But peace in 1945 meant Little League would soon spread far beyond what anyone could have imagined six years earlier when World War II and Little League started.

In cities like Mount Vernon and towns all across America men returned home to families from battlefields in the Pacific and Europe. Virtually all of them had played baseball as boys. Back home now, they started to teach it to their sons. So Little League provided a vehicle for families to become reacquainted. Many men became Little League volunteers. Mothers also were needed at Little League fields. They formed the Mothers' Auxiliary. But Little League baseball wasn't on Mount Vernon's horizon yet at the war's end.

In the spring of 1948 a trip Carl Stotz took resulted in a major event in Little League's history. The organizer of a new Little League in Dushore, Pennsylvania, invited Stotz to bring a team from Williamsport to play an exhibition game, in the hopes of increasing local interest. An editor of the *Saturday Evening Post* who was vacationing nearby attended the game. He liked what he saw and assigned a writer and photographer to cover the national tournament and tell the Little League story. The May 14, 1949, issue of the Post ("Small Boy's Dream Come True") did just that.

No other promotional influence was as important in Little League's history. The founding fathers of Mount Vernon's Little League no doubt saw the story. Another story in *Life* magazine promoted Little League even more. The folks in Mount Vernon may have even seen that one as well. Little League was deluged with inquiries. One of those inquiries came from the folks from Mount Vernon. By 1949 Little League was sprouting nationwide with 867 teams in nearly 197 leagues in over a dozen states. The Little League seed had been planted in Mount Vernon with its first Little League game scheduled for 1950.

All of us who would play Little League baseball in Mount Vernon would soon learn a great deal from our Little League experience. We would learn how to perform under pressure and how to be part of a team; how to win and how to lose. We would soon come face to face with every emotion, winning and losing, disappointments and elation. I never won a championship in Little League but I tried real hard. I guess that's what Little League is all about – trying.

In a way, all of us found some of the basic elements of life in baseball and in Little League. Think about it. You have to show up at a certain time. If you're late, you let the team down. And just like life, there are isolated individual performances that stand out. But in the end, it's what the team did that really matters. How you contributed to the cause was important. When I played Little League, it wasn't something I did because my parents wanted me to do it. It was just fun.

Baseball fans everywhere know that Babe Ruth helped rescue baseball, making it more popular than ever. Who was going to build boys baseball in Mount Vernon? It took a man in Williamsport, Pennsylvania, who stepped on a lilac bush in his backyard to start the ball rolling in Mount Vernon.

2
Founding Fathers

The story of Mount Vernon's introduction to Little League really is about a big leaguer who became a little leaguer.

Anton "Andy" Karl returned to his hometown of Mount Vernon in 1947 after playing professional baseball for 11 years. He was a relief pitcher for the Boston Red Sox, Philadelphia Phillies and Boston Braves. In 1945 he was the Phillies top pitcher, the year he pitched his way to a major league record by relieving in 67 games.

Karl was involved in an event in 1947 which turned out to be an important happening for the youngsters of Mount Vernon. On August 13, while playing for the Braves against the Brooklyn Dodgers at Ebbets Field, the Dodgers held a 'day' for Mount Vernon's Ralph Branca who was having an outstanding season. Since Karl was in town, the city's community leaders included Andy in the ceremonies, too.

Both Branca and Karl each received a $1,000 bond and other gifts. But among the gifts given to Andy that day, the thing he was most impressed with, was a scroll presented to him by the youngsters of the city. He never forgot about it.

A year later, when Mount Vernon businessman, Mike O'Connell, came to Andy to interest him in starting a Little League program, Karl remembered the scroll he received and said he felt that he "owed the kids something". The campaign was underway.

After work at that time, Andy Karl quite often made the short walk from his A.H. Karl and Bros. Inc. plumbing company on Third Street in Mount Vernon to Mike O'Connell's bar and grille right across the street. Most everyone knew it as O'Connell's Restaurant but its actual name was the Blue Bell Restaurant.

Andy Karl

O'CONNELL'S RESTAURANT

O'Connell's—Mt. Vernon's Gathering Place for Businessman's Lunch

BUSINESSMAN'S LUNCH
SERVED 11 A. M.-2 P. M. **75¢** up

DINNERS
SERVED 5 P. M.-8:30 P. M. from **$1.25**

"Nicest Place In Town To Hold Your Small Party"

Dancing Every Saturday Night
PLENTY OF FREE PARKING
253 E. 3rd St.   MO. 7-9759

O'Connell's Restaurant was where the idea for Little League baseball in Mount Vernon took roots.

Behind O'Connell's was a deep drop off where a defunct railroad used to run near Third Street to Columbus Avenue. There were two entrances to O'Connell's, one on Third Street that took you right into the bar. The other entrance was primarily for kids and women and led to a grille room where dinners were served. It was twice as wide as the bar area and had four booths and ten tables and a small area set aside for the band to play. Jeff Borelli was a drummer, and he occasionally performed with friends.

The food wasn't too much to boast about since there wasn't even a full time waiter or waitress there. Danny the bartender would come into the room since he doubled as a cook and brought the hamburgers to the back room grille.

O'Connell's was the kind of small bar where locals went to unwind. Andy Karl was a local and a regular. So were quite a few fellows who loved baseball. There was O'Connell who owned the place, and Jeff Borelli, as well as Joe O'Connor and Bill Real, Larry Tracy and Len Boccardi. They talked about the Dodgers and Giants rivalry and also about Carl Stotz's idea of Little League baseball which was growing leaps and bounds across the country. It was probably in O'Connell's bar where plans for Little League baseball in Mount Vernon were formulated.

O'Connell, who was a successful businessman, had an answering service business in nearby Tuckahoe, New York. He saw the potential of the Little League program and called in Andy Karl, John Sobek and Len Boccardi to see what Mount Vernon could do to start one. O'Connell realized that it was exactly the right program needed, something to keep young boys "off the streets and out of the newspapers."

Together the four men devoted much of their spare time, money and

Mike O'Connell

brains developing the program in Mount Vernon. They called on their friends at O'Connell's to help out setting up four teams that became the second (Port Chester was the first) Little League system in Westchester County.

But it wasn't as easy as all that. Karl recalled when it was just a dream, and a lot of work.

"We were in the hole after the first year," he said. They set out to organize a league with fifty dollars that O'Connell donated out of his own pocket. A local sporting goods man put up the equipment and uniforms. Out of 250 applicants in the first year alone, the organizers narrowed it down, only 60 would play, from the cream of the crop.

"It really mushroomed. It really took hold in the matter of one year," Karl recalled. He became the first commissioner and the others fell into other offices as the program blossomed. O'Connell became vice president. Boccardi, who overcame polio and went into the fuel oil sales business, was secretary and Sobek was treasurer.

Jeff Borelli and Larry Tracy were involved with a popular Mount Vernon softball team called The Sportsmen. Its players and management frequented O'Connell's and got involved with the Little League right away. Borelli, who worked in the textile business, coached the Shamrocks the first year along with Herb Stevens. Larry Tracy got involved in the administrative side right away.

Tracy was the scorekeeper for the league's first game in 1950, but he soon decided that he wanted a more important part in the development of the boys, so he became manager of the Peacocks in 1951. In 1953-54 and part of 1955 he was president of the American League as well as manager. In 1955 he became Little League commissioner and immediately began to make plans for rapid growth in the Little League organization. Under his watch, the league grew from four original teams to six to eight, then to 12 and eventually to 20 teams in two leagues of ten teams each. Tracy's tutelage and direction ran from 1955 to 1962.

Steve Acunto, another pioneer of the league, replaced Tracy as Little League commissioner in 1963. Until then he was a manager of the Indians since the league's first year of play in 1950. He had a long career in athletics and civic affairs. He was the 1960 Olympic chairman for boxing; a director in the People to People Sports Program; a member of the New York State Athletic Commission; boxing director for the city's YMCA; and a member of the Senior Citizens Committee.

Joe O'Connor was also involved with the Little League from the start. He was an accountant for Armour Foods but moonlighted as a bartender at O'Connell's at night. He assisted Bill Real who was the manager of the Panthers. Real was a salesman for Pape's, a wholesaler for food and condiments for restaurants and delicatessens that occupied the space below a bowling alley down the street from O'Connell's bar and grille. Rounding out the first four teams were Carmine Casucci who managed the Pirates and Steve Acunto who was at the helm of the Indians.

Even today, there is a mystery about when Mount Vernon's Little League was chartered. Nancy Raney of Little League Eastern Regional Headquarters checked its archives in 2012 and found that Mount Vernon American was originally chartered with Little League in 1952. She also came across a league called The Little League of Mount Vernon that was first chartered in 1951 by Anton Karl with Little League International. "It is very possible the team was formed in 1949 but not sanctioned by Little League," she said. An article in the *Mount Vernon Daily Argus* in July 1963 noted that the Mount Vernon Little League was franchised in 1949.

Mount Vernon's 1951 Little League application in.

An application submitted by Mount Vernon to Little League Baseball, Inc. in Williamsport just before February 1, 1951 noted that Mount Vernon's officers, Anton Karl, J. O'Connell, Len Boccardi, and John Sobek were duly elected to operate a four team Little League and made application for associate membership in Little League Baseball, Inc. for the year 1951. The application noted that the league would accept applications from boys residing in Mount Vernon, Pelham, Bronxville, and the Bronx. The estimated population of the territory was 70,000. The proposed name of the league on the application was "Little League of MOUNT VERNON, NY., Inc. No.2". The application also listed the names of team managers, William Real, Fred Nelson, Tom Nelly and Steve Acunto. Application "No. 1" was never found.

In the fifties all conversations were about the "boys" and Little League baseball. It wasn't until November 1973 that New Jersey became the first state in the nation to require Little League to allow girls to enjoy that part of Americana. Girls could now play Little League baseball. In Mount Vernon soon thereafter Chrissy Brennan began slugging it out right beside the boys.

Until Little League began in Mount Vernon, parental involvement in youth sports mostly consisted of watching the games. That changed when fathers returned from World War II and got involved with Little League as coaches. Mothers also got involved. By Little League's second season, the Mothers' Auxiliary was formed to raise funds and help with the management duties.

Little by little, more and more mothers came to watch their sons play. Several got involved and devoted countless hours to the program. Women like Mrs. Wilhelmina "Billie" O'Connor, Grace Monahan, Mrs. Bertha Martin were there at the beginning to support the Little League in any way they could. They passed the hat to raise funds to pay umpires at games. They handled countless raffles, bridge games, and cake sales that would help defray costs.

Through the early years, Mount Vernon Little League relied on the efforts and contributions of volunteers, who have always been the backbone of the program, with its army of coaches, managers, umpires, administrators, and fund raisers. Most of the volunteers who were involved from the start stayed with it through the decade of the fifties.

Karl, who was the league's commissioner and president from 1949 to 1968, called the dedication of the volunteers 'fantastic'. "I think most of it is because they enjoyed working with boys. It is quite a thrill to watch a boy develop."

Karl said he saw Little League become the center of interest in a child's life, especially when there were problems at home. "To some of these kids, Little League was everything. They learned the value of working with other boys. It helped a lot to keep boys off the street. They were being taken care of for about eight or nine hours a week."

Many adults who got involved with the league as parent volunteers stayed on after their children grew up. In 1968 Little League honored two people, Mr. and Mrs. C. Joseph O'Connor, who devoted more than 20 years of their lives to the betterment of Mount Vernon boys. In 1950 when Little League started Joe was a coach for the Panthers under Manager Bill Real. O'Connor believed that every boy who wanted to play baseball should have a fair chance on a team, and the boys adored this nice guy who shared their problems and pleasures. Later Joe was a Pony League manager.

His wife, Billie, liked baseball and the youngsters as well. She made out the record cards, wrote letters and began to think about forming a Mothers' Auxiliary unit as well as getting sponsors for the teams. She became president of the first Mothers' Auxiliary and helped arrange parades and motorcades where the boys, dressed in their uniforms, marched through Mount Vernon streets.

Mr. & Mrs. Joe O'Connor devoted more than two decades to the city's Little League in its early years.

The O'Connor's were not alone. Numerous other volunteers helped put Mount Vernon's Little League program on the map. Mrs. Bertha Martin first was involved as secretary of the Mothers' Auxiliary taking over the job from Grace Monahan. When Billie O'Connor retired as president of the group, Bertha Martin assumed that position and helped the league grow even more.

Volunteers have always been instrumental in the growth of the city's Little League program. Pictured left to right are Mrs. Edward Martin, Little League banquet chairwoman, Mrs. Joseph O'Connor, president of the Mothers of the Little League organization, Jack Farrell, New York Yankees press secretary, Andy Karl, league commissioner. The Little League received a $1400 check in 1955 to help defray costs at an end of season banquet.

3

Andy Karl – "Mr. Little League"

Most everyone who tried out for Little League in Mount Vernon on cold Saturday April mornings during the 1950's have dim memories of the experience that we thought would seal our baseball fate forever.

But one lasting memory was seeing a Major League baseball player for the first time up close and personal. There out on the mound wearing a beautiful Boston Red Sox white home jersey with "Red Sox" emblazoned on the blouse stood Anton "Andy" Karl. All of us had to face his pitching on our fateful tryout day.

"I remember him dragging his jersey out of the closest once a year," said his son, Andy Karl Jr., who would go on to have a successful Little League career in the '50s. His father, Andy Karl, was the catalyst for bringing Little League baseball to Mount Vernon more than 60 years ago. He was "Mr. Little League".

Throwing batting practice to hundreds of youngsters wasn't difficult at all for Andy. It may be hard to comprehend in today's game of heavily emphasized bullpens, but there was a time when relief pitching was not a highly specialized art and pitching saves were something else. In the early

1940's, few pitchers made their livings entirely off of relieving. One who did was Andy Karl, and he was one of the early major league specialists in the trade.

He was also the true guiding light in starting a Little League program in Mount Vernon.

In the beginning, folks may have thought that Karl was hired as a figure head to run the program because he played in the major leagues. But that was not the case at all. He was put to the test early on.

When Carl Stotz started Little League he believed the fairest system would be one that provided an opportunity for boys who played together at school or in the same neighborhood to play together on the baseball diamond. That meant that Mount Vernon boys would be geographically assigned to a team. But Mount Vernon, like many cities, was to some degree divided along ethnic, religious and economic lines. Karl objected to Little League's mandate. He didn't want a team composed only of one group, whether it was Italian, Irish, Jewish, black or white. He wanted the boys to mix together.

Karl took action in what he believed. He wrote to Little League headquarters and spoke to officials there. He told them he wanted a waiver from Little League's geographical assignment. Karl won his point. He was a man if you talked to him, through his common sense approach without screaming or threatening, could get his point across. The hierarchy of Little League baseball in Williamsport listened. Thereafter the kids were shuffled on teams. It did not matter whether you came from the North, South, East, or West side of Mount Vernon. It didn't matter what elementary or junior high school you went to. If the manager picked you that is who you played for.

Maintaining a smooth running organization that makes it possible for hundreds of youngsters to acquire baseball skills and enjoy their first real brush with competitive sports, takes a singleness of purpose, a sense of dedication and at times a tough skin. Andy had it all. He also said later in his life that his experience with Little League was more enjoyable than playing in the big leagues.

"I really enjoyed the chance to work with youngsters and to see them develop and come along. This Little League program is wonderful if it is run right at the local level."

The boys who came through the program not only knew Andy but they liked him and respected him, not just as a former major leaguer, but as someone who really knew his baseball and taught them how to play.

Don Cook was one those boys. "What I remember vividly was how generous Andy was with his time. He devoted endless hours to supervising the early years. He would visit with each team at practices; in fact, he pitched many batting practice sessions.

"Fast forwarding the story, Andy helped

Andy Karl spent endless hours running the program and helping the young ballplayers.

me with my college pitching staff at Fairfield University in the 1970's. We stayed in touch over the years."

Quiet, soft-spoken, almost shy, Karl was equally well-liked and respected by the parents who spoke of him with admiration and respect. He was "Andy" to all of them and they turned to him easily for advice and assistance, whether they were coaches or just as parents of Little Leaguers.

"Through Little League, these boys are at least five years farther ahead in their baseball play than I was at the same age," he said. "But more than that, these youngsters are learning early how to compete, and it's a highly competitive world that we're living. And they're learning the value of teamwork and sportsmanship, the need to play the game by the rules, whether it's baseball or the game of life." Karl said this in 1961.

Karl felt a key factor in the success of the program was the age-level of the youngsters. "If you're going to develop kids, you have to start at the youngest age," he said. "Eight is the best age to start learning, but nine is the earliest for competition. If we wait until a youngster is 13 or 14, too many wrong habits have to be overcome."

Andy Karl, center, presents awards to (left to right) Wendell Thompson, Frank Bianche and Fred Casucci. Looking on are Mrs. Joseph O'Connor, president of the Mothers' organization, and Mike O'Connell, league vice president.

Born in Mount Vernon in 1914, he went to DeWitt Clinton elementary school and then Mount Vernon High School. Andy graduated from Manhattan College in 1935 with a degree in industrial engineering. He spent five years in the major leagues, three and one-half with the Philadelphia Phillies from mid 1943 to 1946.

Although saves were not recorded when Karl pitched, he had 22 saves for the Phillies, including 15 in 1945. He was the National League's best reliever that year. In fact, the 15 saves tied the National League record. One of his most memorable outings came in the second game of a doubleheader against the Cincinnati Reds on August 19. Jimmie Foxx, 37, a Hall of Fame slugger, started the game on the mound and pitched seven innings. He turned a 4-1 lead over to Karl, who finished off a 6-2 victory. That was Foxx's only victory as a big-league pitcher.

Throughout his baseball career Karl had a mind of his own. In late June 1943, the Red Sox sent Andy down to Louisville. He refused to report and took up work as a mechanical engineer at a war industry plant in New York. Something was worked out and he was sold to the Phillies. The following year, Andy did it again and refused to report when he was traded to the Chicago Cubs. The trade eventually never took place and Andy stayed with the Phillies.

In 1945, Karl declared that he would only work part-time, when the team was playing in the East, and would thus better be able to concentrate on his plumbing business in Mount Vernon, A.H. Karl and Bros. Inc., located on Third Street. The tall, slim right hander who threw a knuckle ball primarily established his remarkable relief record that year despite the fact that for the first six weeks of the season he pitched only weekends for the Phillies.

It was with the Mount Vernon Scarlets that Karl got his first start in organized baseball. After graduating from Manhattan in 1935, he spent two years hurling for the Scarlets and made such a splendid showing in 1936 he was signed for the Red Sox farm system.

Ten years later, in 1946, many of the veterans who had served during World War II returned to the Major Leagues. Whether it was a higher level of play on offense or that Andy had lost some of his effectiveness, his career started to wind down. The Phillies never used him in 1947 and he was traded early in the season to the Boston Braves. That was his last season. By 1948, when the Braves were winning a pennant, Karl was pitching for the crack semi-pro Brooklyn Bushwicks. Baseball still held appeal. A brief note in the June 20, 1951, *Sporting News,* had Karl pitching for the New York Athletic Club and beating a team from Lafayette College, 6-2.

At the same time, Andy was deeply involved with Mount Vernon's Little League. His daughter Rosemary Karl who lives in New Mexico remembers her dad's involvement in the early years.

"My two brothers and I grew up at 437 Highland Avenue in Mount Vernon," she recalled. "It was right near Hutchinson Field off of Sandford Boulevard. The whole gang from Highland Avenue went to Memorial Field quite often. I remember going to the fields in 1950 to get them ready for Little League tryouts. I picked up paper and helped rake. I must have been nine-years-old."

Rosemary spoke highly about her father's concern for youngsters. "When Mike O'Connell, Larry Tracy and Joe O'Connor came to my father and talked about starting a Little League, they wanted to charge the kids a fee to join. My dad said no. He knew there was a certain percentage of kids who would not be able to pay. He said he would raise funds so the kids wouldn't have to pay. As a result, Little League became open to everyone. My dad believed strongly that it should be open to everyone regardless of race, creed or ability to pay."

Rosemary recalled how upset she got with her father about girls not being able to play in Little League at that time. "That was one of my bones of contention with him. Even back then I felt it should have been open to girls."

Andy Karl in a 1954 interview discussed the benefit of playing Little League baseball. "It's impossible to measure the importance of developing the competitive spirit in youngsters. It's essential not only to the boy, but to the very life-blood of the country. Youngsters today have a far greater advantage than we did. Organized, well-conducted leagues are popping up all over the horizon. Youngsters are foolish who do not take advantage of the opportunity.

"And the parents and elder folks involved in the programs should be commended for their efforts. Were it not for junior teams of this sort, I may never have gone on to the majors. Competitive spirit can't be picked up over night. It must be developed in the boy."

Rosemary Karl wishes that her family could have saved memorabilia from those early days of Little League. Their house burned down in 1969 destroying most everything.

Before moving to New Fairfield, Connecticut, in 1969, Karl was still serving as president of the Mount Vernon Little League. He was on the board of directors of the Boys' Club and was involved with the Lions Club. He died on April 8, 1989, on his 75th birthday, at Scripps Memorial Hospital in La Jolla, California.

4
Men in the Dugout

Whatever good came out of our experience in Mount Vernon's Little League was the result of our managers and their leadership. When we played Little League ball we were greatly influenced by our coaches. In most instances their ideals and aspirations were similar to our own. We shared a common interest in the game. We wanted to excel. We were determined to win.

We might not have realized it then but as kids we often idolized our managers and coaches because they were sources of inspiration. The good managers and coaches were those who recognized that the game really was a vehicle for training and enjoyment, not an end in itself.

Several friends, who played Little League ball, told me they didn't like their managers. It may be because they didn't get playing time since they were most likely eight, nine or ten-year-olds and sat the bench.

So how did we, who played Little League ball, turn out more than 60 years later as a result of our experience in the program? Did we learn some lessons and acquire some habits and attitudes which made us better people at work and at home? I would like to think that we did. While many people believe that participation in Little League baseball is a fine thing for youngsters it is not automatically a desirable experience for everyone.

The heart of our Little League baseball experience was what happened between each of us and our manager. They, more than any single individual, were the most important people in the Mount Vernon Little League program.

Think about this. When we were ten-year-olds, we were seeking to discover meanings about ourselves and others through experiences that largely excluded our parents. This is all part of pre-adolescence. Up to that time we identified with our parents and always looked for their approval and support. Then others began to play significant roles and influenced our outlook, feelings and values. One of those persons was our Little League manager.

What were they like as they taught us to play, soothed our egos, and built our self confidence? They had to disguise their despair and disappointment. The approaches they used differed. Their temperaments were not always the same. The ones who succeeded the best were those who communicated with their players. Those who were influential during the '50s included men like Charlie Cook, Fred Nelson, Steve Wisner, Tom Nelly, Frank Casucci, Ed Martin and Sol Dunsay, Al Coleman, Chet Hurlie, among others.

Here are several who left their mark on many of us:

Bill Real, an excellent baseball man, who kids loved and who was totally dedicated to youth baseball in Mount Vernon. He didn't have sons but he knew the game and was an outstanding teacher. His infield practice was first rate. You had to be a pretty good catcher to hang on to his throws. After three years of managing Little League, he became commissioner of the Pony League. Real was a Little League pioneer.

Bill Real

Jeff Borelli may have been a short man in stature but a giant of a person and also a pioneer of the Little League. He taught the fundamentals as well as anyone. He never yelled or screamed at anybody. He was a gentleman in every respect. Years after his Little League players graduated, he would stay in touch with many of them while monitoring their high school baseball careers.

Larry Tracy did it all. He played a role in the founding of the Little League and was the official scorer at the league's first game. He grew with the job later becoming a successful manager and eventually a league commissioner.

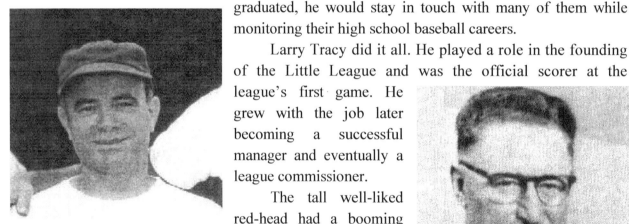
Jeff Borelli

The tall well-liked red-head had a booming voice. If there was a playoff or world series game, he would announce the games. At league dinners he would often show game movies of the season and add his own narration. He knew every youngster's name, how he pitched, and what his batting stance looked like.

Larry Tracy

Joe O'Connor was considered by all those who came in contact with him as just a real nice guy. He was a founder of Mount Vernon Little League and was instrumental in its growth over the next 20 years along with his wife "Billie" who founded the Mothers' Auxiliary.

He believed that every boy who wanted to play baseball should have a fair chance to play on a team, and the boys on his teams adored this nice guy who shared their problems and pleasures.

Joe Tripodi, who owned a grocery store in Mount Vernon, was a teacher and even a better motivator. He was a master at getting his

Joe O'Connor

team motivated and keeping all the players happy. He substituted liberally and gave every kid the innings that they were required to receive according to official Little League rules. He also threw end of the year barbecues at Baker Field for his players and their families.

Steve Acunto, the last surviving founding member of the Little League, for 13 years was a successful manager. He then served as commissioner for three years. Besides his involvement with Little League, Acunto was a boxing legend who inspired students as head coach of boxing at Westchester Community College in Valhalla for 30 years. In 1988, he was inducted into the World Boxing Hall of Fame. Even in his later years, he was in ring demonstrations with the likes of Mohammed Ali, Rocky Marciano and Willy Pep.

Joe Tripodi

I had the good fortune of meeting with Steve at his home while researching this book. I had heard he had a much sterner approach in dealing with his young players compared to many other managers. That may have been the case but I found a warm caring man. It was evident that he was dedicated to his boys. In his late eighties he still recalled many of them quite fondly.

Steve Acunto

Steve truly understood what Little League is all about. In the league's early years, he wrote a newspaper column called "In This Corner" about Little League happenings. He delivered a speech that said it all at the 1955 banquet to honor his Indians team that won the city championship. He said:

Naturally, it is a pleasure to be the manager of a Little League championship club. Each year someone must win wherein someone else loses in the Little League as in all other sports or fields of endeavor. Any manager of a winning club or a championship one will tell you that the formula for winning is: consistent good pitching, hitting, defense and team spirit.

While that is, of course, true, I believe a team must also have a lot of luck to triumph over the other fine teams in the leagues. However, winning is not the real reason for the existence of the Little League, either in Mount Vernon or throughout the nation.

Basically, the specific purpose is to teach our boys that the foremost requisite they will need to play the game of life is to learn to work together in harmony regardless of race, creed, or color, and to win or lose in a sportsmanlike manner in the true American way.

Fundamentally, this is the aim of every manager or coach. If this has been accomplished, as I believe it has in Little League, then we may consider the 1955 Little League year a successful one here in Mount Vernon and everywhere else.

5
Diamonds of Our Youth

If you were a kid and played Little League baseball in the 1950s you had your shrines, Yankee Stadium, Polo Grounds or Ebbets Field. For generations, these three ballparks were where fathers and sons bonded.

But you also had your own diamonds and they were diamonds in the rough. They were ball fields that were simple, basic, with no frills attached. For most of the '50s, our fields of dreams were named Hutchinson, Longfellow and Baker fields.

The infields were usually hard, baked dirt, but thankfully there wasn't any glass. There were no handsome scalloped cutouts around the bases or manicured well-groomed grass. The outfields were mostly splotchy grass, but green. During the regular season there weren't any cyclone fences. Neither were there any lights either except for a special exhibition or World Series game at Hutchinson Field. Finish your game by sundown was the order of the day!

There weren't many better places to spend summer days than on our Little League fields. We grew older, graduated from Little League, and moved on but our baseball diamonds remained, and forever were the stars.

Most of us may not remember days or games from that long ago era. But we recall moments and ball fields. Like clockwork at 6 o'clock at Longfellow Field, a fellow would religiously come by with his hot dog wagon and park his truck near the stone bleachers down the first base line. There also was Tommy Ambrosino's father who sold Treat Potato chips. He would drive his truck to Longfellow and Baker fields and give out bags of chips at games and practices.

Remember running out onto the diamond feeling giddy when the game was about to begin? Remember smacking the pocket of your first baseball glove and chanting the name of your pitcher as your crouched in the infield waiting for a grounder? "Come on Vonnie. Come on Vonnie. Chuck it in there."

The ball fields were our haven. In the winter of 1955, Mount Vernon's Recreation Commission got involved with the ball fields. The commission expanded the Little-Pony-Minor League programs. The Sound Shore League, softball, and the recreation leagues needed playing space. A lively battle was underway between The city's Board of Education and the school system. Baker and the Longfellow fields were made available earlier. Howard Field, located behind A.B. Davis High School on Gramatan Avenue, also became a Little League site.

Did you ever wonder how Baker Field got its name? The Board of Education named it in honor of the late Mrs. Herbert L. Baker, an organizer and chairwoman of the Mount Vernon Recreation Commission, and also for many years chairwoman of the Public Library Board of Trustees. The Baker Field property off of California Road was owned by the Board of Education but used for a long time by the Recreation Commission.

Baker Field, with four baseball diamonds and six adjoining clay tennis courts, is now the site of Mount Vernon High School.

The fields at the intersection of Sandford Boulevard and the Hutchinson River Parkway always weren't known as Hutchinson Field. When Ralph Branca was playing ball there in the '40s it was called Stinson Field, owned earlier by a local farmer named Stinson.

Opening Day ceremonies at Hutchison Field. While the oil tanks remain, the incinerator smokestacks no longer dot the skyline.

What were these baseball diamonds of our youth, our home away from home, like?

Other than opening day and the World Series between the American and National Leagues, all games were played at Longfellow Field up to 1953 season. Longfellow's location at 625 South Fourth Avenue in the southern end of Mount Vernon was a problem for kids who lived in the north and west side of the city. But somehow they made it to games and practices.

In Little League's first year, 1950, all games were played at Longfellow field #1. It was the only field there; quite similar to A.B. Davis' Howard Field on Gramatan Avenue and Memorial Field on Sandford Boulevard. Each had stone bleachers near the field.

A year later, Little League doubled in size from four to eight teams and needed additional fields to play on. Longfellow field #2 came into existence. The fields presented unique and strange challenges. It was generally inferior to Longfellow field #1 which had a grass outfield with trees providing an outfield backdrop. Field #2 had a skin infield like all the fields but the outfield was nearly all dirt.

Longfellow Field recalls a time when cement stands provided the seating.

The background wasn't particularly good when hitting. A sharply hit single at field #2, once it reached the outfield, could roll and roll and turn into a home run.

Going after balls hit to deep left field meant dealing with some sort of a factory or industrial business nearby. A barbed wire fence separated the field from the factory. While not many accomplished it, the goal of many Little Leaguers was pull the ball over the fence for a home run. Even on field #1 to hit a home run required the ball to roll into the trees.

In 1950, the National League used field #1 exclusively. When the new American League began in 1951, the league used field #2. In subsequent years, the leagues alternated using the fields, playing half their games on field #1 and half on field #2.

Hutchinson Field was the site for special occasions like opening day and the World Series. In 1951 a storm fence was erected around the outfield. The scenery was unique on Hutchinson Field's three baseball diamonds. The skin infield was hard. Looking out into right field a group of oil tanks stood tall while an incinerator smokestack occupied territory on the right side of Hutchinson's field #2. The city maximized use of its fields in 1956. Little League's Western League games were played throughout the season at Hutchinson Field. All other play took place on the Baker Field diamonds.

In 1959, Mount Vernon's Little League even found another baseball diamond to play on in early June. The ball field on the Wartburg property near Pelham and Lincoln Avenue was officially commissioned as the Democrats rapped out a 9-6 victory over the Elks.

The words to songwriter Joe Raposo's "There Used To Be A Ballpark", made famous by Frank Sinatra, describe the genteel nature of Baker Field located in the most affluent area of Mount Vernon on California Road. It was a diamond, actually two diamonds that later grew to four diamonds, where the fields were warm and green. Six red clay tennis courts abutted two of the fields near California Road. But just like the song, "There Used To Be A Ballpark", Baker Field and all its diamonds no longer exist. In the early 1960s, the new Mount Vernon High School was built on the site where the kids played their baseball games with a joy hardly ever seen.

6
Mount Vernon Little League Championship Game Scores

1950	Panthers	6
	Pirates	2

1951	Shamrocks	7
	Owls	1

1952	Pirates	13
	Orioles	10

1953	Orioles	1
	Pirates	0

1954	Panthers	3
	Orioles	2

1955	Indians	18
	Community Oil Comets	0
1956	Rotary Club Rams	5
	Braslow Builders	3
1957	Local 338	9
	Lions Club	4
1958	Lions Club	10
	Engine 3	3
1959	Engine 3	12
	Gramatan Men's Shop	0

7

1950 – The First Season

The story of Mount Vernon, New York's inaugural 1950 Little League season had two distinct chapters. The behind the scene work by the league's founding fathers to get the league up and running was the opening one. The actual games and exciting playoffs to crown a first Mount Vernon city-champion was the second.

The buzz for Mount Vernon's newly-sanctioned Little League baseball program for youngsters from eight to twelve years of age began on Friday April 7th when League Commissioner Andy Karl of the Lions Club and advisor Mike O'Connell of Rotary announced in the city's newspaper, *The Daily Argus,* that tryouts would be held on April 29. They would be held on Saturdays and Sundays each week until the season opened. Hutchinson Field # 1 was assigned by the Recreation Commission for all Little League workouts. At the same time with justifiable pride, Karl and O'Connell reported that over $200 had been contributed to set the program into actual operation.

Little League wasn't the main news that would occupy newspaper pages that spring. For days on end reports came in from a world away – Korea. In June the Korean War began. That same month the Russians exploded a nuclear bomb. Months earlier Ted Williams of the Boston Red Sox became the highest paid player in baseball history when he signed for $125,000.

Mount Vernon's Recreation Department jumped on the Little League bandwagon early on. Application blanks, requiring the approval of parent or guardian, were requisites for tryouts. The blanks were available at City Hall. There was immediate interest by youngsters to fill the rosters of the four ball clubs. With the resumption of school following the Easter recess, the call for application blanks rose substantially.

And with each of the four teams carrying a roster of 18 players, a total of 72 positions were open on a strictly competitive basis. By April 7th, over 60 applications were issued. At the same time, a Little League governing board was announced. John Sobek was named treasurer of the board which also included Walter Solinger, Dr. Alfred Gildersleeve and Oliver Westfall. At least two other board members would be designated at a later date.

While Little League may have begun in 1939, there were many families in Mount Vernon who were unfamiliar with the organization. By 1949 it embraced 225 local leagues involving 900 teams and over 13,000 youngsters. Port Chester, New York was the first Westchester County locale to field a Little League team. Mount Vernon was second and looking forward someday to having a team represent the city in the national Little League World Series.

But before they could even dream of that there was a major personnel problem. The League was looking for men to volunteer and work with the boys, as coaches and managers. Karl and O'Connell requested those interested in coaching or managing to attend a league meeting at O'Connell's Restaurant at 253 East Third Street in early April.

On the coldest April 14th on record that also produced one of the most unseasonable snow storms in the history of Westchester County 10 coaches and managers turned up at O'Connell's to complete the guiding staff for the four teams.

The 10 coaches included Bill Real who was instrumental in the formation of the Kiwanis Baseball League in Mount Vernon; Arnold Corwin, president of a local Parent Teachers Association; Bert Abrams, Lions Club officer; Steve Acunto, who was identified in the *Daily Argus* article as a boxing manager; Marty Rosenbaum, a popular city ballplayer; Bob Cassin, Herb Stevens Jr., Ilen Wolfe, Joe O'Connor and advisor Mike O'Connell. Plans were laid out for two coaches to be assigned to each club, while the remaining two would serve as coaches for the whole league, assisting where needed. The committee also appointed Dr. Alfred Gildersleeve, Kiwanis Club secretary, as the official scorer.

In early spring it was evident that there was an immediate need for additional funds to firmly establish the league as a city-wide community affair. Donations of $50 each were provided by the Rotary Club of Mount Vernon, Mount Vernon Trust Company, and the Elks Club. Soon Tom Godfreys Sporting Goods and the Italian Civic Association became donors.

The league also announced that it would follow a unique plan in completing league rosters. All boys at tryouts would be graded on a point basis and the teams would bid for the services of the players, not with money, but with a point-system instead. Everyone wanted to insure a pretty even distribution of top talent among the four clubs.

O'Connell also announced at this historic meeting that teams would be uniformed and all equipment, such as bats, balls, and catcher's gear, would be supplied by the league. The young players were also fully insured. After the four team rosters were completed, the names of the four teams would be chosen by the team players. O'Connell was also looking to the future in announcing that the League hoped to expand to eight teams in 1951. But first there were tryouts and rosters to be filled.

On Saturday April 29 alarm clocks went off early in many Mount Vernon homes. Youngsters could not wait. Mount Vernon's first Little League tryouts would be taking place later that morning. Despite rainy weather, 123 youngsters made their way to Hutchinson Field. Commissioner Karl and his 10 coaches and managers were forced to postpone the first field sessions until the following Saturday when the tryouts would be split up into at least two sections, one for boys aged 8-10 and the other for boys aged 11-12. Coaches would begin an immediate assessment of each youngster's qualifications.

The following week 162 youngsters turned out again. Karl, Bill Real and Tom Nelly staged a session for pitchers and catchers. Frank Casucci, Bob Cassin, Arnold Corwin and Herb Stevens handled infield drills, while Steve Acunto, Tony Carideo, George Fennell, Joe O'Connor and Matty Rosenbaum drilled the youngsters on outfield play and hitting. The youngsters went through their paces before the watchful eyes of several hundred parents.

Following the drills, the candidates were cut to 100 to compete for the 72 slots on the four teams. But before that 25 youngsters would be assigned to each of the four teams. Eventually team managers would cut their clubs down to the 18-player limit. League requirements set by Little League headquarters in Williamsport, PA, allowed a limit of no more than five 12-year-olds on each team, and required at least three 10-year-olds or younger for each club as well.

Opening day was getting close. By mid May officials announced that the season would open on June 10, with four twilight games each week, Monday through Thursday. Competition would be in two rounds, with a league championship playoff. The season would end about August 1, after which an all-star team would be selected to compete in the state finals. The deadline for filing applications for the tryouts was also extended.

The league then added two key members to its executive committee. The two, both Mount Vernonites, were Guido Cribari, sports editor of Westchester County Publishers, Inc., and Brooklyn Dodger hurler Ralph Branca. Cribari would prove to be instrumental in publicizing the Mount Vernon Little League throughout its first season with extensive coverage in the *Daily Argus*. Branca, whose every appearance on the mound for the Dodgers was reported in the *Daily Argus*, also loaned more than his name to the Little League venture. He appeared at Little League games along with several of his Dodgers teammates and helped promote the League at season-ending functions. He even hit his first home run in the major leagues in a 4-3 loss to the Pittsburgh Pirates two days before the Little League opener on June 10.

So on June 10, at long last, youngsters from all corners of Mount Vernon took to the diamonds at Longfellow School for the season openers. The Pirates, coached by Arnold Corwin, took on Bill Real's Panthers. The second game pitted the Indians, coached by Steve Acunto, against the Shamrocks, led by Herb Stevens. A 15-car motorcade officially opened the day's festivities, starting from Sandford Boulevard and South Fulton Avenue where the boys lined up. The parade proceeded along Fulton Avenue to First Street, down First Street to Fourth Avenue, then along Fourth to Third Street.

Before the opening pitch, a VFW color guard participated in flag-raising ceremonies along with The Longfellow School band. The four clubs lined the third base and first base foul lines. Jordan E. Larson, superintendent of Mount Vernon schools, threw out the first pitch. Before the games began, Andy Karl, league commissioner, was given a ball autographed by the managers of the four teams in appreciation of his work for the youngsters.

Play Ball...Historic First Little League Games

June 10 – At game time, some 200 friends, relatives and just plain fans were on hand to watch the pint-size Little Leaguers open their season. When the hits and heartaches of the kids had subsided, the Panthers and Indians slipped into a first-place tie, each by slim one-run victories over the Pirates and Shamrocks, respectively. The Panthers scored in the final inning to win 4-3, while two runs in the fifth saw the Indians come home on top, 2-1.

Firsts was the order of the day. John Branca umpired the first Little League game. From his position behind the pitcher, he called "Play ball!" and Panther pitcher Ralph Merigliano delivered Little League's first pitch to Pirates first baseman Dave Hayes.

Even though Pirate pitcher Charles Burkhardt homered and doubled while striking out ten, he still picked up the loss. Panther third baseman Ed Carrozza delivered to get the winning run across. Bill Allman walked, moved to second on a fielder's choice and romped home on Carrozza's single. It was Carrozza's second hit of the game.

In the nightcap, Phil Ausiello of the Shamrocks struck out ten but lost because of infield errors. Three errors blew apart Ausiello's shutout and cost him a no-hitter in the fifth. Michael Brienza won the decision with Robert Capodicci's final-inning relief stint preserving the win. He struck out the final two batters with the bases loaded to save the victory. Fielding standout was the Indians' John Tripodi. The youngest Little Leaguer that first year was eight-year-old Don Cook who played for the Indians.

Branca, brother of Brooklyn's Ralph, umpired like he would do for many opening season games. Zeke Jewell and Fred Nelson called them on the bases. Len Boccardi was the official scorer. Larry Tracy who was an official scorer throughout the season was assisted by Nelson. There would be more in-depth newspaper coverage of the games in the league's early years than at any other time in the league's history because of Tracy and Boccardi. Both filed extensive stories for the newspaper.

Falco Flirts With Fame – Hurls One Hitter

June 13 – Joe Falco of the Shamrocks flirted with pitching fame. He was hurling no-hit ball until the beginning of the sixth inning when he gave up one hit. He struck out seven and walked nine in the complete game victory. In a bizarre play that is rarely seen, Panthers catcher John Foran, in the first inning, after a fine relay from the outfield tagged out two Shamrocks who were sliding into home at the same time. Foran also got the Panthers only hit.

Whitney Turns in Fielding Gem as Indians Beat Pirates, 10-7

June 17 – All four teams had identical records, one win and one loss before the Indians defeated the Pirates, 10-7. More than 200 people attended the game that featured a home run by Ronald Essemplace of the Indians. Charles Burkhardt, John Cunningham and Bob Ragnone had two hits apiece for the Pirates. Indians second baseman Don Whitney turned in the fielding gem of the evening with a leaping catch.

Ragnone Ks 14 in Pirates Win

June 19 – Bob Ragnone made like Boston Braves strikeout artist Warren Spahn who would lead the National League in whiffs in 1950. Ragnone struck out 14 and walked three in a 3-0 win over the Shamrocks. He also drove in the first and winning run in the fourth inning when Ed Abbatecola doubled to right center and then scored on Ragnone's infield out. Abbatecola collected two of his team's four hits.

1950 – The First Season

Willie Mays Makes Debut and Capodieci Hurls Four-Hitter

June 24 – While Willie Mays was making his professional debut for the New York Giants farm team in Trenton, NJ, Bob Capodieci was throwing a four-hitter as the Indians shutout the Pirates, 9-0. Pat Burke and Joe Monahan each went two for three for the Indians. Wendell Thompson and Burke homered for the winners. Johnny Tripodi saved Capodieci's shutout when he caught a wicked line drive with the bases loaded. A week later, Capodieci won his fifth straight game as he went the route allowing four hits while striking out ten in the Indians 17-1 victory over the Shamrocks. Wendell Thompson and Ronnie Essemplace led the winners' 13-hit barrage, each collecting three hits. Thompson, who wore Joe DiMaggio's number 5, continued to be the league's power hitter. He smashed a triple, double and single.

Merigliano and O'Connor Star in Panthers Win

July 18 – Behind the one-hit pitching of Ralph Merigliano the Panthers downed the Indians, 3-1. The win was Merigliano's second one-hit victory in succession. Fred O'Connor of the winners collected two of the Panthers' three hits, including a triple.

All-Star Team Named

July 20 – Commissioner Andy Karl announced a 14-man team, plus four alternates, to represent the league in the District Little League Tournament. The All-Star squad included five members of the Indians, four from the Shamrocks, three from the Panthers and two from the Pirates. The squad was selected by the four team managers, Herb Stevens of Shamrocks, Bill Real of Panthers, Arnold Corwin of Pirates and Steve Acunto of the Indians, and umpire John Branca and scorer Larry Tracy.

Included on the list were Bob Capodicci and Phil Ausiello, pitchers; Joe Monahan and John Foran, catchers; Ron Innecken, first base; Don Whitney, third base; John Tripodi, shortstop; Wendell Thompson, Tony Montez and Bob DeDonato, outfielders. Also on the squad were Charles Sundberg, shortstop-pitcher; Ralph Merigliano, pitcher-third baseman; Bob Ragnone, pitcher-third baseman; Charles Burkhardt, third baseman-outfielder. Alternates were Eddie Carroza, third baseman-pitcher; Rudy Eisler, catcher; and outfielders Ron Essemplace and Steve Davis.

First Night Game Of The Season

July 26 – Little League staged its first twilight night doubleheader at Hutchinson Field to benefit the camp fund and other activities of the Women's Auxiliary for both the North and South Side Boys' Clubs. The monies raised was for the maintenance of the Clubs' camp at Hopewell Junction, NY, where each year hundreds of city youngsters went to enjoy the outdoor programs at Camp Rainbow.

Ralph Branca and two Dodgers teammates, Eddie Miksis and Wayne Berlardi, acted as judges of the pre-game throwing contests. Wendell Thompson took first in throwing from centerfield to home plate. Fred O'Connor won the home plate to second base competition by hurling the ball into a barrel on his first try. Sixty-two years later O'Connor talked about that experience. "I was a 10 year old and I remember there was a barrel weighted down right on second base," he said. "I remember that I bounced the ball into the barrel. I didn't throw it in on a fly." Later, before a crowd of 700 fans, the Pirates shut out the Shamrocks, 6-0, and the Panthers defeated the Indians, 4-1, in the second game to win the first round title.

Port Chester Tops Mount Vernon in Metro District Playoffs

August 2 – After advancing to the finals of the Metropolitan District Little League playoffs by defeating Inwood City of Manhattan, 3-2, with a sixth-inning rally, the Mount Vernon Little Leaguers lost to right-hander Kevin Bartlik of Port Chester in the finals when he threw a 5-0 no-hitter. It was Bartlik's fifth no-hitter of the season.

In the earlier semi-final game, Ralph Merigliano twirled a two-hitter as Mount Vernon won with a thrilling two-run rally in the ninth inning after being shut out for the first four innings.

Mount Vernon's Charlie Burkhardt opened the sixth inning with a single. Port Chester relief pitcher Joe Martin got Burkhardt on Wendell Thompson's fielder's choice, but an error at first enabled Thompson to move to second. Joe Monahan pinch-hit and smashed one through third, Thompson scoring on the error, tying the game. Monahan went to second on the play and moved to third on Jack Foran's single to right and scored on a wild pitch to end the game.

Thompson Belts Grand Slam, Drives in 5 Runs

August 15 – Wendell Thompson of the Little League Indians and Boston Red Sox slugger Walt Dropo had a lot in common during the 1950 season. Dropo drove in an American League best 144 RBIs. Thompson put on one of the Little League season's best hitting displays in leading his Indians to a 6-4 victory over the Shamrocks, keeping alive the possibility of a playoff for the second round title against the Pirates. In the third inning Thompson hit a grand slam home run. He also pounded out a triple with a teammate aboard to personally drive in five of his team's six runs. The Indians kept alive the possibility of a playoff for the second round with the Pirates if the Pirates dropped their last game to the Panthers. The winner would then meet the Panthers, first round champs, for the Little League crown.

Burkhardt Helps Pirates Wallop Panthers

August 15 – Charlie Burkhardt threw a two-hitter as the Pirates trounced the Panthers, 7-1, in second round playoff play. Roger Boccardi, the losing pitcher, was touched for only four hits, but a combination of errors, walks and stolen bases allowed the Pirates to score seven times. The Pirates led in the second half of season play with a 4 and 1 record. The Panthers, winners of the first half, were last in the league with a 1 and 4 mark.

First Little League Championship Series a Classic

You have to be an imaginative storyteller to dream up what actually happened in the five-game season-ending playoff to crown Mount Vernon's first Little League champion in 1950. For excitement and competitiveness one could say the first Little League World Series is up there with

1950 – The First Season

the greatest playoffs that would take place in the next six decades.

The championship playoffs went the full five game limit. Each time, the Pirates, winners of the second round of play, came from behind to tie the series with the Panthers. The Panthers actually walked away with somewhat of an upset. They won the first round crown only after a playoff with the Indians and then proceeded to take a firm grip on the League cellar in the second round, the second half of the season.

The Pirates on the other hand, played well through the first round and completely dominated the second round play in the league. With this as background, many players, families and fans expected the Pirates to down the Panthers rather easily in this title playoff series. But Manager Bill Real's boys regained their first round caliber of play to defeat the favorites, three games to two, to collect the League crown.

Game 1

In the playoff opener, the Pirates walked off with a 9-4 victory over the Panthers at Longfellow School field. Despite scoring all their four runs in the top of the first inning, the Panthers watched helplessly as the Pirates tied the game in the bottom of the third and scored five times in the fifth inning to ice the victory. The combined pitching of Charlie Burkhardt and Bob Ragnone limited the Panthers to three hits. Burkhardt led the Pirates attack blasting two home runs. Centerfielder Johnny Pagano also collected two hits for the winners including a home run.

Game 2

The Panthers rebounded in the second game with a 3-1 win over the Pirates. Again the Panthers scored early with two runs in the first inning and added another in the third after the Pirates had scored their lone run in the same inning. Both winning and losing hurlers, Ed Carrozza and Bob Ragnone, respectively, hurled three-hit ball.

Game 3

The ballpark changed again for the third straight game. Under the lights at Hutchinson Field, the Panthers edged the Pirates 11-2 in the third game of the best three out of five series. After leading 3-1 going into the fifth inning, the Panthers broke the game wide open by scoring six runs in the next to last inning. Bob DeDonato led the Panthers attack from the lead-off spot. The centerfielder went two for three and scored two runs. He was helped by teammate Mike Bossi who went two for four while scoring three runs.

Game 4

The drama continued as the Panthers and Pirates took the field again for game four of the series. The Pirates needed a win or face elimination. Bob Ragnone hurled a one-hitter as he struck out nine batters and allowed only one walk in shutting out the Panthers 10-0. Both teams were scoreless until the fourth inning when the Pirates exploded for five runs. The Pirates pounded out 12 hits including a double by first baseman Dave Hayes. Hayes, Ragnone, Charlie Burkhardt and Bob McIlvane collected two hits apiece to pace the winners offense.

Panthers Win Mount Vernon Little League Championship

Rip Pirates, 6-2, Under Arcs At Hutchinson Field Yesterday

Panthers defeated Pirates, 6-2, under the arcs at Hutchinson Field last night to take the Mount Vernon Little League Championship.

The winners scored five times in the top of the first frame as a series of walks and miscues made up for a paucity of hits. Big Charlie Burkhardt, the losing hurler, allowed but two hits over the six innings but his mates were unable to get the Pirates back into the ball game as Ralph Merigliano held them to four scattered safeties over the route.

Mark Stokes and Fran Bianche starred afield for the victors, making Merigliano's job all the easier as they hauled in several sure hits.

Bobby Ragnone and Dave Hayes well in a losing cause as they joined pitcher Burkhardt in limiting Panthers to one run after the disastrous first stanza.

The championships playoffs went to the full five game limit. Each time, Pirates, winners of the second round of play, came from behind to tie the series with Panthers.

Panthers actually scored somewhat of an upset. They won the first round crown only after a playoff with the Indians and then proceeded to take a firm grip on the League cellar in the second round.

Pirates, on the other hand, played well through the first round and completely dominated second round play in the league. With this background, many expected Pirates to down the Panthers rather easily in this title playoff series but Bill Real's boys regained their first round caliber of playing to defeat the favorites, three games to two, to collect the League Crown.

Pirates had a mild threat going in the bottom of the last inning but it burned out after one run had scored.

Mike Bossi was the big thorn in the Pirates' skin as he collected one of his team's two bingles and scored two of the six runs.

The box score:

Panthers	ab	r	h	Pirates	ab	r	h
DeDonato, cf	3	1	1	Hayes, 1b	3	0	1
O'Connor, c	2	1	0	Pagano, cf	2	0	0
Bossi, 1b	3	2	1	Ragnone, 3b	2	1	1
Merigliano, p	3	1	0	Burckhardt, p	2	1	0
Bianchi, lf	3	0	0	Abbaticola, lf	3	0	1
Zepes, rf	2	0	0	Davenport, rf	3	0	1
Ruffalo, ss	1	1	0	MacIlvane, ss	3	0	0
Stokes, 2b	1	0	0	Anderson, c	1	0	0
Carozza, 3b	2	0	0	DeSimoni, 2b	1	0	0
				Mayers, c	2	0	0
				Coluntouno, rf	0	0	0
Totals	20	6	2	Totals	22	2	4

SCORE BY INNINGS
Panthers — 5 0 1 0 0 0—6
Pirates — 0 1 0 0 0 1—2
Umpires—Vecchione, Nelson, Pennell.
Scorer—Tracy.

1950 – The First Season

***Panthers, 1950 Little League Champions:** 1, Joe Groccia; 2, Bob DeDonato; 3, Roger Boccardi; 4, Eddie Carrozza; 5, Fred O'Connor; 6, Jack Foran; 7, Bill Altman; 8, Patsy Ruffalo; 9, Mike Bossi; 10, Mark Stokes; 11, Ernie Cioffi; 12, Carmine Casucci; 13, Ralph Merigliano; 14, Bill Seltman; 15, Jim Steinrock; 16, Frank Magarelli; 17, Coach Joe O'Connor; 18, Manager Carmine Casucci; 19, Frank Bianche; 20, Jimmy Carrozza.*

Here, Son, Is Your Application For The City Of Mount Vernon 'LITTLE LEAGUE' In Baseball

_____ Born _____
Player's Name   Month   Day   Year

_____
    Street Address   City   State   Phone No.

Having been informed of the organization of the Little League and the Little League Tournament Association to provide supervised baseball games for boys eight to twelve years of age, I/we, the parents of the above named candidate, do hereby give my/our approval to his participation in any and all of the activities during the current season. I/we do assume all the risks and hazards incidental to the conduct of the activities, transportation to and from the activities; and I/we do further release, absolve, indemnify and hold harmless the Little League and the Little League Tournament Assn., the organizers, sponsors, and the supervisors, any or all of them. In case of injury to my/our son, I/we hereby waive all claims against the organizers, the sponsors or any of the supervisors appointed by them. I/we likewise release from responsibility any person transporting my/our son to or from the activities.

My/our son is NOW _____ years old.

                        Date Signed _____
                                     Month   Day   Year

Father's Signature _____

Mother's Signature _____

Height   Weight   Chest   Waist   Cap Size   Shoe Size   Throws
 In.   Lb.   In.   In.   R☐ L☐

         School _____

         Team _____

                            League Age _____
                           (Do not write here)

(All boys will be protected by accident insurance while officially on the diamond for league games and in traveling to and from the field.)

1950 – The First Season

'Little League' Final Rosters Are Announced

Final rosters for the Mount Vernon Little League were announced today by league president Andy Karl, as all four squads made their final pairings in preparation for the season openers at Longfellow Field Saturday.

The team rosters:

INDIANS
Davis, Tripodi, Cozza, Esemplace, Dunbar, Burke, Whitney, Monahan, Brienza, Nelson, Lupo, Capodicci, DeRosa, Thompson, Weaver, Cook, McCafferty, Galvano.

SHAMROCKS
Floratos, Ausiello, Capone, Casucci, Knox, Robertson, Kain, Morgan, Quinn, Sundberg, Johnson, Foltz, Montez, Eisler, Innechin, Harkins, Elia, Falco.

PIRATES
Ragnone, Hayes, Pagano, Nelly, Davenport, Burkhardt, Abbatecola, Cunningham, DeSimone, Meyers, Colantuano, Bald, Mann, Anderson, Cusick, Puccillo, MacIlvane, Silverman.

PANTHERS
O'Connor, DeDonato, Seltman, Foran, Zopes, Merigliano, Carozza, Casucci, Cioffi, Magarelli, Bossi, Stokes, Bianchi, Ruffalo, Allman, Steinrck, Boccardi, Groccia.

Little League First Game

The Box Scores

1st GAME

Pirates	ab	r	h	Panthers	ab	r	h
Hayes, 1b	3	0	1	O'Connor, ss	3	0	0
DeSimone, 2b	2	1	0	DeDonato, lf	3	0	2
Anderson, 2b	1	0	0	Seltman, 1b	3	0	0
Davenport, cf	3	0	0	Foran, c	3	0	0
Burkhardt, p	3	2	2	Zopes, cf	2	1	0
Abbatecola, rf	3	0	1	Allman, cf	1	1	0
Cun'ham, 3b	3	0	0	Merigliano, p	3	1	1
Meyers, c	3	0	1	Carrozza, 3b	2	1	2
Nelly, lf	2	0	0	Casucci, 2b	2	0	5
Ragnone, ss	2	0	1	Cioffi, rf	1	0	0
				Bianchi, rf	1	0	0
Totals	25	3	6	Totals	24	4	5

SCORE BY INNINGS
Pirates 2 0 1 0 0 0 3
Panthers ... 0 3 0 0 0 1 4

2nd GAME

Shamrocks	ab	r	h	Indians	ab	r	h
Sundberg, ss	4	0	1	Davis, rf	2	0	0
Johnson, 2b	4	0	0	Tripodi, ss	2	0	0
Foltz, rf	4	0	1	Cozza, cf	1	0	0
Montez, cf	3	0	0	Esemplace, lf	2	0	0
Eisler, c	3	0	0	Dunbar, 1b	2	1	0
Innecken, 1b	3	1	0	Burke, 3b	2	1	0
Harkins, lf	3	0	0	Whitney, 2b	2	0	0
Elia, 3b	2	0	0	Monahan, c	1	0	0
Ausiello, p	3	0	0	Thompson, c	1	0	0
Casucci, 3b	1	0	0	Brienza, p	1	0	0
				Capodicci, p	0	0	0
				DeRosa, cf	1	0	0
Totals	30	1	2	Totals	17	2	0

SCORE BY INNINGS
Shamrocks 0 0 0 0 0 1 1
Indians ...... 0 0 0 0 2 x 2

Umpires—John Branca, Zeke Jewell, Fred Nelson. Scorer, Len Boccardi.

Ed Carrozza of the Panthers slides safely home in Mount Vernon Little League's first game. Harry Meyers of the Pirates awaits throw. The Panthers won, 4-3, at Longfellow School field.

Major Leaguers give tips to youngsters before benefit game. Left to right: Don Cook, Eddie Miksis of the Brooklyn Dodgers, Tom McCafferty, Jim Steinrock, Ralph Branca of the Dodgers, Wayne Belardi of the Dodgers, Tom Nelly, Andy Karl, president and commissioner of the Little League.

1950 All Star Team: 1, Coach Joe O'Connor; 2, Charley Burkhardt; 3, Bob Capodieci; 4, Rudy Eisler; 5, Manager Bill Real; 6, Bob Ragnone; 7, Ralph Merigliano; 8, Ron Essemplace; 9, Wendell Thompson; 10, Coach Jeff Borelli; 11, Jack Foran; 12, Tony Montez; 13, Joe Monahan; 14, Charlie Sundberg; 15, Ron Innecken; 16, Phil Ausiello; 17, Ed Carrozza; 18, John Tripodi; 19, Bob DeDonato; 20, Steve Davis; 21, Don Whitney.

1950 – The First Season

The 1950 Shamrocks: 1, Phil Ausiello; 2, Johnson; 3, Fred Casucci; 4, Charlie Sundberg; 5, Johnny Robertson; 6, Ron Innecken; 7, Bruce Leaf; 8, J.J. Falco; 9, Rudy Eisler; 10, Willie Capone; 11, Tony Montez; 12, Mel Foltz; 13, Kain; 14, Manager Herb Stevens; 15, Coach Jeff Borelli; 16, Coach Bob Cassin.

This is to certify

is a member of either

PONY - LITTLE or MINOR LEAGUE BASEBALL TEAM

and is entitled to League Discount at this store on all baseball equipment purchased.

Stephen B. Acunto
MANAGER

TOM GODFREY
Sporting Goods Exclusively
MOUNT VERNON, N.Y.

8
1951 – Expansion

For most of us pre-teens growing up in 1951, we didn't have a worry in the world while our parents had their share of disillusionment. Just six years after World War II ended, America was rearming and planning air raid drills. About three millions Koreans were dead. American war dead stood at 15,000. It was a spring filled with significant events. General Douglas MacArthur was relieved of command in Korea and forced into retirement. Julius and Ethel Rosenberg were convicted of passing U.S. nuclear secrets to the Soviet Union and both are sentenced to death.

The sports world also portrayed some dark days. College basketball players were fixing games and shaving points. Baseball fans, meanwhile, saw the 1951 season get off to an unusual beginning. In April, 19-year-old Mickey Mantle was classified 4-F because of an infection in a leg bone. On May 1, he hit the first of 536 home runs in the American League. Picked to win the National League pennant, the New York Giants were in last place on April 29. In July, Brooklyn Dodgers manager Chuck Dressen said, "The New York Giants is dead." They weren't, just resting. A fellow named Willie Mays woke them up. He played with an enthusiasm that has never been duplicated. "To watch Mays play was to watch Rembrandt paint or Caruso sing," wrote one sportswriter. He turned the Giants around.

Led by feisty manager Leo Durocher and pitchers Sal Maglie and Larry Jansen, the Giants came from 13 games behind in August to tie the Dodgers at season's end. A three-game playoff came down to the bottom of the ninth inning in the third game. With the Dodgers ahead, 4-2, the Giants Bobby Thomson hit a three-run homer off of Ralph Branca to win the pennant for the Giants. It was "The Miracle of Coogan's Bluff."

For some us that event made us insane with grief. My lifelong friend Steve Matthews summed up what many of us felt that day. "October third 1951 leaves me with a very vivid and haunting memory. I was a nine-year-old walking back to my house on Gramatan Avenue listening to the game. Every home seemed to have the game blasting through their open windows. I cried as I heard that Bobby Thomson's home run beat my Dodgers to win the pennant. I have heard Giant announcer Russ Hodges radio call "The Giants Win The Pennant, The Giants Win The Pennant" hundreds of times since that late October afternoon. It still causes a chill through my body."

In Mount Vernon that spring there would be more new rookies playing Little League baseball. Interest in Little League baseball had grown so much that the league now expanded to eight clubs, an increase of four from its first season. The league would run two divisions with the divisional champs meeting for the league title in a playoff series. Little League's first year teams, Panthers, Pirates, Indians and Shamrocks consolidated into the National Division with Len Boccardi as League president. The four new additions, Orioles, Peacocks, Eagles and Owls competed in the American Division headed by Mike O'Connell.

The Indians were thought to have the edge on other clubs what with returning veterans like Johnny Tripodi, Guy Trafford, Joe Monahan, Don Whitney and Tom Neely. The Pirates had six returning players, including Harry Meyers and Joe Colantuono while nine veterans from the Panthers first year squad gave manager Bill Real a solid nucleus to work with. Standouts were Fred O'Connor and Roger Boccardi.

In what was to become almost a yearly ritual as many as three Little League youngsters would compete on the Happy Felton television show telecast before Brooklyn Dodgers games. The first three were Charlie Sundberg of the Shamrocks, John Tripodi of the Indians, and William Crockett of the Orioles. They competed against each other for the shortstop position before a Dodger-Giant game at Ebbets Field.

Twin Double Headers Mark Opening Day

May 19 – The season openers were marked by twin double-headers at Hutchinson Field with the four games preceded by a morning motorcade and pre-game ceremonies at the field that included music provided by the Nathan Hale School band. There was even a procession composed of the eight teams with their coaches and managers, a color guard and group of Little League mothers.

The longest game of the day was the Indians-Shamrock battle that lasted ten innings with the Shamrocks finally scoring a single run in the tenth to win 6-5. Joe Falco picked up the win. He was helped by Charlie Sundberg, Ron Innecken and Willie Capone who had two hits apiece. Guy Trafford took the loss. Joe Monahan led the hit parade.

In another game on Hutchinson Field No. 1, the Pirates defeated the Panthers, 5-2, despite a grand slam home run by Jimmy Steinrock of the Panthers. Bob Cusick was the winner and Roger Boccardi the loser.

On Hutchinson Field No. 2, Tom Miller of the Peacocks threw a no-hitter against the Owls but did not get credit for a shutout as walks and errors combined to produce three Owl runs. The Peacocks won 8-3. The Orioles easily beat the Eagles, 10-2, behind Dick Butchok's pitching. Charlie Luma took the loss.

Charlie Sundberg Two-Hits Panthers for Shamrocks Win

June 22 – Charlie Sundberg of the Shamrocks limited the Panthers to two hits to help his team take possession of first place with a 3-2 record. Sundberg won 1-0. His teammates parlayed four hits, several walks and Panther errors to score its one run.

In an American Division game, the Owls blasted the Orioles, 10-0, to gain a tie for first place with the Orioles. The Owls got 12 hits off of Dick Butchok and Bob Roberts, including doubles by Mickey Rinaldi, Wayne Wright and Bill Crockett. Wright, Bill Masucci, Charlie Luma and Mike Jessup had two hits apiece for the winners. Orioles first baseman Larry Bradford got three of the loser's four hits.

Shamrocks Maintain Lead, Rip Indians, 7-3; Owls Win

June 26 – The Shamrocks lengthened their first place lead in the National Division by beating the Indians, 7-3, at Longfellow Field behind Charlie Sundberg's pitching. The winners collected seven hits as Joe Casucci, Charlie Robertson and Nick Briglia had two apiece. Joe Kopfenstein paced the losers with two safeties.

In an American Division game, the Owls gained a first-place deadlock with the Orioles by blanking the Peacocks, 12-0, on Mike Jessup's two-hit hurling. Mike Rinadi, Wayne Wright and Charlie Luma led the winner's 13-hit barrage with three hits apiece.

Owls Trounce Eagles, 13-2

June 27 – The Owls beat the Eagles, 13-2, at Longfellow Field to gain undisputed possession of first place in the American Division. Charlie limited the Eagles to five hits. Bill Masucci homered to deep left field, doubled, and had a single for the winners. John Von Bargen homered and tripled in three plate appearances for the losers.

All-Star Teams Selected

July 19 – Little League All-Star teams from both the American and National Divisions were selected and compete in an effort to determine the squad that would represent Mount Vernon in the district playoffs in August.

Fourteen players and four reserves were named to each team by the league's managers and coaches at the home of President Andy Karl. Jeff Borrelli, George Fennell and Bill Real were named to manage the National Division, while Bill Costa, Tom Nelly and Bill Pahf would guide the American unit.

Players for the National Division include Joe Kopfenstein, Nick Brigilia, John Pagano, Joe Falco, Ron Innecken, Bob Cusick, Fred Casucci, Don Whitney, Charlie Sundberg, John Tripodi, Bob MacIlvane, Pat Ruffalo, Fred O'Connor and Joe Monahan. Joe Orlando, Harry Myers, Ed Carrozza and Joe Colontuono were the reserves.

In the American circuit, selections included Bill Masucci, Mickey Rinaldi, Charles Luma, Mike Jessup, Tom Miller, Joe Clark, Clarence Sommerville, Andrew DelRusso, Bill Crockett, Tom Nelly, Larry Bradford, John Roberts, Andrew Brooks and Richard DiNunzio. John Von Bargen, Walter Lee, Wayne Wright and Thomas Regan were reserves.

1951 – Expansion

Fred O'Connor and Ed Carrozza No-Hit Indians

July 23 – Fred O'Connor and Ed Carrozza each pitched three hitless innings as the Panthers blanked the Indians, 4-0. While one pitched his half of the no-hitter, the other served as catcher.

The Panthers did all their scoring in the fourth inning on five hits. The win was credited to O'Connor, since Carrozza took over in the bottom of that inning. Magarelli, Pat Ruffalo, and Joe Groccia had timely hits.

The Shamrocks maintained their first place deadlock with the Panthers by beating the Pirates, 6-3. The Shamrocks had an 11-hit outing in support of Charlie Sundberg's five-hitter. Fred Casucci, Ron Innecken, and Johnny Robertson contributed timely hitting. Casucci had two triples while Innecken and Robertson each had a triple and single. Pirate shortstop Bob MacIlvane contributed the evening's fielding gem when he caught a line drive by Sundberg and quickly tossed to first to double off Ed Martin.

Ron Innecken Celebrates Birthday With One-Hitter

The Shamrocks blasted their way into undisputed possession of first place in the National Division by steamrolling the Panthers, 15-0. Hurler Ron Innecken celebrated his birthday by tossing a one-hitter and hitting a three-run home run. He struck out seven. The Shamrocks collected 14 hits including a triple by Johnny Robertson and a double by Fred Casucci. The Shamrocks scored in every inning. It was their fifth win in six second round games.

In another National Division game, the Indians won their first second round game in six attempts. They nipped the Pirates, 3-2, although Pirate pitcher Bob MacIlvane limited them to two hits.

National Trounce Port Chester, 6-1, in District Opener

August 1 – Mount Vernon's National All-Stars took advantage of four Port Chester Nationals errors and added timely hits as they opened the Metropolitan District Little League playoff with a 6-1 trouncing of the home team at Corpus Christi Stadium in Port Chester.

The outstanding pitching of Ron Innecken, who was at his best with men on base, combined with the hitting of first baseman Joe Falco. That highlighted the victory before a home crowd of 300 fans, including more than 200 from Mount Vernon.

A four-run outburst in the third inning was all that was needed to drop the Port Chester team out of the running in the tournament. Two more runs in the sixth was icing on the cake.

In successive middle innings, Innecken wasn't scored on despite putting the first man at bat on third base. He retired the next three batters. He later got out of a bases loaded, no-out situation, with a lone run scoring.

Timely Tribute.....

The following tribute to Mount Vernon's Little League from a father of one of the players appeared in the local newspaper.

Dear Sir:

The turning off of the lights at Hutchinson Field last night marked the closing of the 1951 season of the Little League of Mount Vernon. I was sorry to see it end.

The past year saw my son experience practically all the emotions that will remain constant during his lifetime; hope when he attended the Spring tryouts, pride when he was chosen for one of the teams, disappointment when he to sit on the bench as an un-uniformed substitute during the early season games, ambition when he strived to improve that situation, exultation when he got his first hit, and pain when he got his first baseball-connected "black eye." His mother and I suffered with him through the low spots – he suffered the "black eye" alone – and, in turn, enjoyed the reflected glory of his increased poise and moderate success. Unquestionably, he profited from the experience.

The men who are giving so much of their time to making the Little League program work cannot be praised or thanked too much. From personal observation and close association, I have found them to be selflessly interested in what they are doing to help our boys. The limited funds available to them are being used wisely to teach our youngsters to be good sports, to shoulder bats and to throw baseballs, in contrast to some other countries where boys of comparable ages are being taught to hate, to shoulder guns and to throw grenades.

Sincerely yours,
JOHN H. DOYLE

Panthers Win Exhibition Game Against Clinton, CT

The Panthers walloped the Clinton Connecticut Lions 12-2, in an exhibition game at Hutchinson Field.

Freddie O'Connor and Earl Ford were on the mound for the Panthers and scattered five hits. O'Connor aided his own cause with a homer in a seven-run fourth inning. Other extra base hits included a triple by Steve Kessler and doubles by Richard Caldwell and Kenny Doyle. The Panthers banged out 15 hits.

Plans were made by Panthers manager Bill Real for a home-and-home exhibition series. Both clubs entered a league composed of 14 county teams. The Lions finished second. After the game, played before a crowd of 300 fans, both teams were treated at O'Connell's Restaurant.

Owls Beat Shamrocks, 5 to 2, Deadlock Series

August 27 – Mickey Rinaldi pitched five and two-thirds innings of no-hit ball as his American League Owls defeated the Shamrocks, 5-2, to even the Little League World Series at two games apiece.

Rinaldi was in control as he kept the Shamrocks from hitting the ball past the infield until the sixth inning while striking out eight batters and walking four. In the sixth, after two out, a walk was followed by two singles to centerfield and a double to leftfield, which accounted for the Shamrocks two runs. But Rinaldi bore down and struck out Bruce Leaf to end the inning.

The Owls scored two run in the second inning on three hits. Mike Jessup led off with a single to centerfield. Bruce Gray followed with a line single to left scoring Jessup, who had stolen second base. Gray moved to second on the throw home. Donny Niese, a 10-year-old second baseman, drove Gray home with a single to centerfield. Niese also turned in the fielding gem of the game when he robbed Ron Innecken, the losing pitcher, of a base hit. Innecken slapped a hard grounder between first and second that was labeled "hit," but Niese dove for the ball and while on the ground flipped to first to nip Innecken.

Two more runs were added in the next inning on a pair of singles, a walk and a double by Bruce Gray. The final run scored in the fifth inning as Jessup led off with a single and came home on a single by Wayne Wright.

Shamrocks Capture City Little League Crown By Trouncing Owls, 7 To 1

Sundberg Scatters Six Hits In Final Contest Of Series

By JIM CAPPARELLI

Charlie Sundberg registered his second win in the Little World Series as he led Shamrocks to a 7-1 win over Owls to capture Mount Vernon Little League Championship. The game was played last night at Hutchinson Field before a crowd of approximately 600 persons.

Sundberg, weighing only 80 pounds, was an example of cool proficiency as he toiled on the mound. The twelve-year-old Graham School pupil displayed good control as he walked only two batters in six innings. He ran into trouble twice during the final game and in each instance bore down to escape without any harmful damage.

Sundberg sided his own cause with a single in the fourth inning to drive in two runs. Nick Briglia and Joe Falco drove in two runs apiece for the victors.

Five of the Shamrocks' runs were unearned, due to sloppy fielding. Shamrocks scored in the first frame on a walk, a brace of errors after two were out, and Briglia's line single to left field. Two more runs were added in the top of the third inning. Joe Orlando led off with a double to left field and Innecken walked. Both runners advanced on a wild pitch and both scored as Falco drilled a hit to left.

The game, which had started at 6:45 P.M., was halted at this point and transferred to Hutchinson Field No. 1 to be continued under the lights. After a delay of about 30 minutes, action resumed.

Charlie Luma and Mike Jessup Wright was safe on a fielder's choice to load the bases with one away. Luma was retired at home on Dom Guarino's slow bounder. Jessup scored on a wild pitch.

With a big inning in sight, Sundberg settled down and struck out Donny Neise to end the frame. Owls got two men on in the top half of the sixth inning with two outs but Johnny Alba struck out to end the game.

Sundberg, in going the distance walked one man and struck out four as he scattered six hits. Dom Guarino started for Owls and was relieved by Luma in the fifth inning. Guarino was the losing pitcher.

The box score:

Owls	ab	r	h	Shamrocks	ab	r	h
Niese, 2b	2	0	0	Orlando, lf	3	2	1
Rinaldi, 1b	3	0	1	Sundberg, p	3	1	1
Masucci, 3b	3	0	1	Innecken, ss	0	2	0
DiNunzio, c	3	0	0	Falco, 1b	2	1	1
Luma, p-lf	3	0	1	Briglia, cf	3	0	1
Jessup, cf	3	1	2	Robertson, c	3	0	0
Gray, rf	2	0	1	Casucci, 2b	3	0	0
Wright, ss	3	0	0	Martin, rf	3	0	1
Guarino, p	2	0	0	Leaf, 3b	2	1	0
Alba, lf	1	0	0				
Totals	25	1	6	Totals	22	7	5

SCORE BY INNINGS

```
Owls      0 0 0 1 0 0—1
Shamrocks 2 0 2 3 0 x—7
```

Runs batted in—Sundberg 2, Falco 2, Briglia 2. Earned runs—Shamrocks 2. Left on bases—Owls 8, Shamrocks 4. Hits—5 off Guarino in 4 innings. Struck out—4 by Sundberg. Bases on balls—2 off Sundberg, 4 off Guarino. Wild pitches—Guarino 3. Passed balls—DiNunzio 3. Winning pitcher—Sundberg. Losing pitcher—Guarino. Umpires—Roseff, Rosenbaum, Francese.

Shamrocks, 1951 Little League Champions: 1, Eddie Quinn; 2, Fred Casucci; 3, Charlie Sundberg; 4, Coach George Fennell; 5, Richie Owens; 6, Willie Capone; 7, Ed Martin; 8, Ron Innecken; 9, J.J. Falco; 10, Bruce Leaf; 11, Manager Jeff Borelli; 12, Richie Madden; 13, Roy Larsen; 14, Nick Briglia; 15, Joey Orlando; 16, Johnny Robinson.

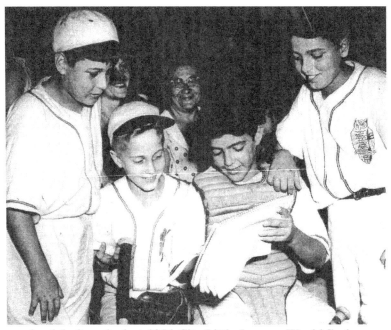

Looking over the scorebook before the last 1951 City Little League World Series game are (left to right) Shamrocks catcher Johnny Robertson and pitcher Charley Sundberg, Owls catcher Dick DiNunzio and pitcher Mickey Rinaldi.

Little League Baseball Clubs Complete Rosters

The team rosters:

PANTHERS

Adolph Carrozza, Al Pignataro, Claude Young, Steve Kessler, Adolph Ferro, Don Page, Matt Cennimi, Dick Caldwell, Art Rosenberg, Dick Deis, Ken Doyle, Bill Schwartz, Ray Schilke, Bob Rankenstein, Earl Ford, Dick Zipes, Ed Carrozza, Fred O'Connor, Patsy Ruffalo, Ernie Cioffi, Jim Stumock, Vernon Zipes, Frank Magarelli, Roger Boccardi, Joe Gioccia.

ORIOLES

Joe Adinaro, Frank Bisignano, Larry Bradford, Andy Brooks, Dick Butckok, Joe Carbone, Bill Crockett, Larry DiLunardi, Ronnie Gerst, Jackie Hess, Dennie Lee, Walt Lee, Frank Localzo, George Poccheance, Tom Pisano, Tom Regan, John Roberts, Marshall Romeo, Dick Siegel, Isaac Wellburn.

PIRATES

Joe Colantuono, Bob Cusick, Harry Meyers, Bob McIlvane, John Pagano, Bob Puccillo, John DeAngelis, Tony Sannicandro, Tom Phelan, Frank Jelinek, Phil Quaranto, Dick Giloth, Bob Scott, John Narducci, Don McMillen, Bob Palisi, Charlie Pellegrino.

OWLS

Charles Luma, Wayne Wright, Mike Rinaldi, Mike Jessup, Dom Guarino, Dick Maguire, Ronnie Chase, Ulisse Marino, Bill Masucci, Hubert Hanbold, Vinnie Colarusso, Marty Todtman, Don Neise, John Alba, Jerry Sarcone, Joe DiBello, Dick DiNunzio, Bruce Gray, Bob Brauner, Pat Kane, Bob Burak, Jim Powell, Don Smith.

INDIANS

Don Cook, Tom McCafferty, Fred Neise, John Tripodi, Mike Brienza, Don Whitney, Bill Weaver, Guy Trafford, Joe Monahan, Tom Neely, Jim Lyons, Joe Kopfensteiner, Jim Kopfensteiner, Billy Grazverde, Bob Gimes, Pete Rohlf, John Fontana, Bill Chavus, Patsy DiSimone, Clark Davis, Bob Heinsohn, Charles Colarusso, George Coleman, John Pignataro.

SHAMROCKS

Mike Briglia, Bob Owens, Jack Wyatt, Dick Madden, Ira Scharaga, Henry Jogell, Ed Martin, Werner Aguilor, Joe Orlando.

EAGLES

H. Allison, A. Stokas, A. Pelligrino, R. Heckett, H. Heckett, R. Eisler, W. Bianco, J. Tucello, A. DelRusso, T. Kelly, M. Shelflar, A. Trafford, F. Marcell, E. Motta, P. Klovekorn, E. Manfredonia, A. McVitty, J. Signarelli, G. Krakie, A. Messenger, F. Chessen, T. Doyle, F. Nelson.

PEACOCKS

T. Miller, J. Rywalt, T. McNamera, T. Mangone, M. Magone, M. Galvano, R. Cassio, J. Seagnelli, R. Schweitzer, S. Naclario, P. Schlosberg, J. Glaser, F. Cordo, R. Dobrish, E. Schimler, T. Pal-, J. Ferrara, J. Clark, J. Brophy, b. erville.

1951 – Expansion

1951 National League All Stars: 1, Joey Monahan; 2, Fred Casucci; 3, Charlie Sundberg; 4, Fred O'Connor; 5, Manager Bill Real; 6, Bob Cusick; 7, John Tripodi; 8, Joey Orlando; 9, Harry Meyers; 10, John Pagano; 11, Patsy Ruffalo; 12, Coach Jeff Borelli; 13, Joe Kopfensteiner; 14, Ron Innecken; 15, Nick Briglia; 16, Joe Colantuono; 17, J.J. Falco; 18, Bob McIlvane; 19, Coach George Fennell.

1951 American League All Stars: 1, Mike Jessup; 2, Tom Regan; 3, Charley Luma; 4, Wayne Wright; 5, Andy Brooks; 6, John Roberts; 7, Mike Rinaldi; 8, Joe Clark; 9, Bill Crockett; 10, Tom Nelly; 11, Walter See; 12, Andy Del Russo; 13, Larry Bradford; 14, Coach Bill Costa; 15, Manager Tom Nelly; 16, John VonBargen; 17, Bill Masucci.

9
1952 – Year of the Pitcher

Nineteen fifty-two was a year of many firsts even for some of the most famous who once called Mount Vernon home. E.B. White who grew up on Summit Avenue first published *Charlotte's Web. Publishers Weekly* listed the book as the best-selling children's paperback of all time. Dick Clark, who did as much as anyone or anything to advance the influence of teenagers and rock 'n' roll on American culture, made his debut on "American Bandstand" on ABC network stations in '52. He was born in Bronxville, moved to the Park Lane apartments at the corner of Lincoln and Columbus avenues, and graduated from A.B. Davis High School, well before Little League baseball found a home in Mount Vernon.

The year 1952 also gave Little League officials something to worry about. When a record 300 boys turned out for Little League tryouts on Saturday, April 14, league directors found themselves with only 10 pitching candidates and just five catchers. Despite that problem, the tryout at Hutchinson Field, handled by all the team coaches and directed by Andy Karl, Bill Real and Jeff Borelli, was the most encouraging in the league's three-year history. Altogether, there were 312 applicants.

League officials commented that this was the first time in their memory that so few candidates were interested in pitching and catching. As one coach said, "Used to be that they all wanted to pitch and especially catch. Now we haven't even got enough catchers for the pitchers, or enough pitchers, for that matter."

Popular *New York Mirror* newspaper sports columnist Jimmy Powers in his *The Powerhouse* column interviewed Andy Karl who said, "Usually they all want to be pitchers or catchers, but Saturday we discovered we had less than 10 pitching candidates and only four or five boys who want to try out for catchers."

Why was there a lack of interest in those positions. Simple, according to Powers, pitchers are as a rule poor hitters. Catchers get more chance to play, but most of the famous big-league hitters are outfielders. He went on to say that the Little League officials seemed to have a bit of a selling job on their hands to get pitchers and catchers.

The ironic part of this story is that if ever there was a "Year of the Pitcher" in Mount Vernon Little League's first decade, 1952 was that year. Pitchers like Larry "Goodie" Bradford, Davey Edwards, Fred O'Connor, Bob Cusick, Dickie Mergenthaler, and Tommy Miller would set the league on fire with their pitching exploits, particularly in tossing no hitters.

Interestingly, the 2012 major league campaign was one in which pitchers could take pride. Seven no hitters were thrown, tying the record for most in one season. But if there ever was "the year of the pitcher" it surely was 1968.

That year Bob Gibson set a modern earned run average record of 1.12 and a World Series record of 17 strikeouts in Game 1, while Series opponent Denny McLain of the Detroit Tigers won 31 regular season games, the only player to reach the 30 win milestone since Dizzy Dean in 1934. Mickey Lolich won three complete games in the World Series, the last player to do so. Luis Tiant of the Cleveland Indians had the American League's lowest ERA at 1.60 and allowed a batting average of only .168, a major league record. Hitting was anemic. Carl Yastrzemski of the Boston Red Sox had the lowest batting average of any league champion when his .301 was good enough for the American League batting title. Mount Vernon Little League batters faced their own "year of the pitcher" in '52.

Larry Bradford Opens Season With a No-Hitter

May 24 – Mount Vernon's Little League pitching onslaught began on opening day. Oriole pitcher Larry Bradford threw his way into the rare no-hit ranks by blanking the Owls, 6-0. In other opening day games, the Eagles beat the Peacocks, 3-1, on four hits. The Shamrocks edged the Panthers, and the Pirates routed the Indians, 7-1.

Actually the first pitch tossed on opening day at Hutchinson Field was thrown by Superintendant of Schools Jordan L. Larson who tossed the hardball to Police Chief William McDonald. Bradford took it from there. He racked up 14 strikeouts and walked only one batter. Only two Owls reached first base, one on a walk and the other on an error.

Tom Miller gave up only two hits as his Peacocks shut down the Eagles, 3-1. He recorded 14 strikeouts and walked two. Fred Corrado led the Peacocks hitting parade with two hits in three at bats, including a home run. Bob Cusick pitched a three-hit, 7-1 win for the Pirates over the Indians. Tony Sanacandra broke a fourth inning, 1-1, tie with a two run homer.

Despite the one-hit pitching of Fred O'Connor, the Shamrocks topped the Panthers, 5-4, on a lone run in the sixth inning. Ed Martin was the winning hurler, giving up six hits but walking only two batters. O'Connor struck out 13 batters but also walked 13.

Dave Edwards Sets Strikeout Record in No-Hitter

May 29 – Indians pitcher Dave Edwards set an unofficial Mount Vernon Little League record in striking out 16 Panthers while winning 6-2 at Longfellow Field. He pitched six innings without giving up a hit. He walked five.

O'Connor's No-Hitter Paces Little League

June 7– Pitching was the story of the four games played at Longfellow Field. Fred

O'Connor's no-hit no-run win for the Panthers over the Shamrocks, 2-0, was the gem. Bob Cusick of the Pirates and Dick Mergenthaler of the Indians both turned in no-hit performances in the same game. The Pirates won, 2-1, on an unearned run. Has that ever happened in the major leagues? On May 2, 1917 Chicago Cubs pitcher James "Hippo" Vaughn and his Cincinnati Reds counterpart, Fred Toney, each struck gold. Vaughn was the losing pitcher despite tossing nine no-hit innings. Toney did the same but won.

In other games at Longfellow, the Orioles blanked the Owls, 4-0, on the one-hit pitching of Joe Adinaro as the Peacocks shut out the Eagles, 5-0, on three hits.

Edwards Hurls 2nd No-Hit No-Run Game

June 14 – Dave Edwards pitched his second no-hitter, a 10-0 win over the Shamrocks. He struck out 13 and walked three. In the two six-inning regulation games he pitched, Edwards ran his strikeout total to 31. In another shutout, Fred O'Connor tossed a one-hitter for the Panthers in blanking the Pirates, 12-0. Patsy Ruffalo had a triple and double, went four-for-four, and drove in two runs.

Tuccillo and Tripodi Homers Help Indians Win

June 19 – Jimmy Tuccillo and John Tripodi provided the big bats for the Indians with each blasting home runs as the Tribe edged out the Panthers, 4-3. Dick Mergenthaler picked up the win giving up two hits. He struck out 11 batters and walked seven.

Bradford Hurls 2nd No-Hit, No-Run Game

June 20 – Larry Bradford of the Orioles did it again. He threw his second no-hitter of the season in beating the Orioles, 7-0, in a six-inning American League game. He struck out 11 and walked five. In addition to his pitching gem, Bradford was virtually the whole show at bat. In four trips to the plate, he hit two home runs and drove in six of his team's seven runs.

Bradford's mound opponent, Bill Bianco gave up 10 hits while striking out the same number.

Edwards Tosses 3rd Straight No-Hitter

June 22 – In the Major Leagues Johnny Vander Meer threw two successive no hitters. Davey Edwards of the Little League Indians did him one better. He pitched his third straight no-hitter but lost the game.

Bases on balls were his undoing. He issued four walks, with the winning run crossing the plate in the sixth inning when he walked Frank Cuomo. The Pirates won 4-3.

Indians third baseman Jimmy Tuccillo hit his second home run in two games to score all his team's runs. Bob Cusick won the game with a six-hit performance. In losing, Edwards raised his strikeout total to 40 in three games. The win gave the Pirates a commanding lead in the league standings with a 4-1 record.

In another National League game, the Shamrocks edged the Panthers, 8-6, with Ed Martin getting the win on an eight-hit performance. He struck out 10 and walked two. John Robertson was the hitting star for the Shamrocks with a triple and double, driving in four runs. Patsy Ruffalo paced the Panthers with a 300-foot home run and double. He drove in four runs.

In the American Division, Tom Miller tossed a two-hitter to lead the Peacocks to a 4-1 win over the Eagles. Art Messenger got both hits, a triple and home run. Joe Glaser lead the Peacocks with a triple and homer.

An outstanding relief pitching performance by Joe Adinaro helped the league-leading Orioles beat the Owls, 5-4. He came on in the fifth inning to shut down the Owls. He also had a triple.

League Leading Pirates Lose to Shamrocks

June 25 – The Shamrocks tripped up the lead-leading Pirates, 5-1, behind Bruce Leaf's two-hitter. A big fifth inning where the Shamrocks scored three runs on only two hits ensured the win. Ten walks off Pirates pitchers Ed Lombardi and Frank Jelinek helped get the win.

Left fielder George Crockett went three for three, banging out two doubles and a home run as the Orioles beat the Eagles, 7-4. Teammate Larry Bradford homered. Joe Adinaro won while giving up five hits.

Orioles Win First Round on Bradford's One-Hitter

June 26 – The Orioles assured themselves of the first round title in the American Division on 10-1 one-hit pitching by Larry Bradford. Bradford also fanned 13 Peacocks. His opponent Tommy Miller, who had previously won four in a row, gave up nine hits. Orioles catcher Tommy Nelly hit the game's only home run while Bradford tripled and George Pacchiana doubled.

In a National Division game, the Pirates defeated the Panthers, 4-2, in a contest that featured five extra-base hits, including a 300-foot homer by Patsy Ruffalo of the Panthers. A triple by Frank Jelinek with two aboard provided the margin of victory. Bob Cusick gave up three hits in the win, striking out eight and walking three. Fred O'Connor took the loss. He struck out eight and walked four.

Pitchers Dominate First Month of Season

June 27 – Three hurlers threw no-hitters during the first month of the season. They allowed an average of less than four hits per game and struck out nearly two of every three batters they faced.

The headliner early on was Indians pitcher Davey Edwards. The 12-year-old left hander relied on a fastball and was praised by his manager Steve Acunto as a pitcher who is "very cool and deliberate, never gets ruffled." Edwards didn't do anything to get ruffled about. In his first three games, he did not give up a hit. He made his first mound appearance just before Memorial Day and beat the Panthers, 9-2, striking out 16 for a record. In his next outing, he notched his second no-hitter beating the Shamrocks, 10-0, while striking out 13. He then posted a no-hitter, but lost to the Pirates, 4-3, as 11 walks hurt his cause. Through three games he had a 2-1 record, 38 strikeouts and 19 walks for the 18 innings he pitched. He also played first base in seven games and batted .400.

An equally impressive record was turned in by Orioles hurler Larry Bradford, a right-hander with two no-hitters and a batting average of .478. His manager Tom Nelly described Bradford "as exceptionally fast". Bradford also had a one-hitter and a two-hitter to his credit. His overall early season record was 4-1. In almost 33 innings of work he allowed but seven hits and had a league-leading 72 strikeouts while walking 22.

He opened the season on May 24 with a 6-0 no-hitter over the Owls. His lone loss came at the hands of Bill Bianco of the Eagles who beat the Orioles, 4-0. Four days later Bradford came back to beat the Peacocks, 6-0, with a two-hitter. That day he tied the league single game strikeout mark with 16. He gained revenge on the Eagles with his second no-hitter in winning 7-0 with 11 strikeouts. His final win was a 10-1 victory over the Peacocks that gave the Orioles the first-round title in the American Division. He also made a relief appearance. He batted .478 including three home runs.

Third of the no-hit, no-run trio early in the season was Fred O'Connor, whose dad, Joe was one of the Panthers coaches. Panthers manager Bill Real noted that Fred has good speed and a fine curve ball. Real pointed out that O'Connor "is probably the best catcher in both leagues." In 1952, O'Connor was in his third season of Little League ball. In 1951, he was a catcher for the Mount Vernon All-Star team that competed in the district playoffs.

O'Connor compiled a rather remarkable record during the first half of play pitching for the Panthers who were at the bottom of the National League standings. His pitching record was 2-3, but all three losses were close. He threw a one-hitter at the Shamrocks on opening day but lost, 4-3, on 13 walks. He tossed a no-hitter, beating the Shamrocks, 2-0, in seven innings, one more than the regulation game for Little League play. He then came back with a one-hitter in beating the Pirates, 12-0, striking out 11. Just before the mid-season break he lost another close game as the Indians beat him, 4-3. on a two-hitter by Dick Mergenthaler. O'Connor gave up six hits. He suffered his third loss, a 4-2 defeat by the Pirates on a three-hitter by Bob Cusick. O'Connor caught when he didn't pitch. He had an even .400 batting average for the first half.

The top winner in both the National and American divisions was Bob Cusick, a left hander who pitched for the Pirates. He won all five of his team's games and was instrumental in getting the Pirates to the top of the National Division. His coach Carmine Casucci said, "He has the best form in the league. He throws hard, has a good fastball and a natural curve."

Cusick allowed only 16 hits in five games while striking out 40 and walking 22. He won his first game, 7-1, his second, 10-4. On June 8, he pitched a no-hitter, striking out 10, to beat the Indians, 2-1. In that same game, Dickie Mergenthaler of the Indians also tossed a no hitter, but lost. That is a rare occurrence even in the Major Leagues. On April 23, 1964, Ken Johnson of the Houston Colt .45s became the only pitcher to lose a complete game no-hitter in nine innings when he was beaten 1-0 by Cincinnati. The winning run was scored by Pete Rose in the top of the ninth inning via an error, groundout, and another error. Cusick batted .333 on 15 trips to the plate.

Another no-hitter pitcher was Mergenthaler, Edwards' teammate on the Indians. The 11-year-old was described by his manager Acunto as "a good curve-baller, a tricky pitcher with a lot of stuff." He was the youngest of the pitching standouts. In four starts, he had a 1-3 record but allowed 11 hits in those 24 innings. He had a no-hitter and two-hitter. He lost his opener 7-1, to the Pirates and two weeks later lost to them again, 2-1. He won his first game, beating the Panthers, 4-3, with a two-hit effort. He lost his third game despite a four-hit pitching effort.

Tommy Miller of the Peacocks was also a pitching star in the American League. The 12-year-old was called by his manager Larry Tracy "a courageous pitcher with a good fastball and excellent control." He had a 4-1 record at the half-way mark without throwing a no-hitter. In his first two starts, he barely missed, beating the Eagles, 3-1, with a two-hitter on opening day and followed that up with a three-hitter in beating the Eagles again, 5-0. He won another game but saw his winning streak end with a loss to Larry Bradford's Orioles.

During their exploits in the first half of the season, these pitchers were threatened regularly by at least four other hurlers. They included Eddie Martin of the Shamrocks who had a 3-1 record while allowing 27 hits; Dom Guarino of the Owls, 1-3, who gave up 26 hits; Bill Bianco of the Owls, 2-2, with a two-hitter; Joe Adinaro of the Orioles, finished with a 3-1 record.

Peacocks and Pirates Triumph

June 30 – The Peacocks took advantage of only two hits into a six-run fifth inning in edging out the Owls, 8-7. In another game, the Pirates turned back the Shamrocks, 6-1.

The Peacocks were trailing, 7-2, when they exploded for six runs. Mike Mangone picked up the win. Pirate hurler Bob Cusick scattered three hits, allowing the only Shamrock run of the game in the first inning. Third baseman Frank Cuomo scored twice for the Pirates and chimed in with a hit.

Mergenthaler Does It Again, No Hits Pirates

July 1 – Dickie Mergenthaler of the Indians had sweet revenge against National League nemesis, the Pirates. He pitched his second no hitter of the season in beating the Bucs who had three times defeated the Indians in first round play. Tom Pisano meanwhile hurled the Orioles to a close, 3-1, win over the Owls in an American Division second round opener. The game was decided on a tie-breaking and winning run in the sixth inning.

Bill Bianco Blanks Peacocks

July 2 – Bill Bianco held the Peacocks to one hit as his Eagles shutout their American Division challenger. Bianco helped his own cause, going two-for-two, while scoring a pair of runs. Right fielder Chessun helped out by scoring a run and getting two hits.

A single by Gene Masucci and a triple by Fred O'Connor helped give the Panthers a two run first inning lead which the Shamrocks failed to overtake. O'Connor won 3-2 giving up only two hits.

Bradford Pitches Third No-Hitter

July 11 – Larry Bradford of the Orioles continued to amaze and confound Little League batters by adding a no-hit win to his pitching accomplishments. He defeated the Eagles, 9-1. Bradford already had two no-hitters, a one-hitter, and one two-hitter. Against the Eagles he struck out 10, walked 11 and went the distance.

Eagles starting pitcher Bill Bianco struck out six, walked seven and didn't give up a hit in his three innings of work. The big blast of the game was a triple by Joe Adinaro of the Orioles in the fourth inning, driving in two runs.

Shamrocks Move into First Place

July 18 – The Shamrocks knocked off the Indians, 8-1, giving them undisputed possession of first place in the National League and dropping the Indians into second. The Shamrocks got only three hits but took advantage of 10 bases on balls and three hit batsmen. Control pitching was what Eddie Martin was all about. He did not walk a single batter. He gave up six hits and had five strikeouts. The Shamrocks broke open the game in the third inning with a six-run rally.

Bases on balls also figured in the Owls 13-2 win over the Eagles. The Owls picked up 11 walks. Mike Jessup hit a grand-slam homer to ice the win. Darkness called a halt after three and a half innings, long enough to make the game official. Dom Guarino won the game.

American and National League All-Star Team Named

July 23– Two Mount Vernon Little League All-Star teams were announced to compete in a 10-team New York Metropolitan District tournament.

National Division players named to the squad were, from the Indians, infielder Johnny Tripodi, pitcher-first baseman, Dave Edwards, infielder Neil Arena and outfielders Jim Tucillo and Jim Kopfensteiner. Shamrocks pitcher-infielder Ed Martin, infielders Steve Brindisi and Bruce Leaf, catcher John Robertson and outfielder Roy Larson.

Panthers were represented by pitcher-catchers Fred O'Connor and Roger Boccardi, infielders Patsy Ruffalo, Steve Kessler and Joe Groccia. Pirates named were pitcher-first baseman Bob Cusick, catcher Howard Meyers and infielder-outfielder Frank Jelinek. The club was managed by Bill Real assisted by Jeff Borelli and Joe Tripodi.

The American League squad was managed by Tom Nelly with help from Bill Paff and Bill Costa.

The squad included, from the Eagles, pitcher-infielder Bill Bianco, catcher Don Cook, outfielder Alex Stokas and infielder Art Messenger. Peacock players were pitcher-infielder Tommy Miller and infielder Fred Corrado. The Owls delegation included catcher-outfielder John Alba, first baseman-outfielder Charley Luma and outfielder Mike Jessup. Orioles on the squad were pitcher-first baseman-outfielder Joe Adinaro, outfielder George Pacchiana, infielder Tom Regan, pitcher-first baseman Larry Bradford and catcher-outfielder Tom Nelly.

American League Blasts Ossining in Tournament Play

August 5 – Behind the two-hit pitching of Tommy Miller, the Mount Vernon Americans reached the Little League District finals by beating the Ossining Nationals, 7-1. Miller's pitching combined with the slugging of Tom Nelly Jr., Larry Bradford, Joey Adinaro and Freddie Corrado were the difference. Nelly scored two runs and had a double and two singles.

Americans Rip Nationals, 6-2 in LL All-Star Tilt

August 8 – More than 1,000 fans sat in on all All-Star Benefit twin-bill of baseball and softball at Hutchinson Field. In the preliminary game, tournament All-Star units from both of the city's Little League divisions met for the second year in a row. The Nationals pushed across single runs in the first and fourth innings to take a 2-0 lead, but the Americans blew the game open in the fourth inning with four runs.

The initial run for the Nationals came on a pair of infield errors and a walk. The second run came in the fourth when Bill Bianco took over the pitching and walked the first batter and then threw a wild pitch sending the runner to second. An infield error pushed the runner, Davey Edwards to third, and he scored on Ed Martin's fielder's choice.

In the bottom of the fourth, with Edwards pitching, two walks paved the way for the four run Americans tally. After retiring a batter on a strikeout, Edwards walked Larry Bradford to load the bases. Tommy Nelly then drove two home with a single, tying the game. After Fred Corrado struck out, Tom Regan drove in two runs on a fielder's choice.

The final two runs came in the fifth inning for the Nationals, both off Freddie O'Connor. With two out, Joe Adinaro walked, and Donny Cook doubled Adinaro home. Bradford's singled scored Cook to make it 6-2, and the game was called in order to get the featured game started.

Edwards Throws Fourth No-Hitter

August – Southpaw Dave Edwards of the Indians pitched his fourth no-hitter of the season as he beat the Pirates, 3-1. He struck out seven and walked three. The Indians scored early. Neil Arena and Vinny Carosella walked. Arena was out trying to score on John Tripodi's single. Singles by Jimmy Kopfensteiner and Art Ettinger knocked in three runs.

Kopfensteiner got his second hit and the game's only extra-base hit when he tripled in the third inning. He was stranded at third.

In an American League game, the Peacocks edged the Orioles, 5-4, on nine hits. Larry Bradford tripled and Tom Nelly and Tommy Regan each doubled for the losers while Miller doubled for the Peacocks. Mike Mangone picked up the win.

Fred O'Connor Highlights Twin Bill at Longfellow

August – Fred O'Connor threw a two-hit, 7-0, shutout for the Panthers over the Pirates. He and Patsy Ruffalo had two hits. In another American League game, the Peacocks won their first game of the second round by beating the Orioles, 8-5. The Orioles were previously undefeated in three starts. Tom Miller picked up the win and Bob Bradford took the loss.

Shamrocks Top Pirates, 3-0, in Pitching Duel

August 14 – The National League Shamrocks whipped the Pirates, 3-0, in an outstanding pitching duel. Each squad had only five hits and both pitchers control was near-perfect. Bob Cusick was the loser despite fanning 12 and issuing two walks. Ed Martin, the winner, did not yield a single walk as he struck out six. Martin was in all likelihood the only Mount Vernon Little League pitcher in 1952 who did not walk a single batter in a game. He did it twice. Against the Pirates he was never in trouble.

The Orioles trounced the Eagles, 8-4, in American League action, scoring two runs in each of the last four innings. Tom Pisano, who struck out 11 and walked eight, was the winning hurler. Bill Bianco took the loss. Joey Adinaro and Larry Bradford hit doubles for the Orioles while Don Cook contributed a double and single for the Eagles.

Panthers and Shamrocks Continue Pennant Fight

August 17– The Panthers and Shamrocks stayed in the pennant hunt together with each getting decisive wins over second division opponents. The Panthers blanked the Indians, 6-0 while the Shamrocks edged out the Pirates, 6-3.

The Shamrock-Pirates game was called after four-and-a-half innings because of darkness. Fred Casucci led the hit parade for the Shamrocks with a single and a double. Carmine DeNisco did the same for the Pirates. Bruce Leaf picked up the win, allowing five hits and issuing only one walk. Bob Cusick was saddled with the loss.

The Panthers breezed with scoring one run in the first and three in the third. Freddy O'Connor and Roger Boccardi combined for the shutout. The Indians started Tom Ambrosino. He looked good early.

Panthers Rip Shamrocks for First Place Tie

August 20 – Freddy O'Connor of the Panthers did it all as he led his Panthers teammates to a 7-5 win over the Shamrocks that pulled the Panthers into a first place tie with the Shamrocks in the National League race.

Besides throwing a four-hitter, O'Connor hit a home run and two triples in four at bats. He drove in five runs and scored two himself. It was O'Connor's second win in two days. The night before he beat the Pirates, 4-0.

O'Connor received support from Joe Groccia who went four for four. Eddie Martin took the loss for the Shamrocks despite throwing a complete game, striking out 12 and issuing only two walks.

In an American League game, the Owls scored all their runs in the second inning in winning 6-2 over the Peacocks. John Alba hit a double and Ronnie Epps tripled to pace the Owls.

Pirates Bow to Shamrocks

August 22 – The Shamrocks moved into first place in the National Division by beating the Pirates, 3-2. The winners ran their season record to 7-2 and took a half-game advantage over the Panthers.

The Shamrocks scored first in a unique way. In the second inning when, with Roy Larson on third base, Pirate pitcher Frank Jelinek was blinded by a cloud of dust. He balked in the run. The Pirates however took a 2-1 lead in the top of the fifth inning when Tom Phelan homered with Carmine DeNisco aboard.

The Shamrocks came right back with two runs. Steve Brindisi singled. John Robertson reached first on an error and Ed Quinn doubled both home. Bruce Leaf of the Shamrocks limited the Pirates to two hits.

Panthers Tie for First With Win

August 25 – Behind Patsy Ruffalo's hitting and Freddy O'Connor's pitching the Panthers defeated the Pirates, 4-1, to move back into a first place tie with the Shamrocks in the exciting National League race. Both team had 7-2 records.

The Panthers and Shamrocks were to meet the next day in a one-game playoff. The winner would face the Pirates, who won the first round title, in a battle for the right to represent the league in the Mount Vernon's Little League World Series. The Orioles clinched the American League crown.

In the first inning, Patsy Ruffalo homered to center field off Bob Cusick to put the Panthers ahead 3-0. O'Connor threw a no-hitter into there were two out in the sixth inning. Bob Cusick hit a fastball into right-center field for a home run, his club's only hit of the night. O'Connor fanned eleven and walked three.

Panthers, Shamrocks Battle to 6-6 Playoff Tie

August 27 – The Panthers and Shamrocks, who wound up with the same 7-2 second round records in the National Division, played to a no decision in what was to have been a playoff for the right to face the Pirates for the Little League championship. The game was called because of darkness after seven innings, with the score tied 6-6. They would meet again to find a champion.

The Panthers scored first in the first inning when Steve Kessler walked. He moved to third on an error and scored on Patsy Ruffalo's single. The Shamrocks scored three runs in the bottom of the first on a walk to Ed Martin, successive singles by Fred Casucci and Steve Brindisi, a walk to Roy Larson and a double by Bruce Leaf.

The Shamrocks increased the lead in the second to 4-1 when Casucci's single brought home Martin, who had walked and reached third base on an error. The Panthers tied it up at 4-4 in the third inning. Kessler, Joe Groccia and Ruffalo single for two runs and then Ruffalo stole home, sliding under the tag of Shamrock catcher Johnny Robertson.

The Panthers scored twice in the top of the fifth to go ahead 6-4. Walks to Tom Cowen and Groccia and a single by Freddie O'Connor contributed to the score.

The Shamrocks in the top of the sixth scored twice when Panthers pitcher Roger Boccardi walked home two runs. With the winning run on third and only one out, Boccardi struck out the next batter.

Then came the play of the game as Bruce Leaf tried to score on a short passed ball but missed home plate and was tagged out after a scramble with catcher O'Connor and Boccardi. Shamrock second baseman Casucci made an outstanding grab of a Ruffalo line drive in the top of the seventh inning with two men on base to halt the last real rally of the game.

Panthers End Shamrocks Season

September 2 – Mount Vernon's 1951 Little League champion Shamrocks ran out the string and saw their 1952 season end. Scoring three runs in the bottom of the fifth, the Panthers beat the Shamrocks, 4-1, to win the National Division playoff and the right to meet the Pirates in a two-out-of-three series for the season crown. The winner would face the American Division titlist, the

Orioles, in the World Series final.

Earlier in the week, the Panthers and Shamrocks battled to a 6-6 tie and another deadlock loomed until the Panthers scored in the fifth inning. Ken Doyle started the rally with a walk. Bill Masucci reached first on an error and both scored when Gary Munsterman and Roy Larson in right field collided while chasing Steve Kessler's second triple.

Kessler scored the final Panthers run on Fred O'Connor's double. All five of the Panthers hits off Bruce Leaf were for extra bases, two triples by Kessler, a double and triple by O'Connor and a double by Joe Groccia.

Kenny Doyle, making his first start, teamed with O'Connor to limit the Shamrocks to two hits, a single by Fred Casucci and double by Johnny Robertson. The Panthers scored first in the bottom of the first inning when Kessler and O'Connor hit back to bat triples after two were out.

The Shamrocks got their run in the top of the third when Eddie Martin walked, moved to second on a balk and came home on Casucci's single. It was the only hit given up by Doyle.

Panthers Beat Pirates, 3-1; Lead NL Title Series

September 3 – The Panthers whipped the Pirates, 3-1, to take a 1-0 lead in the two-out-of-three series in the National Division championship. The Panthers scored first in the top of the third inning when Ray Schilke and Kenny Doyle got on via a walk and an error. They advanced a base each on a passed ball and scored on pitcher Freddie O'Connor's two-out single.

Those runs were enough for O'Connor who pitched a sterling one-hitter. He has been making the difference for the Panthers all season, beating the Shamrocks with a 4-1 two-hitter in the first half playoff.

The Panthers added another run in the fifth with Schilke scoring on four successive walks by Bob Cusick. The Pirates scored in the bottom of the fifth. First baseman Frank Jelinek led off with a double, the only hit off O'Connor. He went to third base on a passed ball and scored while Ed Lombardi, who had walked, was thrown out at second on an attempted steal. Lombardi's walk was the only one yielded by O'Connor, who struck out 12.

Pirates Rout Panthers, 11-1, Tie Playoffs

September 4 – Frank Jelinek pitched a four-hitter as the Pirates easily beat the Panthers, 11-1, to deadlock the National Division playoff at one game apiece.

The winners raked three Panther pitchers for 14 hits. They scored three times in the second inning. Walks to Harry Meyers and Johnny DeAngelis, followed by a fielder's choice and singles by Butch DeNisco and Frank Cuomo accounted for the scores. The Bucs followed that up with four more runs in the third on singles by Jelinek, Ed Lombardi, John Narducci and an error. Four more runs crossed the plate in the fifth inning on singles by DeNisco, DeAngelis, Cusick, and Lombardi, and a walk to Cuomo and a double by Jelinek.

The Panthers scored their only run in the bottom of the fifth inning when Patsy Ruffalo singled. Tom Cowen walked and Roger Boccardi and Steve Kessler hit back-to-back singles.

Pirates in World Series on Lombardi's Pitching

September 6 – The Pirates won the National Division pennant. They beat the Panthers, 2-0, in the rubber game of their pennant playoffs.

Ed Lombardi pitched a one-hitter in the playoff game enabling the Pirates to face the Orioles, who won both rounds of American Division play.

City's 2 LL Tournament Teams Win District Quarter-Finals

Mount Vernon's two entries in the metropolitan district Little League tournament won opening victories in quarter-final games at Nyack and Harrison fields. The Americans beat Nyack, 9-0, behind Bill Bianco's two-hit pitching, while the Nationals had a tougher time in beating Harrison, 7-4.

Bianco allowed only four base-runners all day. He struck out 12 and walked two. He got timely hitting from his teammates. In the first inning, Art Messenger walked, Tommy Nelly reached first base on an error, and Mike Jessup drove the first run home. Joe Adinaro's sacrifice fly to center scored the second run.

Mount Vernon picked up four more runs in the third inning. Nelly opened with a single, Jessup walked, and Larry Bradford tripled both runners in. He scored on Adinaro's hit. A walk to Bianco forced in the fourth run of the inning. Three more runs crossed the plate in the fourth inning. Adinaro singled one run in and Tommy Miller rapped a grounder to shortstop to drive in another run. Fred Corrado singled in the final run.

The Americans shortstop Tommy Regan of the Orioles had a busy couple of days. Along with the Nationals Steve Brindisi of the Shamrocks and Joe Groccia of the Panthers, Regan appeared on the "Happy Felton Knot-Hole Gang" which was broadcast 30 minutes before Brooklyn Dodgers home game. Felton had a different Dodger star work out with and tutor the youngsters who came from hundreds of youth leagues in the New York metropolitan area. Regan edged out his teammates in a brief trial supervised by the Dodgers Pee Wee Reese. Regan returned the next day to meet the Dodgers in the dugout and collect an autographed baseball, plus pointers from second baseman Jackie Robinson.

In the other tournament game, five Harrison errors and 14 Mount Vernon walks helped Mount Vernon's Nationals win 7-4. Bob Cusick picked up the win and had relief help from Fred O'Connor.

The Nationals scored in the second. A walk to Patsy Ruffalo and wild pitch set up the first run with the run scoring when Frank Jelinek's shot to left field resulted in a wild throw. Jim Tueillo's bunt single sent Jelinek to third but he was caught trying to score on a wild pitch. Johnny Tripodi walked with the bases loaded to drive in another run. The Nationals picked up another run in the fourth. Harrison scored two in the third but Mount Vernon pulled away again in the fourth. Tripodi doubled Bob Cusick home and came home himself moments later on Fred O'Connor's double.

In the fifth inning, Cusick loaded the bases with no out. That brought O'Connor out to the mound after he shed his shin-guards and catcher equipment. He got out of the inning while only giving up one run. In a nail biting last inning on the final pitch, the Harrison batter blooped a ball between first and second base. Neil Arena trapped the ball but slipped in the process. Throwing while on the wet ground, Arena pegged the runner out at first to end the game.

Pirates Win National League Championship

September 6 – Behind Ed Lombardi's one-hit pitching, the Pirates captured the third playoff game from the Panthers, 2-0, to win the National Division title and the right to play the Orioles in a three-out-of-five World Series for the Mount Vernon Little League championship.

Never in trouble, Lombardi was constantly ahead of the batters and issued only walk while striking out six. Roger Boccardi went three innings for the Panthers, allowing five hits, two walks, while striking out two. Fred O'Connor took over in the fourth inning and limited the Pirates to only one hit. The Pirates scored first in the second inning when Frank Jelinek singled, was sacrificed to second base, reached third on a wild pitch and scored on an error. Another run came across in the third on successive singles by Bob Cusick, Jelinek and Lombardi.

550 Salute 'Graduating' Little, Pony League Players

September 8 – Honoring some 50 graduates of the Mount Vernon Little and Pony Leagues, more than 550 youngsters, parents and friends gathered at the State Armory.

The star-studded audience included Brooklyn Dodgers pitcher Ralph Branca and Yankee official Jackie Farrell. Branca urged the youngsters to realize the value of the fine coaching they received in the Little and Pony League circuits.

Each graduate received certificates entitling them to engraved belt-buckles. Making the presentations were Andy Karl of the Little League and Ralph Merigliano, vice president of the Pony Leagaue.

The hit of the evening was Little Leaguer Neil Arena who sang "Because of You" and "Anytime" in Johnny Ray style. Chairman of the dinner committee was Mrs. Edward Martin and assisted by co-chairmen Mrs. Michael Mangone, Mrs. Carmine Casucci, Bill Real, Joe O'Connor and Carmine Casucci. The program closed with a movie of the 1952 season with Larry Tracy providing commentary.

Game 1

September 9 – In the first game of the 1952 World Series, George Crockett's fourth inning single drove in Richard Siegel that gave the Orioles a 4-3 win over the Pirates.

Crockett's single, after Siegel had walked and taken second on a passed ball, broke a 3-3 tie. Larry Bradford went all the way for the win. He only gave up two hits and fanned 13. He was in a jam in the second inning when the Pirates scored their three runs. The rally was highlighted by pitcher Frank Jelinek's triple to left field. He scored on a wild pitch and then Bradford walked five in a row.

The Orioles rebounded in the third inning with three runs. Catcher Tom Nelly led off with a single. Joe Adinaro reached first base on an infield error and Tom Regan walked to fill the bases. That set the stage for the game's big hit.

Steve Kablesh, with one out, sliced a ball down the right field line for a bases clearing triple that tied the score at 3-3. Bradford regained his composure and gave up only one walk for the rest of the game. Kablesh and Nelly each had two hits.

Game 2

September 11 – The Pirates deadlocked the Little League World Series at one game apiece with a come from behind victory over the Orioles, 7-6. The Pirates scored five runs in the sixth inning on only one hit.

John Narducci and Tom Phelan started the rally by drawing walks from Orioles starting pitcher Joe Adinaro. Both advanced on a wild pitch before pinch hitter Joe Tripodi also walked to load the bases. Center fielder John DeAngelis hit a chopper through third baseman Tom Pisano's legs and two runs scored.

Catcher Tom Nelly took off his shin guards and came in as a relief pitcher. He immediately hit Mike Margolis. He recovered and struck out Bob Cusick and watched as replacement catcher Larry Bradford picked off Margolis.

Frank Jelinek was then intentionally walked to fill the bases. This strategy backfired when Nelly forced in a third run by hitting Ed Lombardi. Harry Meyers then drove in the tying and winning runs with a double to center field.

Orioles hopes for a comeback where quickly squelched in the bottom of the sixth inning when winning pitcher Cusick struck out the side.

Nelly took the loss even though his hitting put the Orioles into the lead in the first place. He went three-for-three at the plate, including two home runs. He also scored three of his team's six runs.

The Orioles scored first in the opening inning. Walks to George Crockett and Tom Regan, followed by singles by Nelly and Adinaro, and a passed ball accounted for two runs. The Pirates even the scored when Meyers homered to left field. That was followed by walks to Narducci, Tom Phelan, Carmine DeNisco, and John DeAngelis. That tied the score at two apiece.

Nelly put Orioles out in front with his first home run to left centerfield. Cusick then retired the side but not before Regan, who blasted a shot that got him to third, was called out for failing to touch second base. The Orioles made it 5-2 in the fourth, in an inning marked by the game's only double play. George Pacchiana started things by reaching first on an error. Steve Siegel and Dave Walsh followed to load the bases. Tom Pisano attempted to bunt, but Cusick scooped the ball up and threw Pacchiana out at home. A passed ball by Meyers then allowed Siegel and Walsh to score.

Nelly homered in the fifth, putting the Orioles up 5-2. Cusick bore down and retired the side, setting up the sixth inning rally. In pitching a complete game, Cusick struck out six, walked four, and gave up five hits.

Game 3

September 13 – The Orioles scored eight runs in the sixth inning to defeat the Pirates, 10-1, and take a 2-1 lead in the Little League World Series at Hutchinson Field.

Tom Pisano earned the win in throwing a four-hitter and keeping the Pirates off the scoreboard after the second inning. Pisano kept his fastball low and struck out 10 Pirates. The Orioles meanwhile got 10 hits off Pirates pitcher Ed Lombardi, including triples by Tom Regan and Larry Bradford.

The Orioles tied the score in the third when Pisano reached first on an error. He moved to second on Dick Siegel's sacrifice and came home on a single by Tom Nelly. They went up in the fourth 2-1 when Joe Adinaro got on by an error and scored on Regan's triple. That ended the scoring until the sixth inning when the Orioles broke the game wide open.

Nelly, with a year of Little League eligibility remaining, was the hitting star of the series to date. The 11-year-old who both pitches and catches was seven-for-eleven, getting at least two hits in each of the three games.

Game 4

September 15 – The Pirates scored eight runs in the seventh inning to tie the Little League World Series at two games apiece by beating the Orioles, 10-4.

League rules impacted the outcome of the game. Pitching regulations ruled that youngsters could not pitch more than nine innings in one week. Because of this, Joe Adinaro and Larry Bradford of the Orioles and Bob Cusick and Frank Jelinek of the Pirates could only pitch three innings each. As a consequence, Tom Nelly of the Orioles and Jim Forkell of the Pirates each pitched the extra inning and were the respective losing and winning pitchers.

The Pirates took the lead on a Bobby Meyers single in the first inning that scored Frank Cuomo. The Orioles tied it up in the bottom of the first when George Crockett tripled and scored when Nelly hit into a fielder's choice.

In the third inning, two walks, a sacrifice and wild pitch added another Pirates run. The Orioles deadlocked the game and sent it into extra innings in the sixth on Bradford's single. He stole second base and scored on a single by Tom Regan.

The Pirates broke the game open in the seventh inning. A walk, single, passed ball and error sent two runs home. A double and walk loaded the bases, and Mike Margolis was hit by a pitch to force in another run. A walk, single by John Dangles and a double by Cusick sent in five more for a 10-2 lead. The Orioles fought back in the bottom of the seventh but could only score two runs.

Game 5

September 18 – After a nine-inning, three-hour game the Pirates and Orioles finally had to call a halt with both clubs deadlocked at 3-3.

The game was to be the fifth and deciding game of the 1952 Mount Vernon Little League World Series. Each club had won two games, the Orioles winning the first, 4-3, and the third, 10-1, while the Pirates took the second, 7-6, and fourth, 10-4.

In the deadlocked 3-3 game, the Orioles jumped off to a 2-0 lead in the first inning, but the Pirates came back to score one in the third and two in the fifth and took a 3-2 lead. The Orioles tied it up in the bottom of the fifth. The game stayed even to the ninth inning before the game was halted at 9:30 pm, not because of darkness, the lights were long since turned on, but because the youngsters had school the next day.

Earlier, singles by George Crockett and Larry Bradford followed by a double by Tom Regan, scored two runs in the first inning to give the Orioles the lead. In the third inning, the Pirates got on the scoreboard because of two errors. Walks accounted for more Pirates runs in the fifth.

The first two batters walked, but one was erased on a fielder's choice. Frank Jelinek then walked to load the bases. A walk to Ed Lombardi forced one run in. After another fielder's choice, John Carducci walked, forcing in the second run.

Two walks started off the Orioles fifth inning with Joey Adinaro doubling in the tying run.

Pirates Topple Orioles, 13-10, To Win City

Ten Runs In Opening Inning Decide Crucial Sixth Game

Crashing through 10 runs in the 1st frame and then staving off a desperate fifth inning uprising, Pirates captured the City Little League crown Saturday by blasting Orioles, 13-10, in the sixth game of the series. Pirates, who had won the National division title, had mixed wins in the second and fifth games of the five-game series. The two clubs had battled to a nine-inning tie in what was supposed to have been the deciding game, Thursday.

The 10-run first inning for Pirates included four hits, seven walks, two hit batsmen and assorted other baseball doings, such as wild pitch, passed ball, stolen base and two strikeouts.

Starter Joey Adinaro allowed the first seven runs. Two walks, a hit batsman and a single by Lombardi scored the first run. Narducci's single sent in the second tally, and a walk to DeNiesco sent another home. A walk and hit batsman forced in two more, before Pisano came on in relief. A wild pitch and two more free tickets to first sent two more across the plate before Phelan finally made the first out attempting to score on a passed ball. Cusick struck out, but Jelenek doubled two in. A walk and stolen base, followed by Narducci's second straight single sent the 10th man home.

Two More In 2nd

Pirates added two more in the second on three walks, a steal of home by Phelan, another walk and a hit by Lombardi, scoring Forkell. Orioles gained their first runs in the third on three walks. Nelly and Adinaro did the scoring on a passed ball.

In the fifth, Orioles came up with eight runs to put the score at 12-10, with Pirates still in front. A single, followed by four walks forced in two of the tallies and sent Lombardi to the showers, with Jimmie Forkell relieving. Two more runs scored on an infield error, and another came in on two more passes. Adinaro's fly scored two more, while a single by Regan sent the eighth run of the canto home.

In the bottom of the fifth, Pirates scored their final run as Narducci walked, stole second, third and home.

In the sixth, Orioles went out via a strikeout, hit batsman and double play.

The box score:

Orioles	ab	r	h	Pirates	ab	r	h
Crocket, lf	4	1	0	DeAngeles, 3b	1	2	0
Nelly, c-1b	2	2	0	Cusick, 1b	2	1	1
Bradford, 1b	3	1	1	Jelenek, ss	1	2	1
Adinaro, p-2b	4	2	1	Lombardi, p-2b			
Regan, ss	2	1	1	Narducci, c	2	2	2
Pacheano, cf	1	0	0	DeNiesco, lf	3	1	0
Kaolish, rf	2	0	0	Markules, cf	3	1	0
Pisano, 3b-p	3	1	0	Phelan, rf	1	1	0
Bouchard, rf	1	1	0	Forkell, 2b-p	1	2	0
Siegal, 2b	1	1	0				
Totals	23	10	3	Totals	17	13	6

SCORE BY INNINGS
Orioles .... 0 0 2 0 8 0—10
Pirates .... 10 2 0 0 1 x—13

Two base hits—Bradford, Jelenek. Stolen bases—Nelly, Adinaro, Narducci (2), Jelenek, Phelan. Bases on balls—Off Adinaro (4); Pisano (8), off Lombardi (10), Forkell (2). Struck out—By Pisano (9); by Lombardi (4); Forkell (1). Hits—2 off Adinaro in 0 innings; 4 off Pisano in 6 innings, 2 off Lombardi in 5 1/3 innings, 1 off Forkell in 1 2/3 innings. Umpires—Jewel and Borelli.

Pirates, 1952 Little League Champions: 1, Bob Cusick; 2, Mike Margulis; 3, Tom Phelan; 4, Coach Joe Tripodi; 5, Coach Carmine Casucci; 6, Manager Frank Casucci; 7, Coach Jim Forkell; 8, Ed Lombardi, 9, Frank Jelinek; 10, John DeAngelis; 11, Pat Tucci; 12, Frank Cuomo; 13, Harry Meyers; 15, John DeNisco; 16, Jim Forkell, 17, Batboy Joe Tripodi.

No hitters reigned supreme early in the 1952 season. These hurlers threw them (left to right) Fred O'Connor, Tom Miller, Dick Mergenthaler, Bob Cusick, Davey Edwards, and Larry Bradford.

'Little League' Chooses 57 From 300 Baseball Aspirants

Newcomers to Mount Vernon's Little League baseball program, which starts its third season a week from Saturday, were announced today by Commissioner Andy Karl, following the recent "player auction" of the circuit.

More than 300 youngsters participated in tryouts for the league's eight teams, with some 57 selected on the clubs. The National League tapped 35, while the American League, which was organized last year, settled upon 22.

Of the National clubs, Indians chose 14, Pirates 8, Panthers 7, and Shamrocks 6. In the American loop, Owls picked 10, Orioles 5, Peacocks 4, Eagles 3.

In announcing the names of those selected, Commissioner Karl also issued the following statement:

"The fact that only 57 boys were picked from the large group which attended the recent tryouts is not an indication that the boys who were not successful lack ability. The managers were faced with the problem of filling a definite number of vacancies and had to be guided by certain limitations regarding the number of boys they can carry in each age group. The choice was difficult in many cases; some boys who showed above-average ability had to be passed up because there were no more openings in their age groups."

The selections by teams:

NATIONAL LEAGUE

Panthers — Edward Benentt, Thomas Cowen, Paul Stiller, Gilbert Chimes, Gene Masucci, Tom O'Shaughnessy, John Colema.n

Pirates — Frank Cuomo, Joseph Tripodi, Patty Fusco, Edward Lombardi, J. Farkell, Mike Margulis, Patsy Tucoi, Carmine DeNisco.

Shamrocks — Francis Amersang, Charles Hanin, Edward Bruno, J. Bourne, Gary Munsterman, Stephen Brindisi.

Indians — Thomas Ambrosino, Philip Duffey, Leo Stanazak, Anthony Silvestre, Joseph Russo, Larry Briglia, Anthony Petrillo, Vincent Burke, Vincent Carosella, Anthony Cioppa, Robert Romanino, Richard Mergenthaler, Arthur Ettinger, Earl Conti.

AMERICAN LEAGUE

Peacocks — Joseph Angello, Joseph Castro, Raymond Rohrs, Thomas Gherardi.

Eagles — William Bauersfeld, Thomas Shay, John Spina.

Owls — Marty Berg, Peter Dunsay, William Hansen, Anthony Savastano, David Smith, William Thomas, Anthony Bruni, Ronald Epps, Robert Fausel, William Huf

Orioles — Dominick De Angelo, Stephen Kablesh, Edward Kahn, Robert Meyers, David Walsh.

Coach Bill Real explains how to apply a tag at Little League tryouts. More than 300 youngsters turned out at Hutchinson Field.

1952 Indians: 1, Larry Briglia; 2, Bob Romanino; 3, Tony Petrillo; 4, John Tripodi; 5, Neil Arena; 6, Leo Stanazak; 7, Art Ettinger; 8, Jim Kopfensteiner; 9, Dave Edwards; 10, Jim Tuccillo; 11, Vincent Carosella; 12, Tom Ambrosino; 13, Joe Birsso.

1952 – Year of the Pitcher

1952 Shamrocks: 1, Richard Madden; 2, Eddie Martin; 3, Ed Bruno; 4, Steve Brindisi; 5, Fran Amorsano 6, Gary Munsterman; 7, John Bourne; 8, Bill Deemer; 9, Eddie Quinn; 10, Bruce Leaf; 11, Coach Jeff Borelli; 12, Coach George Fennell; 13, Roy Larson; 14, John Robertson; 15, Henry Jagels; 16, Fred Casucci.

1952 National League All Stars: 1, John Bennett; 2, Bob Cusick; 3, John Robertson; 4, Frank Jelinek; 5, Eddie Martin; 6, John Tripodi; 7, Neil Arena; 8, Roger Boccardi; 9, Jim Tucillo; 10, Jim Kopfensteiner; 11, Joe Groccia; 12, Jeff Borelli, manager; 13, Bill Real, coach; 14, Joe Tripodi, coach; 15, Patsy Ruffalo; 16, Dave Edwards; 17, Fred O'Connor.

1952 Panthers: 1, Bill Schwartz; 2, Roger Boccardi; 3, Joe Groccia; 4, Coach Jack Woods; 5, Coach Joe O'Connor; Manager Bill Real; 7, Patsy Ruffalo; 8, Fred O'Connor; 9, Kenny Doyle; 10, Earl Ford; 11, Al Pignataro; 12, John Benney; 13, Gino Carrozza; 14, Ray Schilke; 15, Michael Boccardi.

10

1953 – Orioles Take It All

Now entering its fourth season, Mount Vernon's Little League had more teams and more boys than ever before. Across the country Little League was also growing in popularity. In 1953, the Little League World Series was televised for the first time on CBS. Howard Cosell handled the play-by-play for ABC radio.

In '53, a New York team from Schenectady lost 1-0 to Birmingham, AL in the World Series finals. And did you ever wonder who was the first Little Leaguer who made it to the major leagues? He was Joey Jay, who played in Middletown, CT. He played his first game on July 21, 1953 for the Milwaukee Braves. He would go on to enjoy a 13 year big league career.

And once again in 1953, the New York Yankees took on the Brooklyn Dodgers in the World Series, and once again the Yankees would win, this time four games to two. It was the Yankees fifth straight World Series championship.

And also in '53 we no longer looked at Abner Doubleday as the inventor of baseball. That year historians finally agreed on who invented baseball, Alexander Cartwright.

On April 13, for the first time in 50 years, there was a new city in big league baseball, Milwaukee. The new team took over the Boston Braves franchise in the National League and lost its first game at Cincinnati, 2-0. Four days later, Mickey Mantle, hit a reported 565-foot home run, clearing the bleachers at Griffith Stadium in New York's win over the Senators. The next day Don Larsen made his big league debut. Three years later he would pitch the only perfect game in postseason and World Series history. Tommy Pisano, pitching for the Little League Orioles, would throw a no hitter of his own in the final game of the 1953 Mount Vernon World Series.

In early April more than 70 Mount Vernon officials, managers, and coaches of the Little and Pony leagues were honored by Mike O'Connell at his Blue Bell Restaurant at 253 East Third Avenue. By that time teams were organized and rosters were filled for the May 2 opening day. Both leagues in mid-April gave parents of youngsters who were playing an opportunity to learn more about the baseball programs at a specially called meeting at the restaurant.

Even youngsters who failed to make a Little League roster had something to cheer about in

'53. They found out that a Mount Vernon Minor Little League would run from April 25 through July 1. It would give more boys a chance to enjoy the Little League baseball program, and would serve as a "farm system" for the Little League clubs. Commissioner Andy Karl said players would wear T shirts supplied by the league and the league would run just like a regular minor league with players having the opportunity to move up to the Little or Pony Leagues. Two local firms, Lombardi Insurance Co., and F.C. Garrett Co. helped underwrite the new league.

There was more to celebrate in Mount Vernon in '53. The year marked the 100th anniversary since John Stevens, a merchant tailor from New York City, formed an organization consisting of 300 families for the purpose of settling what eventually would be the City of Mount Vernon.

Mount Vernon, long regarded as the cradle of Westchester baseball, played host to the two finest high school baseball teams in the county in 1953, the only time both clubs would hold that distinction at the same time. Edison Tech was the best team in the Southern Westchester Interscholastic Athletic Conference while A.B. Davis High School ruled the roost in the Westchester Interscholastic Athletic Association. Davis was led by a stocky little shortstop, Jim Carideo, pitcher Cazz Casarella and his battery-mate Jerry Saviola.

To hail the opening of the Mount Vernon Little League season there was a 40-vehicle motorcade on Thursday April 30 through the streets of the city. In the parade were members of the newly formed Minor Little League, the Little League, Pony League, officials, managers, and coaches.

The motorcade began at Sandford Boulevard and South Fulton Avenue, went north on Fulton to Lincoln Avenue, west on Lincoln and around the Circle to Gramatan, south on Gramatan into Fourth Avenue to Third Street, east on Third to Fulton and back to the original starting point where it disbanded. A sound truck led the procession playing the official Little League march. The Mothers' Auxiliary even had a car in the parade carrying Mrs. Joe O'Connor, president; Mrs. Edward Martin, recording secretary; Mrs. Ray Schilke, corresponding secretary; Mrs. Mike Mangone, treasurer; and Mrs. Frank Falco, vice president. Sixteen pick-up trucks, each one holding one team of the new Minor League with managers and coaches followed.

There were more boys and teams participating in the baseball programs than ever before. In 1952 the Pony and Little Leagues handled 180 boys. A year later the three leagues enabled 450 boys to play. When the Little League boys took the field for the May 2nd opener at Hutchinson, 128 of them were divided into a two division loop with four teams in the National and the same number in the American. After opening day at Hutchinson Field, all Little League games were played at Longfellow School.

Before that season opener, spectators hunched their shoulders against the cold as the boys milled about in a state of excitement. They threw baseballs, batted and ran around. One first baseman sneered confidently beneath his cap as he stopped a chiding rival dead with a "put up or shut up" offer to bet ten cents on the game's outcome. Dogs romped playfully adding a nice note of confusion to the proceedings.

At the end of the season, more than 750 boys, mothers and fathers turned out for a gala Little and Pony League banquet at the Glen Island Casino. Highlight of the evening was an appearance by three New York Giants, Whitey Lockman, Dusty Rhodes and Davey Williams. Lockman offered advice to the youngsters in his keynote address. He said, "Each time you walk off the ball field, be able to say you gave your best."

Eddie Martin Stars on Opening Day

May 2 – Not even bad weather could discourage Little Leaguers, especially Eddie Martin of the Shamrocks, from opening the 1952 season at Hutchinson Field.

In the National Division, the Shamrocks came from behind to beat the Panthers, 5-4, in what was a battle of pitchers. Both hurlers accounted for three hits, but all of Martin's were for extra bases. He homered and hit two doubles. On the mound, he gave up only two walks and struck out 14. Loser Ken Doyle struck out nine and walked seven as he came within one inning of chalking up the victory. The Panthers led all the way until the sixth when the Shamrocks put three hits together, two of them doubles, and pushed across the winning run.

The 1953 was a good season for the Martin family. Besides Eddie Martin's outstanding play, his mother Mrs. Edward Martin, at the close of the season, was installed as president of the Mount Vernon Little and Pony League Mothers Auxiliary. Retiring President Mrs. Joseph O'Connor was presented with a watch. She in turn gave Mrs. Martin a gavel, symbolic of her new office. Both ladies received orchids from Pony League Commissioner Bill Real and Little League Commissioner Andy Karl.

In another opening day game, The Orioles took the Eagles, 4-0, in what was technically the official opening game. Losing pitcher Harry Allison held the Orioles to three hits while striking out 11 batters, but fell prey to his own bases on balls. He gave up eight walks which converted into the winning margin of four runs by the Orioles.

Tom Pisano's clutch pitching won the game for the American League champions. With two men on base he struck out the two final batters in both the first and third innings. Catcher Don Cook of the Eagles had two hits.

The Owls lost to the Peacocks, 4-1, when the Peacocks took advantage of Ronald Epps' five walks. Joe Glaser, the winning pitcher, struck out 13 and walked just one batter.

The Pirates downed the Indians 4-3 to close out the day's schedule. Both Bob Puccillo of the Indians and Dick Mergenthaler of the Pirates had identical records of 11 strikeouts and 10 bases on balls, but Mergenthaler had the breaks and came away with the win.

Oriole John Dalisa Blanks Owls on 2 Hits

May 8 – The Orioles shutout the Owls 4-0 behind John Dalisa's good pitching and tight defense. Dalisa struck out eight in his first starting assignment. Tom Nelly homered for the Orioles and Tom Pisano had two doubles while teammates Joe Carbone and Dave Walsh had one apiece. Ron Epps was charged with the loss.

Harry Allison Strikes Out 20 in Eagles Win

May 9 – The Eagles and Owls in the American Division battled for 11 innings before the Eagles came away with a 3-1 win. Harry Allison struck out 20 batters as he and Ulisse Marini dueled at 1-1 for nine innings before both had to stop pitching in accordance with Little League rules. Jimmy Heckett, who had three hits including two doubles, came on in relief and gained the victory.

How good was Allison's and Marini's pitching performances? Consider this. What was the greatest pitched game ever in the major leagues?

Usual games include the 26-inning, 1-1 tie pitched in 1920 by Joe Oeschger of the Boston Braves and Leon Cadore of the Brooklyn Dodgers; Harvey Haddix's unprecedented 12-inning, 1959 perfect game that he lost in the 13th; and Sandy Koufax's 1965 perfecto in which losing pitcher Bob Hendley of the Cubs allowed one hit and two base runners. These games were remarkable in their own right. Yet the epic confrontation between the Braves' Warren Spahn and the Giants' Juan Marichal on July 2, 1963 could have been the best. There was nothing to compare it to.

On that day, a pair of future Hall of Famers, one with his best days behind him, the other with his career blossoming before him, engaged in a battle never seen before or since. Spahn, already an icon, had debuted during World War II and was in the midst of his 13th and final 20-win season. Marichal was en route to his first of six 20-win seasons.

The two men battled through 15 scoreless innings before the game was decided in the 16th. It remains the last time any two pitchers have pitched shutout ball for so long in the same game. Both men threw more than 200-plus pitches.

Ed Martin didn't have to pitch 16 innings to pick up his second win of the season on May 9 when his Shamrocks beat the Indians, 9-4, for their third straight win in as many starts. He only went the required six innings and helped his cause with two hits including a triple. Teammate Steve Brindisi doubled while Indian catcher Art Ettinger tripled. Bob Puccillo was the losing pitcher. Earlier in the week, the Shamrocks Steve Brindisi shutout the Pirates 3-0 in his first mound appearance of the season. He allowed three hits.

In another game, the Pirates took it out on the Panthers beating them 16-2. Pitcher Tom Ambrosino limited the Panthers to four hits while striking out 11. His teammates pounded out 12 hits with catcher Jim Forkell getting three.

Orioles Tom Pisano Rules Roost Over Peacocks

May 11 – Oriole hurler Tom Pisano ruled the roost or at least that portion belonging to the American division of the Little League, as he struck out a dozen Peacocks in a 5-0 shutout win.

Pisano was razor sharp as he held the Peacocks to two hits and gave up but one walk. He also picked up the only extra base hit of the game with a double. Joe Glaser was charged with the loss.

Third Straight Loss Hung on Panthers

May 17 – The Indians Anthony Silvestre tagged the Panthers with their third straight loss, beating them, 14-2, while giving up only three hits.

In other games, Joe Glaser of the Peacocks also threw a three hitter, beating the Owls, 11-1. That same afternoon, the Pirates came from behind with three runs in the seventh inning to top the Indians, 6-4. Ed Lombardi came on to relieve Dick Mergenthaler to pick up the win.

The Orioles won their third American League game despite an Eagle sixth inning rally which fell one run short at 3-2. Harry Allison pitched a complete game for the win. First baseman Ernie Motta drove in two runs for the winner.

Puccillo Hurls 2 Hit Shutout

May 22 – The Indians Bob Puccillo pitched two hit ball in blanking the Panthers, 7-0, as he struck out 12 and gave up only one walk. Tom Cowan got the only two hits for the Panthers, a double and single. Dan Lorusso led the Indian hitters with a triple as the tribe picked up five runs in the third, one in the fourth and one in the fifth.

Mickey Mangone had an easy time of it on the mound for the Peacocks as they pounded out a 15-8 win over the Eagles in an American League contest. His teammates Tom Gherardi, Joe Castro, Bob Zuccaro, Joe Glaser and Mangone all had extra base hits.

Orioles, Pirates, Shamrocks, Eagles Grab Wins

May 25 – The Eagles broke a 3-3 deadlock with a solo run in the sixth inning to edge the Owls, 4-3. With the bases loaded, Eagle Johnny Stina laid down a perfect bunt to squeeze in the winning run. Left fielder Bill Huff had three doubles while Tom Ruffalo had a double for the Owls. Eagles pitcher Harry Allison held the Owls to six hits while striking out 11.

The Orioles scored three runs in the third inning to top the Peacocks, 3-1. Ed Kahn, Tom Nelly, and Dom D'Angelo each drilled two doubles for the winners. Tom Pisano was the winning pitcher while Joe Glaser was charged with the loss.

The Pirates collected 11 hits in blasting the youthful Panther team, 11-2. Buc John DeAngelis had a pair of doubles while teammates Ed Lombardi and Dick Mergenthaler had one apiece. John DeNisco homered for the winners. Vin Carosella picked up the win.

The Shamrocks downed the Indians, 5-2, as John Bourne and Fred Casucci hit a double and triple, respectively. The Shamrocks scored four times in the second inning to overcome a two run deficit. They added another run in the fourth inning. Eddie Martin picked up the win in throwing a complete game while scattering eight hits.

Pirates Clip Shamrocks 11-1

June 1 – The Pirates had little trouble beating the Shamrocks, 11-1, as Ed Lombardi and John DeNisco blasted home runs. The Bucs scored all their runs in the last three innings. Lombardi had three of the team's 15 hits off losing pitcher Eddie Martin. Dickie Mergenthaler picked up the win.

In another game, the Orioles swamped the Owls, 16-4, as Dom DiAngelo paced the attack with a three-run home run. Tom Pisano pitched a four-hitter for the win.

Pat Tucci Drives in Winning Run for Pirates

June 2 – Pat Tucci's hit broke a scoreless tie in the fourth inning as the Pirates scored twice to defeat the Indians, 2-0. Ed Lombardi was the winning pitcher, striking out three, walking two, while giving up four hits. Bob Puccillo took the loss.

Owls Chalk Up First Win of Season

June 8 – The Owls picked up their first win of the season in American League play by topping the Eagles 8-4. Both clubs collected seven hits. Ulisse Marini was the winner.

The Shamrocks overcame a 5-3 deficit when they scored five runs in the fourth inning and one more in the fifth to beat the Indians 9-5. Steve Brindisi clouted two home runs and a single and scored three runs for the winners. Eddie Martin tripled for the Shamrocks and was the winning pitcher.

The Orioles scored 10 runs in beating the Peacocks. George Pacchiana, John Dalisa and Nick DeAngelo set the pace for the Orioles with a double, double, triple, and homer, respectively. Pete Fox was the winning hurler in pitching a complete game while striking out six.

The Pirates put up a football score as they blasted the Panthers 22-4 in a three hour National League game. The Bucs scored 19 runs in the second inning as they bombed Panthers hurlers for ten singles, three doubles, a triple and home run. Tom Ambrosino was the winning hurler. The Panthers in 1953 fielded the youngest team in the league.

Joe Glaser Wins Pitching Duel With Ernie Motta

June 10 – Joe Glaser of the Peacocks waged a pitching duel with the Eagles Ernie Motta and came out on top, 3-2. Glaser limited the Eagles to four hits, one more than his teammates were able to pick up off Motta. Peacocks first baseman Joe Castro hit a two run triple in the third inning when the winners scored three runs. Catcher Bob Schweitzer brought in Castro with the winning run. The Eagles Bill Bauersfeld also tripled.

The Shamrocks came from behind with two runs in the last inning to nip the Panthers, 8-7. Gary Munsterman went the distance to pick up his first Little League win. Ed Bruno's single to centerfield drove in the winning run. Tom Cowen hit a grand slam homer for the losers. The win gave the Shamrocks second place in the first round of the National Division with a 7-2 record. The top spot belonged to the Pirates with a 8-1 mark.

Peacocks Take 6-5 Win Over Owls

June 15 – The Peacocks took a close 6-5 win over the Owls as Joe Glaser helped out with a pair of singles and a double. Don Niese and Tom Ruffalo hit doubles for the losers. Mickey Mangone picked up the win while Ron Epps was charged with the defeat.

Dalisa's Three RBIs Seals Orioles Win over Eagles

June 19 – Johnny Dalisa drove in three runs to insure the Orioles 4-1 victory over the Eagles. The Orioles iced the game in the third inning when Dave Walsh and Ed Kahn hit back to back singles and Tom Nelly and Dalisa followed with doubles. Tom Pisano hurled a complete game to pick up the win. He struck out a dozen batters. Ernie Motta took the loss.

The following night Steve Brindisi of the Shamrocks shutout the Panthers in an 18-0 rout. Teammate Fred Casucci had four hits and Brindisi helped his own cause with three. Every Shamrock player had at least one hit.

Another shutout was thrown by Ulysse Marini as the Owls downed the Peacocks 4-0. Don Niese paced the winners with a triple and a single. Marini gave up four hits.

Petrillo, Martin, Cook, Walsh Lead Teams To Victories

June 22 – Tony Petrillo threw a one-hitter as the Indians tamed the Panthers 14-4. He struck out 17 batters. A bunt single by Jack Coleman was the only blemish. Petrillo's teammates Dan Lorusso, Art Ettinger and Bob Puccillo provided the hitting in the win.

The Shamrocks had an easy time of it in beating the Pirates 8-2. Pitcher Eddie Martin kept the Pirates at bay with a neat five hit performance on the mound. Martin struck out eight and walked but one. He also homered to drive in three runs. Pete Fiore doubled as the club piled it on in the closing innings. The losing hurler was Eddie Lombardi.

Don Cook led the Eagles with a homer in the third inning that helped the club to a 7-1 win over the Peacocks. Harry Allison was in complete control on the mound for the Eagles. He gave up two hits including a first inning Joe Glaser triple.

Dave Walsh's home run with one aboard was the highlight of the Orioles 7-4 win over the Owls for their tenth win of the season. Johnny Dalisa helped out the Orioles with a triple that drove in two runs. He also picked up the win.

Harry Allison Tosses 1-0 Shutout in Eagles Win

June 26 – In a tight pitching duel between Harry Allison of Eagles and Tom Pisano of the Orioles, Allison came out on top in throwing a 1-0 shutout. He struck out 13 and gave up three hits. Tom Pisano was even stingier in the hit department. The Eagles got only one hit off him.

Mike Hirsch threw a complete game in picking up the first Little League victory of his career, a 6-5 Pirates win over the Panthers. He fanned three and gave up only three hits. He got solid support from Denis Rocchio who homered and had a pair of singles. Frank Cuomo's double scored two runs. Cuomo also followed that up with a steal of third base and then of home in the big six run third inning. Lou Gazverde was charged with the loss.

Fred Casucci led a 10-hit attack with a three run homer in the fourth inning as the Shamrocks beat the Panthers 8-2. Steve Brindisi went three-for-three at the plate and Barry Lipton picked up two hits for the winners. Eddie Martin fanned 13 for the win.

The Owls scored six runs in the fifth inning to beat the Peacocks 7-4. Carl Silverman's two run double for the Owls was the only extra base hit of the game, although the Owls had nine hits in the win. Ron Epps was credited with the victory. He struck out 11. Mike Mangone took the loss.

The Indians beat the Pirates 7-3 for their first victory of the season over the Bucs. Both teams could only muster three hits apiece. The Indians, however, got the big hit when Joe Russo cleared the bases with a double. Bob Puccillo went all the way for the win. Dick Mergenthaler picked up the loss.

Pacchiana and Martin Lead Orioles, Shamrocks to Wins

June 29 – George Pacchiana pitched the Orioles to an 8-0 win over the Peacocks. He gave up four singles while striking out seven. His teammates had 13 hits off losing pitcher Joe Glaser. Dave Walsh led the way with a double and a single.

In another contest, The Shamrocks blasted the Indians 10-4 with Ed Martin providing most of the hitting. He belted a triple, double and single. Steve Brindisi was sharp on the mound for the

Shamrocks, giving up but one walk. The win was the fourth in a row for the Shamrocks without a loss in the second round of League play.

The Eagles meanwhile were busy topping the Owls 10-8. Don Cook led the way with a double and a home run for the winners. Teammates Johnny Spina and Jim Heckett each hit a triple. Frank Bisignano homered for the Owls. Ernie Motta picked up the win.

Pirates Hand Shamrocks First Loss in 2nd Round

June 30 – The Pirates won 2-1 and handed the Shamrocks their first loss in the second round of play.

Ed Martin of the Shamrocks and Pirates hurler Dick Mergenthaler were locked in a tight pitching duel until the fifth inning when the Pirates scored when Johnny DeAngelis stole home after he tripled to left field. Martin put his club back in the game in the sixth inning when he smashed a two out, two strike curveball for a home run. The Pirates nailed it down, however, in the bottom of the seventh when Frank Cuomo singled, stole second and scored on an overthrow.

At the same time the Pirates were winning, the Orioles dumped the Owls 9-4 behind Joe Carbone's triple and Nick DiAngelo's double and single. The Orioles scored five runs in the third inning to overcome a 4-1 deficit. Tom Pisano came on in relief in the fourth inning for the Orioles and pitched hitless ball for the remainder of the game.

In another game, The Indians dumped the youngest team competing in the Little League, the Panthers, 12-4. Tony Petrillo picked up the win striking out 11. Left fielder Len Henderson had two hits and scored two runs for the winners.

Eagles Pick Up Two Wins on Cook Home Runs

July 2 – The Eagles blasted the Peacocks, 14-0, behind Harry Allison's two-hit pitching performance. He struck out 14 batters along the way. Catcher Don Cook had a two run homer in the first inning. Lou Nange pitched in with a double and Allison helped his own cause with three singles.

The Eagles picked up another win the night before edging the Owls, 5-4. Cook continued to wield a hot bat. He belted two home runs and a double. Eagles pitcher Ernie Motta tripled. Pete Dunsay tripled for the losers while Bob Fausel had a double and single. Motta went the distance for the win. The Eagles pushed across the winning run in the sixth inning to break a 4-4 tie. Bob Cruickshank was charged with the defeat.

Brindisi Picks up Shamrocks Win

July 3 – The Shamrocks beat the Indians 5-3 as Steve Brindisi limited the Tribe to four hits. Eddie Martin had the only extra base hit of the game when he homered in the second inning. It was Martin's second homer in as many games. Gary Munsterman had a pair of singles for the winners.

Brindisi faltered somewhat in the last inning when he walked three to set up two of the Indians runs. He pulled himself together and fanned the last two batters to avoid further damage. Bob Puccillo was the losing pitcher.

Tom Nelly, Dave Walsh and Steve Kablesh provided the hitting as the Orioles beat the

Peacocks 11-3. Orioles catcher Tom Nelly hit a pair of home runs and a single. Walsh also homered and Kablesh came through with a double. The ball was flying out of the Longfellow Field ballpark as Joe Glaser homered and tripled for the Peacocks and Tom Gherardi doubled. George Pacchiana went the distance for the win. Mike Mangone was charged with the loss.

Bob Puccillo No-Hits City Island Civic Association

July 6 – In an exhibition game, Bob Puccillo threw a no-hitter for the Indians in beating the City Island Civic Association, 2-0. Puccillo never was in any trouble as he fanned 11. He also drove in the first run of the game. Teammate Joe Russo homered for the second run. Tony Petrillo had a double.

Some Funny Happenings

July 7 – News coverage about Little League baseball during its first decade was extensive in Mount Vernon's newspaper, particularly in the league's first five years. Here are a few unique and sometimes funny happenings involving youngsters during the 1953 season.

Indian pitcher Tony Petrillo took time off during a game to pull out a bothersome and loose tooth. He came to the sidelines to do it and went right back to the mound and won the game.

Panther infielder Tom O'Shaughnessy had a hard hit ground ball take a bad hop in front of him, bounce off his head and into the Johnny Bennett's glove who then made the putout.

Pirate Joe Tripodi got quite the surprise at a practice when he picked up his mitt and was stung by a bee who crept inside.

Pirate John DeAngelis went after a hard hit ball in a close game only to be caught short in amazement. The base clearing blast had rolled into a deep hole and required the long arm of one of the Pirate coaches to retrieve it. That is not all. The batter was called out on an umpire appeal for not tagging first base.

Panther Mike Boccardi made the jump from team mascot to regular second baseman. Pirate players DeAngelis and John DeNisco between the two of them scored eight runs by stealing home.

Peacocks Outslug Owls, 12-11; Shamrocks Win

July 8 – The Peacocks rallied for five runs in the last inning to edge the Owls, 12-11. Joe Castro, Bob Schweitzer and Larry Troncone each had triples for the Peacocks and pitcher Mickey Mangone added a double.

The losers scored by the long ball. Carl Silverman tripled and Kevin Olifers and Bill Thomas homered. Despite giving up 11 runs, Mangone went the distance while striking out five.

In another contest, the Shamrocks beat the Panthers, 7-5, with Ed Bruno's solo home run in the sixth inning highlighting a solid attack. Steve Brindisi and Eddie Martin came through with a pair of hits for the winners. Brindisi picked up the win. He struck out 10. Ken Doyle homered and singled for the losers. Bill Schwartz tripled and Jack Coleman doubled for the Panthers.

Bucs Win To Tie Shamrocks in Little League Race

July 10 – The Pirates beat the Shamrocks 3-2 to move into a first place tie with the losers in the National League race. Winner Dick Mergenthaler and Eddie Martin hooked up in an outstanding pitching duel. Mergenthaler limited the Shamrocks to four hits while fanning 10. Martin was touched for eight hits and struck out eight. The winners broke a 2-2 deadlock when they pushed across a run in the seventh and last inning to hand Martin the defeat.

The Peacocks, meanwhile, rallied in the closing innings to take a 4-2 victory from the Eagles. Larry Troncone led the winning hit parade with a pair of singles. Don Cook had a double and single for the losers. Joe Glaser limited the Eagles to three hits. He fanned nine and walked two. Ernie Motta was charged with the defeat.

It was also reported that Little League officials asked spectators to refrain from leaving the stands during games to talk to players or umpires. With the races in both the National and American divisions coming down the end, followers of the various teams attended games in greater numbers and were offering "more active" encouragement.

Lombardi, Puccillo Star as Pirates Edge Indians

July 13 – The Pirates had 10 hits in beating the Indians, 5-3, and moved into a first place tie with the Shamrocks in the National Division.

Buc hurler Ed Lombardi helped his own cause with a home run, a pair of singles, and four RBI's. Teammates Joe Tripodi tripled, Tom Ambrosino doubled, and John DeNisco had three hits.

Indians pitcher Bob Puccillo blasted two homers while Len Henderson doubled and singled. Both hurlers pitched well. Lombardi struck out a dozen to pick up the win. Puccillo had ten strikeouts in a losing effort.

In another contest, the Eagles downed the Orioles 5-1. Eagles third baseman Jim Heckett hit a three run homer in the fourth to give his team a commanding lead. Bob Pisano and Harry Allison of the Eagles hooked up in a fine pitching duel. Both fanned eight.

The following night, Tony Silvestre pitched the Indians to a 3-2 victory over the Shamrocks. Silvestre hurled a tight game, fanning ten while giving up only three hits, two of them doubles by Ed Martin, the rival pitcher. Silvestre's single in the fifth inning brought home teammate Len Henderson with the winning run and bounced the Shamrocks out of a first place tie with the Pirates. Martin took the loss.

Panthers Upset Bucs; Force Playoff

July 15 – What truly can be considered an upset, the youthful and last place Panthers stalled the Pirates pennant drive by beating them 5-3, forcing them into a playoff game against the Shamrocks.

Panthers pitcher Billy Schwartz hooked up in a pitching duel with the Pirates Dick Mergenthaler. Trailing 3-2 in the sixth inning, Schwartz got his break when his teammates loaded the bases on a hit batsman, a walk, and a single. Eight-year-old Mike Boyle then rapped a triple to right to drive in three runs and sink the Pirates. Schwartz picked up the win fanning 10 while Mergenthaler took the loss in striking out 12.

In another game, Johnny Weis' perfect squeeze bunt brought home John Gorrebeck with the winning run as the Eagles edged the Owls, 3-2. The Owls led 2-1 going into the sixth inning, but Don Cook homered to tie the score. Weis' squeeze bunt gave the Eagles the second round championship. Ron Epps homered for the losers while striking out 10. Willie Huff picked up the win. He held the losers to three hits and fanned 14.

Pirates Win Little League N.L. Pennant

July 16 – Dick Mergenthaler helped his teammates out of a tight game when he hit a three-run home run in the bottom of the last inning to give the Pirates a 7-4 win over the Shamrocks and undisputed rights to the National League title.

The Bucs were leading by three going into the sixth inning when the Shamrocks scored four runs to take the lead. In the bottom half of the sixth, the Bucs rallied, when with one out, John DeNisco singled. Frank Cuomo's long single brought DeNisco home with the tying run. Mike Margulis got on via an error and then came home on Mergenthaler's home run.

In the second inning, DeNisco hit his fifth home run of the season. Vincent Carosella reversed an earlier defeat by going the distance to pick up the win. Steve Brindisi was charged with the loss.

In an American League game, the Orioles beat the Eagles 2-1 in the first of three playoff games. Tom Nelly homered in the third inning to give the first round champion Orioles the lead. The Eagles scored in the fifth on a pass and a pair of singles by Tom Shay and Johnny Weis.

The tight well-pitched game saw losing pitcher Harry Allison strike out 11 and give up only four hits. Winner Tom Pisano fanned eight and held the Eagles to five hits.

The night before, the Peacocks clubbed the Orioles 20-6. Orioles centerfielder George Pacchiana hit a grand slam homer in the third inning. Joe Glaser doubled and singled for the winners while teammate Tom Gherardi had two singles. Joe Castro was the winner.

Orioles Win American League Crown

July 18 – The Orioles knocked off the Eagles, 7-1, to win the American League championship and a chance to play the Pirates in the 1953 Mount Vernon Little League World Series.

The Orioles showed some great pitching by Tom Pisano and John Dalisa in the two game set against the Eagles. But in the 7-1 win, George Pacchiana drove in two runs. Pitching was the chief stock and trade of the Pirates, whose staff was anchored by Dick Mergenthaler, the National League's leading pitcher. In addition, they had other top notch hurlers such as Ed Lombardi, Vincent Carosella, and Mike Hirsch.

The series, based on a three out of five schedule, would see the Orioles seeking to prevent a second straight city title for the National League pennant winning Pirates.

Orioles Trip Pirates, 2-1 in Series Opener

July 22 – Mount Vernon's Little Leaguers were little in name only as the American League champion Orioles edged National League pennant winning Pirates, 2-1, before an estimated 1,200 people at Hutchinson Field at the World Series opener.

It was the largest crowd to witness a local sports event since the Thanksgiving Day Edison

Tech vs. A.B. Davis football game.

Outstanding pitching by Oriole Tommy Pisano and Pirate Dick Mergenthaler highlighted the match up in which none of the runs were earned. Each pitcher limited the opposition to four hits. Pisano struck out eight and walked three while Mergenthaler relied on two curves, slow and slower. He fanned 11 and walked one. During one stretch he struck out five batters in a row.

The Orioles got on the board first in the second inning. Johnny Dalisa walked. When he attempted to steal second the throw beat him but his slide jarred the ball loose from the glove of Pirate second baseman Joe Tripodi. After retiring the next two batters on strikeouts, George Pacchiana singled to center to drive in the run.

The Pirates tied the score in the bottom of the second. Ed Lombardi beat out an infield hit. A wild pitch and passed ball moved him to third base. With two out, another passed ball allowed Lombardi to score and tie the score.

In the fourth inning, Dalisa singled to left field. The throw-in got by the infield allowing Dalisa to race to third base. Pisano then hit to Pirate third baseman Frank Cuomo who made a neat across the body grab of the grounder. While Cuomo tossed out the runner, Dalisa beat the relay across the plate with the winning run.

Mergenthaler choked off any Orioles rally the rest of the way. The Pirates had scoring opportunities also. Two walks and an infield hit loaded the bases in the fourth inning but catcher Mike Margulis grounded out to end the inning.

In the fifth inning, Johnny DeAngelis stretched a single to center field into a double but Pisano fanned Tom Ambrosino to close out the inning. A two out single by Vince Carosella and a passed ball lifted Pirates hopes in the sixth inning but second baseman Joe Carbone collared Cuomo's shot to end the game.

Pirates Deadlock Series with Win

July 25 – The Pirates deadlocked the Little League World Series at a game apiece by beating the Orioles 7-6 before an overflow crowd of 300 people at Hutchinson Field 3.

Trailing the Pirates 7-1, the Orioles stormed back to score five runs in the bottom of the fifth inning. In the sixth and final inning, they got the first two men on base only to have Pirate pitcher Ed Lombardi bear down to stop the tying run from crossing the plate.

Poor defensive play by the Orioles allowed the Pirates to take a 3-1 after two innings. In the third, nine Pirates came to bat. Four runners scored. After successive singles by Frank Cuomo, John DeAngelis, and Vince Carosella loaded the bases, Carmine DeNisco singled to left to drive in the first two earned runs of the series. Mike Margulis then walked and Jim Forkell drove in the sixth and seventh runs.

Oriole pitcher Johnny Dalisa settled down over the next three innings, allowing one hit the rest of the way.

In the fifth inning, the Orioles came back. George Pacchiana lined a home run over the left field fence.

The next two hitters hit comeback pitches to the mound but Dom D'Angelo kept things going with a single to center field. Bob Meyers then walked. The runners moved up on a passed ball and D'Angelo scored when catcher Tom Nelly got on by an error. A single then cut the lead to 7-4.

Johnny Dalisa walked to load the bases for second baseman Joe Carbone. Carbone doubled to cut the margin to 7-6.

Excitement grew when long-ball hitter George Pacchiana batted for the second time in the inning. He bounced to Pirate third baseman Frank Cuomo who threw him out.

With one out in the Oriole sixth, Steve Kablesh reached first on an error. D'Angelo reached first when Pirate pitcher Dick Mergenthaler threw late trying for a force at second base. Lombardi then got Meyers to hit a force play grounder to second.

National and American Teams Enter LL Tournaments

Mount Vernon Little League officials took the edge off of the 1953 World Series by interrupting it with tournament play as reflected in the following four stories. By introducing all-star teams and games at this time, the importance was taken away from Little League's strongest point, regular season play and a youngster's pride in working for his regular-season club. More than a week elapsed between the second and third World Series game.

NL Beats City Island Behind Mergenthaler 3-Hitter

Dick Mergenthaler hurled the Mount Vernon National League All Stars to a 2-0 win over City Island in the national tournament opener. He gave up only three singles while striking out 10. He fanned the first five batters in the game and only walked one over seven innings.

Facing a scoreless deadlock going into the fourth inning, the National League scored twice. Steve Brindisi opened with a single to left field. Fred Casucci struck out. Ed Martin got to first when City Island was unsuccessful in catching Brindisi going into second base. Vincent Carosella singled to load the bases. A pitch got away from the City Island catcher and in his attempt to cut down Brindisi at the plate, he threw wildly and Martin kept on running to score the second run.

City Island tried to rally in the fifth inning. They loaded the bases on an error and two soft singles. The National League got out of the inning on a force play at second base.

AL Tops Bronxchester, 7-4; Nelly Homers

Trailing 3-2 going into the fifth inning, the American League All Stars rallied for five runs to beat Bronxchester 7-4.

Catcher Tom Nelly's two run homer gave the National Leaguers a 4-3 lead. Before the inning was over three more runs scored. Bob Fausel batting behind Nelly homered. Bronxchester pitcher Carmine Giordano gave up two runs in the first inning but then tossed hitless ball over the next three innings. Ron Epps went all the way for the win giving up nine hits.

The National Leaguers scored in their first turn at bat. After Nelly forced Don Niese, Fausel doubled and Don Cook singled for one run. With two out, Joe Carbone singled home Fausel. Cook tried to score on the hit but was thrown out at the plate on a strong throw by left fielder Paul Lizzo.

Bronxchester rallied to lead 3-2. That scored stood over the next three innings, thanks to a strong throw to the plate by National League left fielder Joe Glaser that cut off a fifth inning rally. Then in the fifth, Niese got on by an error. Nelly homered into deep left centerfield. Fausel followed with his own home run. Bronxchester changed pitchers and Cook immediately singled.

Carbone brought Cook home on a single and moved around to third base on the throw to the plate. He scored the final run, beating a throw home on George Pacchiana's shot to third.

The game ended when the tying run came to the plate for Bronxchester. He hit a hard drive to the left of second base but National League second baseman Don Niese cut over, knocked the ball down, and recovered in time to toss out the runner.

Port Chester Beats American League 8-7

Mount Vernon's American League All Star team rallied and overcame a 6-1 Port Chester American League lead only to see Port Chester push across a seventh inning run to win 8-7 knocking the Mount Vernon club out of the regional tournament.

After two innings of well played ball, Mount Vernon faltered in the third. Walks, mental errors, and a two-run wild pitch enabled Port Chester to pick up four runs without a hit. Mount Vernon got one back in the fourth to cut the lead to 4-1. But Port Chester stretched the lead to 6-1.

Mount Vernon rallied and scored four in the fifth inning. After three straight hits, Don Niese lined to the Port Chester first baseman who threw wildly trying for a double play. Tom Nelly then hit his second tournament home run and Mount Vernon trailed 6-5. Port Chester pitcher Bill Fado homered in the fifth to increase the lead to 7-5.

George Pacchiana opened the Mount Vernon sixth with his second straight hit. Joe Glaser followed with a single. After John Dalisa flied out to left field, Niese singled in Pacchiana. Nelly doubled to tie the score.

Pacchiana who relieved Tom Pisano set down Port Chester in the last of the sixth. That was when both managers agreed to halt the game as darkness descended. When it was judged sufficiently dark, the lights went on at Corpus Christi Field in Port Chester.

Port Chester reliever Bob Lichti stopped Mount Vernon in the seventh. Lou Feretti opened the bottom of the inning with a double. After a ground out, a single to right field drove Feretti home with the winning run.

Port Chester Tops National League 8-5

A first inning grand slam home run broke the back of the National League All Star attack as they lost 8-5 to Port Chester in a national tournament game. The defeat knocked the Mount Vernon team out of the Little League qualifying championships.

With both the National and American League teams eliminated, the Mount Vernon World Series was scheduled to resume on August 4.

The fielding gem in the National League loss came in the third inning. The Nationals had Johnny DeAngelis on first and second when Bob Puccillo hit a sharp bounding ball up the middle. The Port Chester second baseman grabbed it, stepped on second and threw to first for a double play. DeAngelis kept on running and the first baseman nailed him at the plate for the third out and a triple play.

Mount Vernon scored two in the first inning when DeAngelis singled with one out. He advanced to third on Steve Brindisi's double. Puccillo brought DeAngelis home on an infield grounder and Brindisi scored when the first baseman threw the ball away in an attempt to nail

DeAngelis at the plate. Port Chester rallied and scored five runs in the bottom of the first including Lou Ferretti's grand slam. Port Chester scored three more in the third. A single, a double, and a walk loaded the bases. Ed Lombardi, who relieved starter, Ed Martin, was greeted with a double that brought two runs in. Another single scored Port Chester's final run.

In the top of the fifth inning, the National League rallied. Three singles by Johnny DeNisco, DeAngelis and Brindisi loaded the bases. Puccillo's fly to right field scored two runs when the catcher let the ball get away on the throw home. Another error on an infield play to first on Martin's grounder brought Brindisi in with the third run. Vincent Carosella singled to center field put men on first and second. Tom Cowen's sacrifice advanced the runners, but Lombardi's line drive to shortstop ended the inning and the threat.

Orioles Beat Bucs 8-1; Lead Series 2-1

August 4 – The Orioles took advantage of Pirates errors in the first inning and then went on to rack up an 8-1 victory in the third game of the Mount Vernon Little League World Series.

The American League champion Orioles made three Buc miscues pay off in the first inning. Two Orioles got on via errors and then John Dalisa singled to load the bases. Tom Pisano's routine grounder was bobbled on the throw to first and two runs scored. Pisano later scored when Joe Carbone was safe on a fielder's choice.

The Pirates scored their only run of the day when third baseman Frank Cuomo singled in the bottom of the first inning. He stole second and then scored on Ed Lombardi's single.

The Orioles scored four more runs in the third inning. Pisano started it with a double. He moved to third on a fielder's choice that failed to work. Dave Walsh walked and George Pacchiana singled Pisano home. Carbone then scored on an error. Two more runs scored when Steve Kablesh walked and Ed Kahn singled. The Orioles final scoring came in the fourth inning when Carbone and Pacchiana hit back to back doubles.

Vin Carosella started for the Pirates and was relieved by his cousin Tom Ambrosino in the third inning. Ambrosino allowed but one run and three hits the remainder of the game. Pacchiana was credited with the win.

Orioles Defeat Pirates To Capture City Little League Championship

Tom Pisano Hurls No-Hitter To Hard Fought Mound Duel

The Pirates lost a baseball game last night. Unfortunately for them the loss enabled the Orioles to claim the Mount Vernon Little League Championship. Nevertheless, it was a game that one team had to lose.

Tom Nelly shouldered his way into the limelight shared by the two opposing hurlers, Tom Pisano and Dick Mergenthaler. Pisano pitched a masterful no-hitter, sending ten Bucs down on strikes and yielding but two free passes. Mergenthaler had a one hit shutout going until Nelly led off the bottom of the seventh with a long double to right field. The hustling Oriole catcher took third when the ball was fumbled on the throw to the infield. The Oriole brain trust called for the bunt and Johnny Dalisa laid one down. It was as simple as that. The Pirate infield froze and Nelly raced in with the winning tally.

Tight From Start

The weather at game time seemed suitable for mid-October football. As the innings rolled by the darkening skies threatened to postpone the whole business. From the start it was apparent that neither club intended to yield an advantage. Pisano fanned the first two Pirates to face him and got the third on an easy infield out. Mergenthaler took his cue and followed suit, racking up a strikeout and nailing two batters on easy grounders.

The Orioles got what looked like a rally going in the second, but an alert Pirate defense immediately put the damper on the threat. Dalisa made first on an infield error, but was cut down in an attempted steal of second on a perfect throw from catcher Mike Margulis to second baseman Joe Tripodi. Joe Carbone came up with a two-out single that bounded up against the fence in right center, but another fine throw to Tripodi nailed him flat footed as he tried to stretch it to a double.

Pisano Rolls

Again in the fourth inning the Orioles got a man on base via an error, but Mergenthaler put the pressure on to fan the next batter and end the inning. All the while Pisano was rolling along in complete control of the Pirate offense. The Oriole hurling ace was racking up at least one strikeout an inning. Finally, after fanning two in the fifth, he walked his first man. An infield out, however, left one dead Buc at first base.

Mergenthaler issued his initial base on balls in the bottom of the frame, but he personally took charge of the matter by catching an easy pop-up for the third out.

Nelly Breaks Monotony

The spectators had adjusted themselves to the pace of the game and expected the mound duel to continue into extra innings when Nelly opened up the seventh with his blast to the outfield. With an amazing suddenness the contest was decided. Nelly stood on third and his mates had three chances to get him home. Dalisa cut the suspense short moments later with a perfect bunt down the first base line. The right side of the Pirate infield converged on the ball, but it scooted by them. Nelly scooted home and that was the ball game.

Pirates	ab	r	h	Orioles	ab	r	h
Tripodi, 2b	2	0	0	DiAngelo, rf	3	0	0
Rocchio, ss	1	0	0	Kahn, lf	3	0	0
Cuomo, 3b	3	0	0	Nelly, c	3	1	1
Lombardi, rf	2	0	0	Daliso, 3b	3	0	1
Carosella, 1b	3	0	0	Pisano, p	2	0	0
DeAngelis, cf	1	0	0	Carbone, 2b	2	0	1
DeNisco, lf	1	0	0	Facchiana, 1b	1	0	0
Margulis, c	2	0	0	Walsh, ss	2	0	0
Mergenthaler	2	0	0	Kablesh, cf	2	0	0
Ambrosino, 2b	2	0	0				
Forkell, rf	2	0	0				
Totals	21	0	0	Totals	21	1	3

SCORE BY INNINGS

Pirates 0 0 0 0 0 0 0—0
Orioles 0 0 0 0 0 0 1—1

Runs Batted In—Dalisa 1. Earned Runs—None. Two Base Hits—Nelly. Left On Bases—Pirates 2, Orioles 2. Bases On Balls, Off—Pisano 2, Mergenthaler 1. Struck Out, by—Pisano 10, Mergenthaler 4. Hits, Off—Pisano 0 in 7 ins.; Mergenthaler 3 in 7 ins. Scorer—Mergenthaler. Time of Game—2½ hours.

1953 – Orioles Take It All

LITTLE LEAGUE

NATIONAL LEAGUE

SHAMROCKS
Uniform No.
1. JOHN BOURNE
2. FRANCES AMORSANO
3. EDDIE MARTIN
4. GARY MUNSTERMEN
5. RONALD CUNNINGHAM
6. RONALD REZZA
9. PETE FIORE
10. STEVE BRINDISI
11. JOHN FAVA
12. EDDIE BRUNO
13. ROBERT BLOUNT
14. FRED CASUCCI
15. TOM ROMININO
16. BARRY LIPTON
17. WILLIAM DEEMER
18. GEO. FENNELL, Bat Boy

JEFF BORELLI, Mgr.
MR. WALSH, Coach
MR. EMMERLUTH, Coach

PIRATES
Uniform No.
8. THOMAS AMBROSINO
6. VINCENT CAROSELLA
12. FRANK CUOMO
13. JOHN DE ANGELIS
10. CARMINE DE NISCO
11. JAMES FORKELL
18. MICHAEL HIRSCH
14. EDWARD LOMBARDI
15. MIKE MARGULIS
5. RICHARD MERGENTHALER
7. DENIS ROCCHIO
4. JOSEPH TRIPODI
2. PATSY TUCCI
1. CARL VIGGIANO
17. PAUL WIENER

JOE TRIPODI, Mgr.
JAMES FORKELL, Coach
CARMINE CAROSELLA, Coach
ED. MERGENTHALER, Coach

PANTHERS
Uniform No.
13. JOHN BENNETT
18. MICHAEL BOCCARDI
4. MICHAEL BOYLE
12. JOHN COLEMAN
16. THOMAS COWEN
5. KENNETH DOYLE
10. LOUIS GASVERDE
14. WILLIAM HELLER
8. GENE MASUCCI
15. THOMAS O'SHAUGHNESSY
2. JACK O'SHAUGHNESSY
1. RAYMOND SCHILKE
9. WILLIAM SCHWARTZ
3. PAUL SQUILLACOTE
7. PAUL STILLER

JACK WOODS, Mgr.
JOE O'CONNOR, Coach
AL COLEMAN, Coach

INDIANS
Uniform No.
1. PETER BARTOLINI
3. LARRY BRIGLIA
18. EARL CONTI
10. PAUL CUGNO
17. ARTHUR ETTINGER
9. RICHARD GROSS
5. DANIEL LORUSSO
7. ANTHONY PETRILLO
13. ROBERT PETRONE
2. ROBERT PUCCILLO
14. ROBERT ROMANINO
15. JOSEPH RUSSO
8. ANTHONY SILVESTRI
12. ANTHONY TOBACCO
4. MARK WEINSTEIN

STEVE ACUNTO, Mgr.
DAN LORUSSO, Coach
FAUST CARDILLO, Coach

AMERICAN LEAGUE

PEACOCKS
Uniform No.
6. ROBERT CASSIO
8. JOSEPH CASTRO
11. THOMAS GHERARDI
4. NICK GIORDANO
5. JOSEPH GLASSER
12. MICHAEL MANGONE
10. THOMAS MANGONE
9. THOMAS McNAMARA
15. RICHARD MOCCIO
2. JACK PARETA
3. RAYMOND ROHRS
13. DONALD ROSS
7. ROBERT SCHWEITZER
14. LAURENCE TRONCONE
1. ROBERT ZUCCARO

JOE MOCCIO, Mgr.
MIKE MANGONE, Coach
JOHN GHERARDI, Coach

OWLS
Uniform No.
6. THOMAS CAPODIECI
7. FRANK BISIGNANO
12. ROBERT CRUIKSHANK
2. PETER DUNSAY
8. RONALD EPPS
15. ROBERT FAUSEL
9. PATRICK KANE
11. ULISSE MARINI
4. DONALD NEISE
13. JAMES PELLEGRINO
5. JOHN RIGANATI
14. ANTHONY SAVASTANO
3. THOMAS RUFFALO
1. WILLIAM THOMAS
10. CARL SILVERMAN

FRANK DI MARGO, Mgr.
JOHN GRECES, Coach
WALTER BERNHARDT, Coach

ORIOLES
Uniform No.
8. JOHN BARTOLINI
9. JOSEPH CARBONE
3. LARRY CASARELLA
1. DOMINICK D'ANGELO
7. JOHN DALISA
4. DAVID FOX
13. PETER FOX
14. STEPHEN KABLESH
2. EDWARD KAHN
15. THOMAS NELLY
11. ROBERT MEYERS
12. GEORGE PACCHIANA
10. TOMMY PISANO
6. LAURENCE TOWNSEND
5. DAVID WALSH

TOM NELLY, Mgr.
WILLIAM COSTA, Coach
GEORGE JACOBS, Coach

EAGLES
Uniform No.
13. JOHN ALLEN
1. HARRY ALLISON
6. WILLIAM BAUERSFELD
8. DONALD COOK
15. WILLIE HUFF
5. JOHN GORREBECK
2. JAMES HECKETT
14. ERNEST MOTTA
9. LOUIS NANGE
7. RUSSEL ROSEN
12. THOMAS SHAY
10. MICHAEL SLANE
4. JOHN SPINA
3. PETER SWENSON
11. JOHN WEIS

CHARLES COOK, Mgr.
HAROLD BAUERSFELD, Coach
ERNEST MOTTA, Coach

The Orioles Tom Nelly comes into third base in World Series game. Pirate third baseman Tom Ambrosino awaits the throw.

Peter Fiore of the Shamrocks makes it a close play sliding into third base.

Pirates And Shamrocks Dominate National League L.L. All-Stars

ED MARTIN

DICK MERGENTHALER

JOHN DE ANGELIS

Front running Pirates and Shamrocks of the National League All-Star team, selected by coaches and managers.

Led by curve baller Dick Mergenthaler whose 6-1 mark paced the Bucs to their first round title, the Pirates placed six players on the select nine. They are John DeAngelis, John DeNisco, Vincent Carosella, Ed Lombardi, Mike Margulis and Mergenthaler.

A quartet of Shamrocks is headed by Eddie Martin who owns a 6-3 mound mark plus the reputation of being a timely hitter. He has two homers to his credit. Along with him are Pete Fiore, Fred Casucci and Steve Brindisi.

Two Panthers and a pair of Indians will also play with the All-Stars. Ray Schilke and Tom Cowan are the Panther representatives while Bob Pucillo and Dan LoRusso are the Indian choices.

Joe Tripodi, who skippered the Pirates to the first round title, will handle the All-Star reins. His regular coach, James Forkell of Pirates and Manager Jeff Borelli of Shamrocks, will assist as coaches.

1953 National League All-Stars: 1, Coach Jim Forkell; 2, Jim Carosella; 3, Dan Lorusso; 4, Bob Puccillo; 5, Mike Margulis; 6, Fred Casucci; 7, League President Larry Tracy; 8, Coach Jeff Borelli; 9, John DeAngelis; 10, Ed Lombardi; 11, Ray Schilke; 12, Tom Cowan; 13, Manager Joe Tripodi; 14, Dick Mergenthaler; 15, Ed Martin; 16, Peter Fiore; 17, Steve Brindisi; 18, John DeNisco; 19, Batboy Joey Tripodi.

1953 Pirates: 1, Coach Vin Carosella; 2, Vincent Carosella; 3, Tom Ambrosino; 4, Mike Margolis; 5, Coach Jim Forkell; 6, Dick Mergenthaler; 7, John DeNisco; 8, Frank Cuomo; 9, Ed Lombardi; 10, John DeAngelis; 11, Paul Wiener; 12, Denis Rocchio; 13, Joe Tripodi; 14, Jim Forkell; 15, Carl Viggiano; 16, Mike Hirsch; 17, Pat Tucci; 18, Manager Joe Tripodi.

1953 – Orioles Take It All

1953 Indians: 1, Paul Cugno; 2, Bob Romanino; 3, Earl Conti; 4, Tony Petrillo; 5, Art Ettinger; 6, Bob Petrone; 7, Peter Bartolini; 8, Tony Tobacco; 9, Manager Steve Acunto; 10, Anthony Silvestri; 11, Richard Gross; 12, Bob Puccillo; 13, Coach Faust Cardillo; 14, Mark Weinstein; 15, Joe Russo; 16, Dan Lorusso; 17, Coach Dan Lorusso; 18, Batboy Steve Acunto III.

1953 Peacocks: 1, Joe Glasser; 2, Manager Joe Moccio; 3, Nick Giordano; 4, Bob Schweitzer; 5, Tom Gherardi; 6, Don Ross; 7, Coach John Gherardi; 8, Joe Castro; 9, Richard Moccio; 10, Larry Troncone; 11, Batboy Ken Glasser; 12, Mike Mangone; 13, Jack Pareta; 14, Tom Mangone.

1953 Shamrocks: 1, Gary Munsterman; 2, Peter Fiore; 3, Tom Rominino; 4, Ed Bruno; 5, Frances Amorsano; 6, Ron Cunningham; 7, Bobby Blount; 8, John Fava; 9, Manager Jeff Borelli; 10, Barry Lipton; 11, Fred Casucci; 12, Billy Deemer; 13, Coach Walter Emmerluth; 14, Steve Brindisi; 15, Eddie Martin; 16, Coach Don Walsh; 17, Jack Bourne.

1953 Panthers: 1, Michael Boccardi; 2, John Bennett; 3, Kenny Doyle; 4. Coach Joe O'Connor; 5, Gene Masucci; 6, Manager Jack Woods; 7, Coach Al Coleman.

1953 – Orioles Take It All

Little League coaches, left to right, Jim Forkell, Jeff Borelli, Joe Tripodi, and Larry Tracy.

Little Leaguers meet New York Giant stars, left to right, Dusty Rhodes, Whitey Lockman, and Dave Williams. The major leaguers autographed their programs for, left to right, Fred Casucci, Lou Nange, and Mike Shane.

11

1954 – Pirates Win 2nd Word Series

Mount Vernon's Little League and Major League Baseball's American League both made big changes in 1954. After a hiatus of 51 years, big league baseball returned to Baltimore to stay. The lowly St. Louis Browns suffered from anemic teams and low attendance for a number of years. So as part of the first major league realignment since 1903, the Browns moved to Baltimore and became the Orioles.

Meanwhile, about 204 miles north of Baltimore in Mount Vernon youngsters were enjoying the Davy Crockett national fad as sales of "coonskin" caps soared. At the same time, while we as youngsters never realized it, the idea of a world war was increasing. The United States detonated a hydrogen bomb in the South Pacific and Supreme Court Chief Justice Earl Warren ordered the states to proceed to enforce Brown v. Board of Education whereby racial separation in public schools is unconstitutional. In 1954 we were first inoculated with Dr. Jonas Salk's polio vaccine.

Early in '54 plans were made in Mount Vernon to accommodate at least twice as many boys for the 1954 season as it had in 1953. Two new four-team leagues were organized, bringing the total number of clubs in the city from 8 to 16. At least 180 more boys could now play Little League baseball. In 1954, Little League baseball expanded to more than 3,300 leagues. Besides opening the ranks for players in Mount Vernon, the expansion created an even greater need for coaches. The call went out throughout the city.

At a meeting to announce expansion plans, Andy Karl was named commissioner for another term, while Larry Tracy and George Fennell remained as presidents of the National and American Leagues, respectively. Joseph C. O'Connor was named to head up the new Eastern League (Wildcats, Rams, Lions, and Jesters) while Tom Nelly became president of the Western League (Comets, Bulldogs, Cubs and Tigers). The list of managers for both new leagues was also announced. Mike Angelestio, Eddie Martin, Ernie Altieri and Sol Dunsay headed up Eastern League teams while Steve Wisner, John Koenickie and James and John Mazzarella skippered Western League clubs.

Some 242 boys counted off the days until the Little League season officially got underway on

May 1. The Orioles looked forward to a season where they would have to beat off determined challenges from the Eagles, Owls and Peacocks if they were to repeat the 1953 double trick of winning both the American League pennant and the city championship. Over in the National League the defending champion Pirates figured to have plenty of trouble with the Shamrocks, Indians and Panthers. Both of the new divisions would feature wide open races.

On Friday night April 30 the beat of the Mount St. Michael Academy band drums resonated throughout downtown Mount Vernon as the city was ushering in opening games of the season with a parade. The city's center turned into a page of out the popular Broadway show, *The Music Man.* A colorful cavalcade of players, parents, sponsors, coaches and officials accompanied by a color guard from the Mount Vernon Fire Department smartly stepped down Gramatan Avenue. City folk, kids and parents alike, lined the streets waving and shouting. Whoever marched in that parade could never forget the route. The line of march began at A.B. Davis High School down Gramatan Avenue, up Fourth Avenue to Third Street and left to Fulton Avenue where the parade disbanded.

A color guard from the Nautical Cadets headed the marchers followed by the Fire Department Band. The commissioners car followed carrying the parade's grand marshal, Bill Skiff of the New York Yankees, one of that organization's chief scouts in the New York-New England area. Following that were minor league players. The Little League was next in line, headed by a car carrying the presidents of its four divisions. The lineup seemed never to end. More city organizations followed and then a group of girls, sisters of the players who were dressed in red-white-and-blue costumes. They headed the Mothers' Organization which included parents of boys who were playing in either the Minor, Little, or Pony Leagues. Fava Post, American Legion, had a delegation of twirlers march ahead of the Mount St. Michael band. Finally, a car which the leagues offered in their fund-raising campaign closed the parade.

Pirates Down Panthers, 3-2, on Hirsch's Double

May 1 – Mike Hirsch's long sixth inning double to left field gave the Pirates a 3-2 victory over the Panthers on opening day. Virgil Trucks of the Chicago White Sox and Panthers pitcher Lou Gazzverde were working on separate no-hitters at the same. Both had their hopes dashed in the sixth inning. The Pirates broke up Gazzverde's bid in the sixth with a walk, a single and Hirsch's two bagger.

In other opening day action, Ed Bruno sparked the Shamrocks to a 4-2 triumph over the Indians. Bruno drove in three runs with a double and triple. Len Henderson led the losers' attack with two singles and a triple. Both Gary Munsterman and Tony Petrillo, the winning and losing pitchers, respectively, chalked up eight strikeouts.

In the third of five contests on opening day, the defending champion Orioles romped to a 12-2 decision over the Peacocks. Stephen Kablesh, Ed Kahn, and Larry Townsend led the attack with seven hits between them. Jack Pareta's double for the losers' cause was the only extra base hit of the game. Great defensive play enabled George Pacchiana to pick up the win.

Tony Cioppa's home run led the Cubs to a 19-9 win over the Comets. Harry Manchester and Lou Zuccarelli had two and three hits, respectively for the Cubs. Bart Sagarin pitched a complete game win. Lew Mains fanned 11 in the Wildcats 9-2 defeat of the Jesters. Alan Daniello led the hitting attack for the winners going two for four.

Shamrocks' Munsterman Whitewashes Indians, 3-0

May 22 – The Shamrocks took undisputed possession of first place in the Little League National League by defeating the Indians, 3-0. Gary Munsterman threw a one-hit shutout for the winners. Bob Cruikshank pitched the Owls to a 4-3 victory over the Eagles, fanning twelve and walking three. Ernie Motta of the Eagles struck out ten and issued four walks. In other contests, the Tigers handed the Bulldogs their first loss in a close 6-5 game. Bob Delmonico pitched the Comets to a 13-9 triumph over the Cubs.

Joel Mazzarella Homers Twice in Bulldogs Win

June 1 – The Owls put together a three run rally in the bottom of the sixth inning to edge the Mount Vernon Little League champion Orioles, 10-9, at Baker Field. Kevin Olifiers went four for four including a home run. The Pirates tagged the Indians with a 6-4 defeat. Although outhit, the Bucs managed to move the runs across when it counted and were led by Ed Lombardi, Joe Tripodi and Tom Ambrosino.

Lose play spoiled Shamrock hurler Tom Gasparini's mound debut as the Panthers posted a 6-4 triumph. Gasparini didn't allow an earned run while giving up but four hits in six innings. Gene Masucci picked up the win for the Panthers.

In Western League action Joel Mazzarella clouted two home runs as the Bulldogs trounced the Cubs, 14-2. Meanwhile, the Jesters finished on the short end of a 13-5 count against the Rams. Carl Viggiano and Bob Leggieri hit homers for the winners. Augie Alegi tripled for the Jesters as Leggieri picked up the win while Ed Abate took the defeat despite racking up 13 strikeouts.

Shamrocks Win First Round of National Little League

June 5 – The Shamrocks defeated the Pirates, 10-8, to capture the first round of the city's National Little League. Pete Fiore, Tom Gasparini, Francis Amorosano and Ed Bruno provided the hitting in the Shamrocks attack.

They hit Pirate hurler Mike Hirsch hard in the first two innings as the Shamrocks scored nine runs. It was too late when relief pitcher Tom Ambrosino came in and limited the winners to one hit and one run over the last four innings despite his teammates rallying for eight runs led by Jim Forkell, Frank Cuomo and Pat Tucci.

In another game the Panthers edged the Indians, 4-3, in extra innings to gain the league's second place slot. Joe Brescia tripled and had two singles for the Panthers. Gene Masucci pitched six innings for the winners but needed relief help from Ray Schilke. In an American League contest, Ernie Motta threw a two hitter to lead the Eagles to a 4-0 blanking of the Orioles in an American League game. Motta fanned 15 batters along the way. The Owls blasted the Peacocks, 15 to 4, behind the strong hitting of Tom Ruffalo who had two triples.

Indians Top Pirates, 8-4

June 11 – The Indians topped the Pirates for an 8-4 National Little League win with Bob Romanino, Dick Gross and Ted Cardasis leading the way. Paul LoGuercio pitched well in his mound debut for the Pirates but suffered from poor fielding help behind him. The Pirates weren't the only team suffering from bad fielding the same day. At Wrigley Field in Chicago, the New York Giants and Chicago Cubs combined for nine errors.

Orioles Win First Round in American League

June 14 – The City champion Orioles took the first step toward retaining their Little American League title when they defeated the Owls 5-1 in a playoff game. The win gave them the first round championship. George Pacchiana went all the way, allowing five scattered hits and striking out ten. Dom D'Angelo and Dave Smith paced the attack.

Pirates Win Game for Eddie

June 17 – Eight-year-old Eddie Anderson in the hospital recovering from an injury felt a whole lot better thanks to his Pirate teammates. They promised him a victory in their first second-round game. In true storybook fashion, they came through, stopping the Indians, 6-3. Anderson's teammates also sent their injured teammate an autographed baseball. Mike Hirsch scattered six hits and received hitting support from Jim Forkell and Pat Tucci. While Hirsch hurled a six-inning complete game, the same day Philadelphia Phillies pitcher Robin Roberts went 15 innings in a Phillies win over the St. Louis Cardinals.

Future Pirate Titles Founded on Youth Movement

June 17 – The National League champion Pirates employed one of the smallest infield combinations during the season. Eight-year-olds John Merola and Eddie Anderson played second base and shortstop, respectively. To balance the infield, ten-year-old Joey Tripodi moved to third base. The senior member of the infield was Jim Forkell, the catcher. Carl Viggiano held down first base.

The "whiz kids" did not play the entire game. It was a Pirate practice to use a platoon system. When the older boys came in, only Tripodi remained. A *Daily Argus* story reported that Merola and Anderson were "still too young to save the game with long homers and great defensive plays, but they are learning fast. They are both deft bunters and do not hesitate to flag down a hard-hit ground ball or to tag out an ambitious base runner." The youth plan was not a new thing with the Pirates. In 1953, despite a drive for the National League title, the team played Tripodi, then nine-years-old, and ten-year-old Denis Roccio at least two innings in every game.

Tony Petrillo Hurls 2-Hitter in Indians Win

June 21 – The Shamrocks suffered an 11-1 defeat at the hands of the Indians as Tony Petrillo hurled a two hitter while striking out six and walking two. Losing pitcher Pete Fiore wrecked Petrillo's no-hit bid with a single in the fifth inning. Ted Cardasis, Earl Conti, John DeFeo and Petrillo each had at least one extra base hit for the Indians.

Over in the American League, the Orioles shut out the Owls, 2-0, behind the three-hit pitching of George Pacchiana while Bill Bauersfeld helped his Eagles teammates defeat the Owls, 4-2. Bauersfeld had two hits and compiled 15 strikeouts.

Bulldogs Hold League Lead; Bucs Win on Cuomo's Triple

June 23 – The Bulldogs won their first two games in second round league play to maintain their division lead. John Corke meanwhile blanked the Tigers, 6-0, and later crushed the Comets, 21 to 8, as Joe Mazzarella, Roy Pizzarella and Joel Mazzarella each hit home runs.

Another Saturday game saw the Pirates edge the Shamrocks, 4-3, on Frank Cuomo's triple in the seventh inning with one teammate aboard. Tom Ambrosino came on in relief to pick up the win. Buc starter Ed Lombardi fanned six during his six innings on the mound.

The Panthers posted a couple of league wins by edging the Shamrocks, 4-3, and trimming the Indians, 7-4. The Panthers scored a tie-breaking run in the sixth inning and then held off the Shamrocks after they loaded the bases in the bottom of the same inning. Second baseman Mike Boyle made a sparkling play on Gary Munsterman's hard hit grounder to save the victory.

The Tigers rallied in the last inning to beat the Cubs, 11-7, even though Tony Cioppa tripled and homered for the Cubs. In another league game, the Comets blasted the Bulldogs in a 25-3 victory. Winning pitcher Mike Simon made like Washington Senator Harmon Killebrew, who made his first major league appearance the same day, when Simon cracked the game wide open in the second inning with a grand slam home run. Ten more runs followed before play moved into the third inning. Simon homered again along with teammates Bob Wisner and Vonnie Wickens.

Pirates Lose; Peacocks Tops Orioles, 10-9

July 2 – The Pirates lost to the Panthers 2-1.

Pirate hurler Ed Lombardi had the game wrapped up until the Panthers took advantage of a two out fielding error in the fourth inning and scored the winning runs. John Bennett, Lou Gazverde, Ray Schilke and Jack Coleman led the hit parade for the Panthers. Winning pitcher Gazverde struck out seven and walked one. Lombardi fanned nine and gave up two walks.

In an American League game, the Peacocks tripped the Orioles 10-9 for their first victory of the second round. Don Ross was the difference for the Peacocks, hitting a home run and three singles. Teammate Larry Troncone also homered. Winning pitcher Nick Giordano's fine relief pitching kept the Orioles at bay during the final inning.

Ed Lombardi Fans 14 in Upending Indians

July 5 – The Pirates finally broke their three-game losing streak and climbed back into the National League race by upending the Indians, 3-0. Ed Lombardi fanned 14 and gave up but two scratch hits. He had his eyes set on a no-hitter until Len Henderson hit a Texas League single in the fifth. The Bucs have one more game left and that is with the current league-leading Panthers. The Panthers meanwhile have three more games. If the Panthers lose one they guarantee the Bucs a tie.

Also over the Independence Day holiday weekend, the Comets posted a couple of wins, one a 6-4 victory over the Tigers, the other a 6-5 defeat of the Cubs. John Geberth and Bruce Fabricant homered in the first game as Ed Smith picked up the win. Phil Napolitano picked up the second game win.

Indians Still Contenders in National League Race

July 9 – The Indians split half their six games in the second round of the National League pennant race but remain serious league contenders.

Throughout the season, their hitting has been led by Bobby Romanino, Dick Gross, and John Duno. Bob Petrone and Peter Lombardi have also shown some promise at the plate. On the defensive side, Tony Tobacco has shown real catching potential while John DeFeo is fast becoming one of the best third basemen in the league. Earl Conti, at first base, and Ted Cardasis also rate applause for their defensive play while Len Henderson and Jim Ferraro have been tough on the base paths. Handling the pitching has been Tony Petrillo. Steve Acunto has piloted the team since its inception. Assisting him are coaches Tony Romanino and Dan Lorusso.

Cuomo and Ambrosino Homer as Pirates Cruise

July 15 – The National League champion Pirates gave up a run to the Panthers in the first inning but rallied to win, 7-2, to cinch second round honors. Ed Lombardi tossed a one hitter but waited until the fourth inning before his teammates sewed up the game with three runs. They added another three in the fifth. Frank Cuomo and Tom Ambrosino homered. The Panthers loan hit was a double by Gene Masucci. The Pirates now enter the league three-game playoff against the Shamrocks.

The Orioles kept their American League pennant hopes alive by beating the Peacocks, 7-2 at Baker Field. George Pacchiana broke up a 1-0 game in the third inning with a three-run home run. Teammate Larry Townsend also homered while losing pitcher Tom Mangone did the same for the Peacocks.

While the Orioles were winning, the Eagles broke a two-game losing streak coming from behind to beat the Owls, 7-6. Five walks and single to right field by Mike Slane in the sixth inning settled the issue. John Weis homered for the Eagles as Ernie Motta picked up the win.

Bulldogs Win Western League Championship

July 16 – The Bulldogs knocked the Tigers out of contention with an easy 18-1 win at Longfellow Field. The Bulldogs wrapped up the second round crown to go along with its first round pennant.

Roy Pizzarello led the Bulldogs with a grand slam home run and a triple.

Mount Vernon Little League To Expand

July17 – The Mount Vernon Little League received news from National Little League headquarters in Williamsport, PA that the Mount Vernon organization must expand to a five loop arrangement for the 1955 season. Little League national headquarters requires one league per 15,000 population so that would require five leagues for the city's 75,000 people.

Pacchiana Fans 15 Eagles in Orioles Win

July 19 – The battle for the city's top honors is expected to narrow down to a contest between last year's rivals, the Pirates and the defending champion Orioles. Both clubs won opening games in their respective league playoffs.

The Pirates downed the Shamrocks, 11-3. Denis Rocchio, with a homer and two singles, Ed Lombardi, with two triples and a single, and Paul Wiener and Frank Cuomo, with a pair of base hits each, were the Buc batting leaders. Francis Amorosano homered for the Shamrocks and Gary Munsterman had two singles.

Defensive play was outstanding on both sides. Amorosano pulled down a 275-foot drive off the bat of Lombardi, which was one of the longest hit balls seen in the Little League during the season. Lombardi picked up the win with an eight strikeout, five hit, two walk performance.

The Orioles beat the Eagles, 6-1, in the American League playoff feature. George Pacchiana held the losers to three hits while fanning 15. The Eagles scored on a Larry Townsend double that drove in two runs and Dom D'Angelo came up with an identical bases loaded situation in the second inning and drove in two more runs.

Ross and Giordano Star as Peacocks Top Orioles

July 21 – The Peacocks tripped the Orioles, 10-9, for their first victory of the second round. Don Ross was the difference maker with a home run and three singles for the winners. Teammate Larry Troncone also had a home run and single. Winning pitcher Nick Giordano's fine relief pitching kept the Orioles at bay during the final inning.

Mains Helps Wildcats To First in East Little League Playoff

July 22 – On the same day the New York Yankees were signing free agent Ralph Branca who would appear in five games in 1954, the Wildcats got away winging in the first game of the Eastern Little League playoff drubbing the Rams, 12-2, at Baker Field.

The Cats iced the game when they scored five runs in the second inning. Lew Mains was outstanding in relief striking out 10 and walking only three. In addition, he went two-for-two. Bob Tramontano, playing third base for the Wildcats, also singled. In the field, Jimmy Domato, Vinnie Rocco and Al Daniello each came up with fine defensive plays to help the Wildcats cause. Carl Viggiano spoiled Mains' shutout, hitting a home run in the fourth inning.

Orioles Still Pack Big Bats

July 27 – It has become a tradition in Mount Vernon Little League to think of the Orioles when mentioning teams with the ability to fashion runs in wholesale lots. Last year, the Orioles rolled to a city a championship. Many thought that the tradition might die when the Orioles lost several key players when the league expanded this year. The Orioles also lost manager Tom Nelly. Nelly became president of the new Western Little League and Faust Cardillo took over as Oriole boss.

And now another season is over and the Orioles are American Little League champs and driving for another city title. Again, hitting is a byword with the club. Dom D'Angelo, George Pacchiana, and Larry Townsend pack the big bats, but everyone on the roster, including pitchers, is capable of breaking up a game. Defense is not neglected, with center fielder Ed Kahn and versatile

Steve Kablesh, who plays anywhere but third base and pitcher, leading the defense.

Dave and Pete Fox, Artie Trapp, and Larry Casarella are among the boys who will form the nucleus of the 1955 Orioles. Casarella is the younger brother of former Paramount and A.B. Davis mound ace Caz Casarella.

Leggiere Out-Pitches Mains in 2-1 Rams Win

July 27 – In a stirring pitching duel with only four hits in the game, the Rams defeated the Wildcats, 2-1, to win the Mount Vernon Eastern Little League championship. Bob Leggiere out-pitched Lew Mains in a neat mound struggle, limiting the Wildcats to one hit. Mains, the Wildcats leading hurler, allowed only three hits, one a double by Leggiere.

Leggiere struck out 10 and walked one. Mains fanned six and walked two. The Rams scored early, with one run in the first inning and another in the second. The Wildcats threatened in the sixth when they scored their lone run.

Tourney Over for City's LL; Port Chester and New Rochelle Win

August 2 – Mount Vernon's Little League turned their thoughts and bats to the forthcoming city championships after an unsuccessful weekend in national tournament play. The Mount Vernon Americans lost to the New Rochelle Centrals, 8-6, while the city's Nationals lost, 4-1, to Port Chester's Americans.

No Surprise – Pirates and Orioles Advance in City Series

August 10 – There was no surprise. Both pre-season favorites, the Pirates and Panthers, advanced in opening round robin games for Mount Vernon's Little League championship.

The National title holding Pirates won convincingly, 9-2, over the Western Division winners, The Bulldogs. The American League champion Orioles beat the Eastern League Rams, 8-5. The Pirates face the Rams and Orioles take on the Bulldogs in their next game.

The Pirates broke open their game against the Bulldogs in the sixth inning. Until then, the game was tied 1-1. The Pirates scored eight runs. Patsy Tucci, Tom Ambrosino, Carl Viggiano and John Forkell led the hit parade. Forkell's triple drove in three runs. The Bulldogs only managed three hits by Phil DeRosa, John Corke and Nino Fiore. Taking advantage of those runs was winning pitcher Ed Lombardi who fanned 10 and walked only two. Joel Mazzarella picked up the loss.

Steve Kablesh highlighted the Orioles attack with four hits including a double. George Pacchiana, the winning pitcher, homered and also had two singles. Teammate Dom DeAngelo had three singles. Ed Kahn homered for the losing Rams.

Bucs and Orioles on Collision Course

August 11 – Playoff games are nerve wracking. The Orioles perspired plenty to keep pace with the Pirates. At stake is a trip to the finals. While the Pirates easily beat the Rams, 10-0, the Orioles had to come from behind to down the Bulldogs, 8-7.

Tom Ambrosino threw no-hit ball for almost five innings while his teammates scored all their runs by the time the fifth inning opened. Denis Rocchio and Ambrosino led the offense, each with a pair of hits. Carl Viggiano and Bob Leggiere had the only Ram hits.

Joel Mazzarella almost defeated the Orioles by himself, hitting a home run and a double while driving in five of his team's seven runs. His hitting, combined with John Corke's pitching, had the Orioles on the ropes, 7-6, after three innings. But the Orioles rallied and tied the score in the fifth. The Bulldogs then loaded the bases with two out in the sixth inning against Oriole reliever Larry Townsend. Townsend got the next hitter to hit on the ground but it took a nice pickup by Bob Meyers to corral a bad throw and get Townsend out of the jam. Dave Smith clinched the Oriole victory in the bottom of the sixth inning when he doubled and eventually scored the winning run.

Bucs Whip Orioles, 4-1, To Take Series Lead

August 13 – The same night Bob Feller tamed the Baltimore Orioles for his 259th lifetime victory, the Mount Vernon Little League Orioles lost to the Pirates, giving the Bucs a distinct advantage in the scramble for the year's crown. The Pirates 4-1 victory makes up for last year's loss of the city championship to the Orioles.

Losing pitcher George Pacchiana was throwing a no-hitter as he coasted into the bottom of the sixth inning with a 1-0 lead. Carl Viggiano's bunt single spoiled that. The Orioles were within one out of taking home the victory when a walk, single, and a wild pitch enabled the Pirates to tie the score on Frank Cuomo's hit. Hurler Ed Lombardi made sure the decision was his by belting a 2-1 pitch over the centerfield fence.

In the series other matchup, the Rams knocked off the Bulldogs, 13-3. Winning pitcher Bob Leggiere hit a pair of home runs as he went three for four at the plate. His curve ball helped him fan nine while walking only three. Teammate Jim Fraser had a home run, triple and double.

Older Leagues Romp Over Eastern and Western Loops

August 16 – The Pirates and Orioles of the older National and American Leagues easily beat the Rams and Bulldogs of the newer Eastern and Western circuits.

The Pirates trounced the Bulldogs, 10-2, while the Orioles were blasting the Rams, 14-1. Chances are the city champion will not be crowned until Friday night when the Orioles get their second chance against the Pirates. The Orioles used outfielder Eddie Kahn to pitch. He made it look easy. He also had two doubles as did Dom D'Angelo. George Pacchiana blasted another home run for the winners.

Pirate pitcher Mike Hirsch came home from an Adirondack Mountains vacation and was welcomed back by his teammates. He responded by scattering eight hits. Third baseman Frank Cuomo went four-for-four and Jim Forkell added a couple of singles and a double.

Mrs. Edward Martin Re-elected as Mothers' President

August 18 – Mrs. Edward Martin was re-elected president of the Mount Vernon Pony-Little-Minor League Mothers organization at a meeting held at the Boys' Club. With a tally of 61 to 21 votes, Mrs. Martin was elected to her second term in office. Mrs. C.B. Edwards was named vice president; Mrs. Eric Lindfors, recording secretary; Mrs. Michael Mangone, corresponding secretary; and Mrs. Alfred Rocchio, treasurer. Mrs. Charlotte Innecken was chairwoman of the nominating committee.

Viggiano Homers as Rams Tie Series

August 18 – The Rams drubbed the Pirates, 7-1 at Baker Field. The upset, coupled with the Orioles win over the Bulldogs, throws the race for city honors into a turmoil. Tomorrow's playoff finale will decide the championship. The Bucs and Orioles are tied with 4-1 records.

The Pirates failed to come up with the brand of ball that gave them four consecutive National League pennants. They put together but five hits, two singles by Frank Cuomo, a pair of doubles by Jim Forkell and a double by Tom Ambrosino. For the Rams it was Carl Viggiano, with a home run and a double, and Jack Williams, with a single and a double, pacing the attack. Bob Leggiere took credit for the Rams win, fanning six and walking six. Ambrosino was charged with the loss.

Pacchiana Ups Playoff Batting Average to .769

August 19 – Sparked by an 18 to 1 trouncing of the Bulldogs, the Orioles face a showdown test against the Pirates. The Orioles had seemed out of the running for the city Little League championship after the Pirates defeated them early in the playoffs. But since the Pirates recent loss, the race is a toss-up.

Dom DeAngelo went all the way to pick up the victory for the Orioles, striking out six while limiting the Bulldogs to five hits. George Pacchiana blasted his fourth home run of the series. His three for four record at bat pushed his playoff batting average to .769. Pacchiana leads all batters in both home runs and batting. The Orioles also have Larry Townsend who went four for four against the Bulldogs. Steve Kablesh, runner-up to Pacchiana in batting, went three for four while Bob Meyers went four for four.

As the Pirates and Orioles were getting ready for their championship game, another New York state Little League team was hoping to get to the 1954 Little League World Series championship in Williamsport, PA. A team from Schenectady got there and would eventually become the first Empire State team to win a championship at Williamsport. During the Little League World Series a team from Lakeland, FL would compete. On that team was John "Boog" Powell who later would star for the Baltimore Orioles. Powell gave up 15 runs in three innings against Schenectady.

Pirates Edge Orioles, 3-2

Cop Little Loop Title As Losers' Rally Fails

They had to sweat out a tension-packed final inning to do it, but National Little League Pirates took their second city championship and first under Manager Joe Tropodi by nipping American League Orioles 3-2, at Baker Field last night.

Trailing 3-0 going into the sixth inning, Orioles rose up to score twice and have the tying run thrown out at the plate. Even then the tension held until pitcher Eddie Lombardi got hard-hitting Bob Meyers to bounce into the final out.

Sidearming his fastball with uncanny accuracy, Lombardi ran through Orioles' batting order for the first four innings. Only a walk on a 3-2 pitch to John Bartolini in the third separated him from a perfect game.

Pressure On Pacchiana

Meanwhile his mates kept the pressure on opposition pitcher George Pacchiana. Frank Cuomo opened the second inning by lining the first pitch down the right field line and over the fence. No one had a tape measure, but the drive was estimated at 185 feet.

Two more Bucs pattered over the plate in the fourth. Patsy Tucci led off by doubling inside third base. He moved to third on a wild pitch and came in when shortstop Steve Kablesh picked up Tom Ambrosino's grounder and tried to nail him at the plate. The throw went wild and Ambrosino wound up on second. A few passed balls later he was across and Pirates led 3-0.

The way Lombardi was pitching, the 3 looked like 300. That is until the fifth when the handwriting began to be scribbled on the wall.

First Oriole Hit

Larry Townsend got the first Oriole hit, banging a medium speed curve into left. Meyers rapped back to Lombardi who engineered a snappy 1-6-3 double play. Catcher Dave Smith singled to right but Bartolini fanned to end the inning.

With one down in the sixth, Ed Kahn kindled Oriole hopes by singling to right. Lombardi gave up his second walk of the game, to Steve Kablesh. Dom D'Angelo singled on the ground to left scoring Kahn and sending Kablesh to second. D'Angelo and Kablesh moved up a notch on the throw to the plate.

Manager Tripodi placed discretion before valor and ordered an intentional pass to George Pacchiana. Townsend then rifled a sharp grounder into the hole between short and third and all runners scampered like hookey players from a truant officer.

No One Knows

How he got there no one knows, but shortstop Denis Rocchio managed to get a glove on the ball and slow it down. He scrambled after it as Kablesh came across the plate. D'Angelo cruised around third—hesitated—then started in with the tying run. It wasn't even close. Rocchio collared the ball, wheeled around, sized up the situation at a glance, and threw to catcher Jim Forkell who tagged the oncoming D'Angelo. Lombard mustered his reserve strength and got Meyers on a sharp hopper to second baseman Joe Tripodi.

ALL - STAR SLANTS: No major league scouts were noticed but the Pony League had at least three managers in the crowd making mental notes.... Townsend carboned Willie Mays with a vest-pocket catch of Lombardi's lofty hoist in the third.... Because of the importance of the game, Commissioner Andy Karl brought in a third umpire from Rams-Bulldogs game and filled in that contest on the bases.... Crowd of around 350 was swelled to at least twice that size when Rams-Bulldogs spectators topped over en-masse to watch the final two innings.

Pirates	ab	r	h	Orioles	ab	r	h
Tripodi, 2b	3	0	0	Kahn, cf	3	1	1
Rocchio, ss	2	0	1	Kablesh, ss	2	1	0
Lombardi, p	2	0	0	D'Angelo, 3b	3	0	1
Forkell, c	3	0	0	Pacchiana, p	2	0	0
Cuomo, 3b	3	1	1	Townsend, rf	3	0	2
Tucci, rf	3	1	1	Meyers, 1b	3	0	0
Ambrosino, cf	2	1	0	Smith, c	2	0	1
Viggiano, 1b	2	0	1	Bartolini, 2b	1	0	0
Wiener, lf	2	0	0	D. Fox, lf	2	0	0
Totals	22	3	4	Totals	21	2	5

SCORE BY INNINGS

Pirates .... 010 200—3
Orioles .... 000 002—2

Runs batted in—Cuomo, Ambrosino. Double play—Lombardi to Rocchio to Viggiano. Earned runs—Pirates 2, Orioles 2. Left on bases—Pirates 3, Orioles 5. Home run—Cuomo. Sacrifice

1954 – Pirates Win 2nd Word Series

Pirates, 1954 Little League Champions: 1, Coach Ed Mergenthaler; 2, Paul LoGuercio; 3, Mike Hirsch; 4, Frank Cuomo; 5, Jim Forkell; 6, Manager Joe Tripodi; 7, Ed Lombardi; 8, Tom Ambrosino; 9, Coach Jim Forkell; 10, Lou Lobes; 11, Carl Viggiano; 12, Paul Wiener; 13, Joe Tripodi; 14, Bob Merola; 15, Denis Rocchio; 16, George McLean; 17, Pat Tucci.

Comets: 1, Coach Jerry Delmonico; 2, Manager Steve Wisner; 3, Larry Ferruzzi; 4, Jeff Geberth; 5, Phil Napolitano; 6, Ed Smith; 7, Mike Simon; 8, Bruce Fabricant; 9, Bob Delmonico; 10, Bob Wisner; 11, Vonnie Wickens; 12, Joe Urana; 13, Fred Peterson; 14, Ricky Miller; 15, Harold Peterson.

242 Boys Count The Hours As Opening Day Approaches

Some 242 boys are counting off the days until the Little League gets the 1954 baseball season officially underway May 1. Two

NATIONAL LEAGUE
Shamrocks
Francis Amorosano, Salvator Alcide, Robert Blonnt, John Bourne, Edward Bruno, William Deemer, George Fennell, Peter Fiore, Thomas Gasparini, George Ivers, Richard Lord, Louis Nordone, Gary Musterman, Thomas Romanino, Paul Vetrano.

Pirates
Thomas Ambrosino, Edward Anderson, Frank Cuomo, James Forkell, Michael Hirsh, Louis Lobes, Edward Lombardi, Paul Lo-Guercio, John Merola, Denis Rocchio, Joseph Tripodi, Patsy Tucci, Carl Viggiano, Paul Weiner, John Wren.

Indians
Peter Bartolini, Larry Briglia, Earl Conti, John De Fiero, John Duno, James Ferrara, Richard Gross, Leonard Henderson, Peter Lombardi, Anthony Petrillo, Robert Petrone, Robert Romanino, Andrew Siegenfeld, Anthony Tobacco, Mark Weinstein.

Panthers
John Bennett, Michael Boccardi, Michael Boyle, John Bradford, Joseph Brescia, John Coleman, Thomas Cowen, Louis Gasverdi, William Heller, Dennis Hurlie, Gene Masucci, Thomas O'Shaughnessy, Jack O'Shaughnessy, Raymond Schilke, Paul Squillacote.

EASTERN LEAGUE
Wildcats
Peter Altieri, Bobby Bankenstein, Billy Bankenstein, Henry Carideo, Alan D. Daniello, James Domato, Henry Hess, Lewis Mains, Thomas Edward Mascaro, Vincent Rocco, Harold J. Stamler Jr., Robert Tramontano, Robert Trupin, Dick Tursi, Jon Tursi, Robert Vetrano, Albert Wieland, Joe Zuzzolo.

Rams
Andrew A. Bush, Charles F. Censullo, Leslie Cheikin, Peter De Vito, George De Vito, James D. Fraser, Thomas R. Leggiere, Robert T. Leggiere, David A. Monaghan, Christopher Rezza, Michael Smith, Robert George Snyder, Carl F. Viggiano, Leonard Weistrop, John R.

EASTERN LEAGUE
Wildcats
Peter Altieri, Bobby Bankenstein, Billy Bankenstein, Henry Carideo, Alan D. Daniello, James Domato, Henry Hess, Lewis Mains, Thomas Edward Mascaro, Vincent Rocco, Harold J. Stamler Jr., Robert Tramontano, Robert Trupin, Dick Tursi, Jon Tursi, Robert Vetrano, Albert Wieland, Joe Zuzzolo.

Rams
Andrew A. Bush, Charles F. Censullo, Leslie Cheikin, Peter De Vito, George De Vito, James D. Fraser, Thomas R. Leggiere, Robert T. Leggiere, David A. Monaghan, Christopher Rezza, Michael Smith, Robert George Snyder, Carl F. Viggiano, Leonard Weistrop, John R. Williams.

Lions
Ronald F. Blake, Nicholas Ceglio, John W. Cumming, Patsy De Mone, Charles William Dunsay, Cary Fields, Frank Fiore, Leonard A. Kashner, John Koennecke, Robert J. Luth, Daniel Monteferante, Lawrence S. Reed, Roy H. Sussman, Dick Wasserstrom.

Jesters
Edmund Abate, August Alegi, Robert Bisordi, Ray Blumenfeld, Gino P. Bossio, Lloyd Burak, Pat Carbone, Richard Francisco Jr., Robert L. Friedman, Robert Guarino, John Limato, William A. Malone, Dominick Masucci, Kenneth Rabasca, Joseph Sicuranzo.

AMERICAN LEAGUE
Eagles
John Allen, William Bauersfeld, Alton Brooks, Frank Castaldo, Thomas Carroll, Michael Joyce, Anthony Kane, Russell Kohl, Ernest Motta, Louis Nange, Fred Riggio, Michael Slane, Thomas Shay, John Weis, Stephen Wexler.

Owls
Robert Bell, David Cirin, Thomas Capodicci, Robert Cruickshank, Ken Glaser, Chester Holmes, Patrick Kane, Kevin Olifiers, James Pellegrino, Thomas Ruffalo, John Riganati, Peter Sista, Carl Silverman, Anthony Savastano, William Thomas.

Peacocks
John Antonelli, Charles Auricchio, Donald Bugsch, Joseph Castro, Nicholas Giordano, Dennis Eliason, Jack Liebespack, Peter Leifert, Richard Merigliano, Thomas Mangone, Richard Moccio, Jack Pareta, Donald Ross, Lawrence Tromcone, Joseph Wasserman.

Orioles
John Bartolini, Larry Casarella, Dominick D'Angelo, David Fox, Peter Fox, Stephen Kablish, Edward Kahn, John Manganello, Victor Magnatta, Robert Meyer, William Pelliccio, George Pacchiana, David Smith, Arthur Trapp, Lawrence Townsend.

WESTERN LEAGUE
Comets
Robert Delmonico, Bruce Fabricant, Lawrence Ferruzzi, Jeffrey Geberth, John Geberth, Ricky Miller, Phillip Napolitano, Axel Orbert, Fred Peterson, Harold Peterson, Michael Simon, Edward Smith, Giovanni Wickens, Robert Wisner, Joseph Urana.

Bulldogs
John D. Corke, Philip De Rosa, Arthur Ebert, Anthony Fiore, James Manna, John Magner, Joseph Mazzarella, Joel Mazzarella, Michael L. Nagelberg, Donald Nicita, Stephen Pittari, Roy Anthony Pizzarello, George Reynolds, Edward Reynolds, Richard A. Spindler.

Cubs
Anthony Cioppa, August Colarusso, Edmund De Blasio, Stephen De Feo, Ross Epstein, Robert John Grosch, Gary William Jossen, Eugene Earl Kilpatrick, Frank Lasorsa, Louis A. Lisella, Harry Manchester, George H. Pignataro, Bart Stephen Sagarin, Arthur (Buster) Smith, Louis F. Zuccareili.

Tigers
Carl Richard Anderson, Edward D. Chappetta, William Cromwell, Charles J. De Luca, James Lacerra, James Lyons, Pat Manto, Robert S. Mayer, Thomas McNamara, Richard A. Pregiato, James Robinson, Paul Richard Wackermann, Roger Lewis Wackermann, Robert Woolrich, Raymond Woolrich.

1954
World Series
Batting

	AB.	R.	H.	Avg.
Kablesh, Orioles	15	5	10	.667
Pacchiana, Orioles	15	8	10	.667
Viggiano, Rams	16	12	10	.625
Cuomo, Pirates	17	6	10	.588
Leggiere, Rams	16	6	9	.563
Townsend, Orioles	16	6	8	.500
Forkell, Pirates	16	4	7	.438
Manna, Bulldogs	14	5	6	.429
Fraser, Rams	18	6	7	.389
Kahn, Orioles	16	8	6	.375

(Limited to 12 or more turns at bat.)

Home Run Leaders

Pacchiana, Orioles — 4
Leggiere, Rams — 2
Cuomo and Lombardi, Pirates; Viggiano, Williams and Fraser, Rams — 1 each.

1954 National League All Stars: 1, Pat Tucci; 2, Lenny Henderson; 3, Anthony Tobacco; 4, Ray Schilke; 5, Frank Cuomo; 6, Gary Munsterman; 7, Gene Masucci; 8, Tom Ambrosino; 9, Ed Bruno; 10, Tony Petrillo; 11, Lou Gazverde; 12, Jim Forkell; 13, Ed Lombardi; 14, Coach Jeff Borelli; 15, Manager Joe Tripodi.

1954 Bulldogs: 1, Phil DeRosa; 2, Steve Pittari; 3, Bob Bourque; 4, Roy Pizzarello; 5, Jim Manna; 6, Joe Mazzarella; 7, Nino Fiore; 8, Coach Nino Fiore; 9, Coach Roy Pizzarello; 10, Manager Mazzarella; 11, John Sealy.

1954 Lions: 1, Harry Szamler; 2, Johnny Koennette; 3, Patsy DeMone; 4, Larry Reed; 5, Billy Dunsay; 6, Cary Fields; 7, Ronnie Blake; 8, Nick Ceglio; 9, Manager Sol Dunsay; 10, Peter Dunsay; 11, Lenny Kashner; 12, Coach Frank Blake.

Frank Cuomo went three for five against the Shamrocks in helping the Pirates win the 1954 National League pennant.

HERE MA, SIGN!

Parents of grade school youngsters get used to having things brought home for them to sign. There are report cards, notes from the teacher, absence notes, and other documents of that type. Over recent years here, they have added another to that list— Little League baseball applications.

Each season, though, league officials report that there are a number of parents who hesitate before signing for their youngsters. They do not know what Little League is. Is there a fee? Will they have to buy uniforms? Is it commercial? Is there supervision? Many a well-meaning parent would like more information before entrusting a child to a new and strange program. Hence this explanation.

Little League baseball is not commercial. They say that it is big league baseball adapted to the mental and physical capacities of boys twelve years of age and under. That's wrong. Big league baseball today is a business, out to make money and in competition with the movies, TV and horse racing. Little League does raise money, but unlike the majors, it puts all of its profits back into the clubs. Not since the late Colonel Jacob Rupert could the big show make that statement. Little League needs money to pay umpires, help care for the fields, make up the difference between the cost of equipment and the sums given by sponsors.

It doesn't cost parents a cent. Everyone tries out for teams and players are chosen on ability. Batting and fielding averages count, race, religion, financial standing do not. The kid who owns a baseball does not necessarily pitch. Carefully selected managers and coaches decide who plays where.

Little League is not a perfect organization, but neither is any other group organized for youngsters. We don't know of any perfect parents either. But parents whose sons stick a Little League application under their noses and say, "sign," need not hesitate. The program is designed to teach baseball and citizenship and no youngster ever got too much of either.

Since it has been here, Little League has become an active force in the community. Witness the letters which come into its headquarters, one from Police Chief William McDonald in thanks for being made an honorary member, one from the Mount Vernon Hospital after the League sent them the flowers from its annual dinner, one from a father explaining how much Little League has done for his son, and a similar one from a league umpire who also teaches in the city school system. These people would hardly hesitate in signing an application and neither would the parents whose sons have gone through a Little or Minor league season.

1954 – Pirates Win 2nd Word Series

The tall and short of it in Mount Vernon baseball. Tha is 6-foot 5-inch John VonBargen who played in the Pony League. The smaller fellow is Joe Tripodi of the Pirates.

12

1955 – City Leagues Consolidate

The biggest changes for Mount Vernon Little League in 1955 came not on the diamonds but at its headquarters. Also in '55, young Brooklyn Dodgers fans in the city would never have to say again, "Wait Til Next Year". The Dodgers finally beat the Yankees, 4 to 3, in the World Series.

It was also the year that the biggest vaccination project ever undertaken in Mount Vernon took place. Many of us were among the 2053 public school children and 700 parochial school youngsters who received the Salk anti-polio vaccine. We also started brushing our teeth with newly introduced Crest toothpaste and began eating Special K for the first time. Late in the year the Tappan Zee Bridge opened to traffic at Tarrytown, NY for the first time.

In Mount Vernon, in a sweeping reorganization, the entire Little League, Pony League, and Minor League, was consolidated into an organization, The Little League of Mount Vernon, New York, Inc. Under the new arrangement, Little League Commissioner Andy Karl became director of the entire program. Three commissioners were elected to head its branches: Larry Tracy for the Little League, Fred Nelson for the Pony League, and Len Boccardi for the Minor League.

A board of directors was created including Karl, Boccardi, Nelson, Tracy, Bill Real, Tom Nelly, Mike O'Connell, Joe O'Connor, Andy Borelli, Harry Sundberg, and Mrs. Edward Martin, president of the Mothers' Organization. The elected officials of the board were Karl as president; Borelli, vice president; Mrs. Joseph O'Connor, secretary; Ralph Merola, treasurer, and Edward Mergenthaler, publicity director.

Karl appointed O'Connell as finance chairman, with a committee made up of Nelson, Boccardi and Mrs. Martin as co-chairwoman of the sponsors committee. Real headed the by-laws section, Edward Willing became the group's attorney, and Nelly its equipment chairperson. Operational costs, including that of the projected new Little League, made it necessary for the three leagues to become sponsored, the first time for the Little League.

The sponsored teams were: National League: Pirates (Perry Soda Company), Shamrocks (Lombardi Insurance Company), Panthers (Nutex Cleaners), Indians (Republican Club). American League: Orioles (Fava Post), Owls (42nd M.P.s), Peacocks (Gramatan Men's Shop), Eagles

(Embassy Radio and Appliance). Service Club League: Wildcats (City Club), Rams (Rotary Club), Jesters (Kiwanis), Lions (Lions Club). Western League: Cubs (Town Fotoshop), Tigers (Topps Cleaners), Comets (Community Oil Company), Bulldogs (B'nai Brith).

By late February 1955, there was still snow on the ground but applications were coming into Mount Vernon's Recreation Commission for use of its ball fields. A lively battle was underway for playing space between the expanded Little-Pony-Minor League program, the Sound Shore League, softball, and the recreation leagues.

The city's Board of Education and the school system cooperated and made available Baker Field and the Longfellow fields. Howard Field, located behind A.B. Davis High School on Gramatan Avenue, also became a Little League site.

Over the first two weekends in April, tryouts were held at Hutchinson Field where each player was numbered and went through fielding and hitting drills. They were graded by managers who knew them only by numbers. On Monday night April 11, 82 boys were selected from more than 400 candidates for the Little League to fill vacancies on the league's 16 teams. One much sought after pitcher became the property of the Eastern League Lions. He was Andy Karl Jr., son of the director of The Little League of Mount Vernon.

Also playing Little League baseball for the first time in 1955 was nine-year-old George W. Bush, who played his first of four years at Central Little League of Midland, Texas where he was a catcher on the Cubs. He was the first Little League graduate to be elected President of the United States.

When Mount Vernon Little Leaguers took to the diamond on opening day they soon became aware of The Little League Pledge, written in 1955, by an official of Little League. It was not, and has never been, required to be recited by any person involved with Little League baseball or softball but the text of the Little League Pledge has remained unchanged since its inception. It is:

I trust in God
I love my country
And will respect its laws
I will play fair
And strive to win
But win or lose
I will always do my best

Opening Day With Mayor Joe

May 7 – While Mount Vernon Mayor Joseph P. Vaccarella didn't lead the Major Leagues in wins like Robin Roberts did in 1955, he showed his best fastball when he threw out the first ball on opening day to kick off each Little League team's 18-game schedule. The Lions, Panthers, Bulldogs, Wildcats, Owls, Orioles and Comets picked up victories.

In the Service Club league the Lions beat the Rams, 12 to 6, on John Konnecke's power hitting. Louis Nargi made a spectacular catch with two runners on base to give his Owl teammates a 6 to 3 win over the Eagles. The closest game of the day came out of the National League where Ray Schilke pitched and hit the Panthers to a 4 to 3 victory over the Pirates.

Vaccarella on opening day proclaimed the week of June 6-12 as Mount Vernon Baseball

Week to recognize the city's citizens conducting the program that had 600 youngsters playing in Little League, Pony League and Minor League baseball on the city's diamonds.

Fraser Throws Year's First No-Hit Game

May 13 – The Rams Jim Fraser may have read about how Sam Jones pitched a 4-0 no-hitter as his Chicago Cubs defeated the Pittsburgh Pirates the day before. So Fraser went out and threw the first no-hitter of the season when he shutout the Wildcats, 10-0, at Longfellow Field. He faced only 22 batters, walking three and striking out nine. Second baseman Bob Snyder speared two line drives to keep the no-hitter intact. Fraser helped his own cause with a homer. Mike Funke went three for three with a single, double and triple. In other games, the Bulldogs John Seeley beat the Comets, 6 to 5, despite a two-run homer by the Comets Phil Napolitano. The Indians Tony Tobacco outpitched the Panthers Ray Schilke, 4 to 3.

Manna No-Hits Cubs

June 4 – The Pirates Mike Hirsch had visions of throwing a no-hitter but the Shamrocks John Nordone wanted no part of it. He drove a clean single through the right side of the infield to ruin the bid. The Pirates, one of the youngest teams in the league, went on to down the Shamrocks 7 to 3. Bob Bisordi's three hits, including a triple, helped the Jesters defeat the Lions, 13 to 4.

Little League hitters were having a tough time catching up with pitchers during the early part of the season. While Hirsch missed his no-hitter, Jim Manna of the Bulldogs did not. He threw a no-hit, no-run game in beating the Cubs. He led his club with a double and a home run in the 14-0 victory. In other contests, Tom Mangone's triple and double led the Peacocks to a 4 to 3 win over the Owls. The Indians Ted Cardasis singled, tripled and hit a grand slam homer in the Tribe's 17 to 3 win over the Pirates. Mike Simon's four hits, one a homer, was enough batting power for the Comets to streak past the Tigers.

1,200 Youngsters Step Lively To Honor Baseball

June 9 – Nearly 1,200 youngsters representing many city baseball leagues participated in a 40-minute parade watched by several thousand people along Gramatan Avenue.

The youngsters marched five-abreast to the beat of the Washington, Nichols, and Graham Junior High School bands from A.B. Davis High School, down Gramatan Avenue, up Fourth Avenue to Fourth Street. The Anthony T. Fava Post American Legion band also accompanied the marchers. The Westchester Cadets were also featured. Besides the Minor, Little, and Pony League representatives, there were four teams from the Boys Club, about one hundred marchers from the Police Athletic League, the city championship Edison Tech baseball team and the Mount Vernon Softball All-Stars.

Daniello Strikes Out 10 in Wildcats Win

June 14 – The Wildcats scored a run in the bottom of the sixth to edge the Lions 7 to 6 as Alan Daniello held on for the win while striking out ten batters. Cary Fields, with seven strikeouts, was tagged with the loss. The Wildcats were helped by Al Rogliano and Jim Domato with three hits apiece. In another squeaker, the Bulldogs beat the Cubs 5 to 3 as John Seeley and Phil DeRosa combined to limit the Cubs to one hit. DeRosa also homered and doubled.

Joe DiMaggio Is Still Playing

June 15 – Yes, Joe DiMaggio is playing centerfield for the Indians. The eleven-year-old "rookie" came up from Mount Vernon's Minor League to play for the Indians. It was reported in *The Daily Argus* that he is a cousin of the New York Yankees great.

Second Round Little League Play Begins

June 16 – Second round play got underway with the Eagles, Indians, Comets, Lions, and Elks winning. The Eagles got to Orioles starter Larry Casarella for seven runs in the second inning and went on to a 15-5 triumph. Ernie Motta homered and went three for three for the winners. Teammate John Weis went two for two and also homered. Oriole Dave Smith went three for three with a home run.

The defending city champion Pirates only could come up with one hit as Indians pitcher Andy Siegenfeld went all the way in a 12-0 triumph. Mike Hirsch was the loser. Triples by Tony Tobacco, Dino DiFillipo and Earl Conti paced the winners. Young George Bochow got the lone Pirate hit in the inning. Harold "Red" Peterson made his first start for the Comets, limiting the Cubs to three singles, as the Comets won easily 10-1. Ted Johnson of the Lions tossed a two-hitter but 15 walks kept him in hot water before his teammates bailed him out with six runs in the last two innings as the Lions topped the Rams, 8-6. Dick Honeck's homer and Bob Luth's double helped in the comeback. Jim Lewis took the loss for the Rams.

The unbeaten Elks got their second straight win in the Eastern League in beating the Americans, 13-5. The win put them in undisputed possession of first place. The losers outhit the Elks, 10 to 5, but 11 walks offset the batting. Bob Crescenzo's homer for the Elks was a factor. The National League's Indians staged a comeback to edge the Shamrocks. In a pitching duel, Bob Piselli topped Tom Gasperini. Tony Tobacco and Ted Cardasis each had two hits with Cardasis driving in the winning run in the sixth inning. The win put them in a first place tie with the Shamrocks with each posting a 6-2 record.

Tobacco and Cardasis Star in Little League Play

June 18 – Anthony Tobacco struck out 10 and gave up only one hit as the Indians topped the Panthers 7-1. Teammate Ted Cardasis doubled, tripled and homered for the winners. Two weeks earlier, Cardasis singled, tripled and hit a grand slam in a game.

Opening second round play, the Shamrocks beat the Panthers 11-5 while the Eagles won a battle of the birds when they trounced the Peacocks, 22-2. Ernie Motta was awesome at the plate for the Eagles, accounting for nine RBI's with a homer and a pair of triples. In other American League games, the Owls downed the Orioles 10-3. Tom Ruffalo and Bob Bell accounted for all the Owls hits with each player hitting a home run. Bob Cruickshank started his first game since an injury and decisively beat the Peacocks, 21-4. The Lions edged the Jesters 13-11 in the Service

Club League with Dick Honeck and Larry Reed homering for the winners. Jim Fraser and Tom Shannon supplied the hitting as the Rams downed the Wildcats 11-4.

Ernie Motta Has a Dream Week

June 20 – The Eagles Ernie Motta had a week Little League players only dream about. The little man with a big fastball chalked up a no-hit, no-run victory as the Eagles grounded the Owls 7-0. Two days earlier he drove in nine runs with a homer and pair of singles in a single game. Motta missed a perfect game by two batters and both of them reached base by walks. He struck out 12 and never was in any trouble as he got help from teammates John Weis who homered and Richard Brooks who doubled.

The Rams topped the Wildcats 13-9 in a Service Club division game that saw Jim Fraser homer and triple for the winners. Teammate Al Nelson did the same. Bob Gilhooley picked up the win.

And a Child Will Lead Us

June 21 – The Tigers may have defeated the Cubs 9 to 3 but the Cubs John Tornberry, eight and half years old, limited the Tigers to only one run in five innings of relief work. The Tigers scored eight runs in the first inning. Tom Gasparini hit a home run and pitched the Shamrocks to a 7 to 5 win over the Indians.

Perry's Pirates blasted the Panthers 10 to 4 before a large crowd at Baker Field as Bob Merola, Joey Tripodi and Denis Rocchio led a 13-hit barrage. The Peacocks scored five runs in the fifth inning to beat the Orioles 11 to 8 despite the fact that the Peacocks had only nine players available because many of the players were sick or sitting out injuries. Phil Buglione and Richard Moccio led the rally that ended a Peacock slump.

Simon Hits 7th Homer of Season in Comets Win

June 25 – Mike Simon of the Comets hit his seventh home run of the season in the sixth inning to lead the Comets to 4 to 3 victory over the Bulldogs. The win gave the Comets the first round crown in the Western Division while over in the National League the Indians pounded out an 11 to 4 win over the Panthers and the Shamrocks downed the Pirates 5 to 1. Both winners were tied for the league lead. Ted Cardasis drove in five runs for the Indians on three hits. Jack Bourne doubled and tripled for the Shamrocks.

The Peacocks fell one run short in losing to the Owls 7 to 6 in the American League. In another one-run game, the Orioles nipped the Eagles 6 to 5 behind Larry Townsend's clutch pitching. The weekend play saw a three-way tie with the Rams, Wildcats and Lions all occupying first place in the Service Club League. The Lions squeezed by the Jesters 8 to 7 and the Wildcats beat the Rams 11 to 4.

Eagles Bang Out 20 Hits in Victory

July 2 – The Eagles kept its win streak alive with a 16 to 4 win over the Orioles as Ted Rizzo of the winners had four of the team's 20 hits. In the Service Club League, the Jesters defeated the

Rams 18 to 8. Ricky Yarobino led the Jesters with a pair of home runs. Augie Alegi and Bob Friedman also homered for the winners while Al Nelson, Jim Fraser, Tom Shannon and John DiMenna hit homers for the Rams.

In the Western League, the Comets and Tigers played a thriller with the Comets pushing three runs across in the fifth inning to win. Mike Simon continued his torrid hitting for the Comets in blasting his eighth home run of the season.

Indians Win National Title in Beating Shamrocks, 7-1

July 12 – The Indians were waiting for this win for quite a while. In fact, they have been trying to win the National League crown since 1950. They finally won the pennant with a 7 to 1 victory of the Shamrocks.

Steve Acunto's squad won the first round National League title earlier in the season and did it again in the second round behind the four-hit pitching of Bob Piselli. He had a shutout going into the last inning when he was nicked for the lone run. The Indians were led by third baseman Earl Conti who had a pair of singles and a double. Ted Cardasis doubled with the bases loaded to start a four run first inning rally and Tony Tobacco added a triple.

This was a long road for the Indians managed by Acunto. He and the Indians have been part of Mount Vernon Little League since its very first day. He said that this 1955 club was the best hitting squad in the team's history. The Indians leading hitter was Ted Cardasis with a .803 batting average. Other top-ranking performers were first baseman Earl Conti, pitcher Bob Piselli, shortstop-pitcher Bob Petrone and catcher-pitcher Tony Tobacco. Acunto singled out two other factors for the club's success. First is the assistance provided by his coaches, John Cardasis and Anthony Romanino. Second was the rooting support from the players' parents.

Meanwhile, the Rams assured themselves of at least a tie in the Service Club League as they downed the Jesters, 5 to 1. The Rams took the second round title behind the three-hit pitching of John DiMenna and the home runs from Andy Bush, Jim Lewis and Jim Fraser. Mike Simon hurled a two-hitter and helped his cause with three hits as the Comets beat the Tigers 14 to 4. In another game, Tom Ruffalo had three hits and led the Owls to a 14 to 4 win over the Eagles.

Townsend Fans 10 Hurls One-Hit Shutout in Orioles Win

July 14 – A single by Tom Mangone kept Larry Townsend from pitching a no-hitter as his Orioles beat the Peacocks behind Townsend's 10-strikeout pitching. Bill Pelliccio and David Fox homered for the Orioles.

In the National League, the Pirates and Panthers ended their seasons with the Panthers winning 11 to 2. The Panthers scored seven runs in the first inning and romped home behind Mike Boyle's four-hit pitching and the hitting of Tom Cowan who tripled and singled.

Zuzzolo, Tursi, Castaldo Lead Wildcats To League Title

July 19 – The Wildcats defeated the Rams, 8-6, in the Service Club division to win the league's second round play. The victory came on the heels of the Wildcats finishing in a three way tie for the first round title. A big third inning in which the Wildcats scored six runs was enough.

Doubles by Joe Zuzzolo, John Tursi and Ralph Castaldo led the assault. Trailing 8 to 1, the Rams cut the lead to two runs on homers by Bob Snyder and Tom Leggiere.

Wickens Rides Comets To Western Loop Crown

July 20– The Comets captured the Western League championship by beating the Bulldogs, 10 to 4. The Comets added this second round playoff win to their first round victory and won the title with a season record of 15 and 4.

Manager Steve Wisner and coach Bob Cassin sent Vonnie Wickens to the mound and he came through with a two hitter. He posted 11 strikeouts and worked himself out of trouble with a blazing fastball. In the third inning, he struck out the first batter and then loaded the bases with three consecutive walks only to fan the next two batters.

John Sealy pitched for the Bulldogs and allowed only four hits but two were home runs. Wickens clouted a three-run homer in the second inning and Bruce Fabricant unloaded a two-run homer in the first. Fabricant also doubled and walked in his two other trips to the plate and scored three times. James Manna and Phil DeRosa were the only Bulldogs who nicked Wickens for hits.

The champion Comet nine included Wickens, Fabricant, Bob Delmonico, Joe Urana, Al Radogna, Phil Napolitano, Greg Weber, Clarence Lee, Larry Ferruzzi, Harold Peterson, Fred Peterson, Rick Miller, and Jeff Geberth.

Home runs by Jim Fraser, John DiMenna, Jim Lewis, Tom Shannon and Al Nelson gave the Rams a 13 to 9 win over the Lions in the Service Club League. Fraser also had 12 strikeouts in the first round playoff.

National All Stars Blank New Rochelle, 5-0, in Tourney Play

July 25 – Mount Vernon's National League team advanced in tournament play by defeating the New Rochelle Atlantics, 5-0, at City Park in New Rochelle before a crowd of 600 fans. Anthony Tobacco threw a shutout, striking out ten, walking one and scattering six hits. Mount Vernon scored in the third inning when Bobby Blount singled to center. Tom Gasparini followed with a hit and went all the way to third when the center fielder threw wildly to third and Blount scored. Ray Schilke doubled in a run to make the score 3-0.

Gasparini homered to right center field in the fifth inning and Ted Cardasis followed with his four bagger. Interestingly, Cardasis traveled 250 miles to play in the game. He was vacationing with his family in the Adirondacks.

A No-Hitter for DiMenna in Wildcats in Playoff Game

August 1 – The Rotary Rams raced to an 8-0 win in the first playoff game for the Service Club Little League championship defeating the Wildcats behind the no-hit pitching of John DiMenna.

DiMenna had the best day of his young career as he struck out a dozen batters and shut down the Wildcats inning after inning without any trouble. He helped his own cause with a double as the Rams got eight hits off losing pitcher Al Daniello. Andy Bush and Mike Funke also doubled and Bob Gilhooley and Tom Shannon both managed a pair of singles.

In the opening game of the American League playoffs the Owls beat the Eagles, 9-3, as Tom Ruffalo threw a three-hitter to beat the Eagles Ernie Motta. Marcel Olifers paced the winners with two homers and single.

Rams and Owls Clinch League Championships

August 2 – The Rotary Club Rams and the Owls both became league champions, the Rams finishing first in the Service Club loop and Owls in the American circuit.

It was the second win in two starts for the Rams over the Wildcats in the best two out of three playoff series. The Rams put together 16 hits in a 10-5 victory. Picking up the victory was Rams' starter Jim Fraser who gave up six hits but struck out ten.

Andy Bush, Fraser, Bobby Snyder, Tom Leggiere and Bob Gilhooley gave the Rams a six run lead in the first inning and that was all Fraser needed. The Wildcats came within one run. But in the fourth inning the Rams tacked on two more runs. Bush doubled twice and Fraser, Snyder, and Gilhooley also doubled. Vinnie Rocco, Ralph Castaldo and John Tursi tried to keep the Wildcats in the game with doubles but that wasn't enough. The win marked the second consecutive pennant for the Rams and manager Ed Martin. On both occasion, the Wildcats finished in the runner-up slot.

The Owls meanwhile made it two-for-two over the Eagles in winning 6-2. Bob Cruickshank tossed a one-hitter with the Eagles Bob O'Hara getting an infield single. The Owls had home runs from Tom Ruffalo and Marcel Olifers with Ruffalo also turning in some fine plays at shortstop.

Owls and Comets Combine for 30 Runs in Playoff Wins

August 8 – The Owls and Comets scored a combined 30 runs in winning their Little League playoff games. The American League champion Owls hammered the Rams, 18-0, and the Western League Comets beat the Eastern League Elks, 12-3.

The Owls 18 runs were scored on 18 hits with 10 of them going for extra bases. Overshadowing the power was the pitching of Bob Cruickshank who limited the Rams to a pair of singles off the bats of Jim Fraser and Tom Shannon. Tom Ruffalo of the Owls had four hits including two home runs and a double while his teammate Marcel Olifers also had four hits, all doubles.

The Comets had an easy time also. Harold "Red" Peterson went the distance and gave up only three hits.

Comets Streak Past Owls for 3rd LL World Series Win

August 10 – The Western League Comets climbed another rung on the ladder leading to the city Little League championship as they easily beat the American League Owls, 12 to 3. Harold Peterson's choice as a starter by manager Steve Wisner and coach Bob Cassin was a shrewd move. Peterson baffled Owls hitters with an assortment of slow pitches.

Shortstop Bob Delmonico and center fielder Fred Peterson, brother of the pitcher, helped out with fine defensive plays. The Comets trailed, 3-2, going into the fourth inning when Owl pitcher Bob Cruickshank ran into trouble. Ricky Miller opened with a single, Greg Weber reached first on a fielder's choice, Delmonico walked, Vonnie Wickens singled, and Phil Napolitano singled. With two outs the Owl pitchers walked five more Comets. By the time the damage was over, seven runs crossed the plate and the Comets sent 13 batters to the plate. The Comets collected five hits off Cruickshank, Ted Thompson and John Riganati. Wickens had two including the game's only homer. Chester Holmes spoiled Peterson's bid for a no-hitter with a sharp single in the second inning.

The National League champion Indians also stayed on the undefeated side by beating the Eastern League Elks, 8-1. The Indians had 10 hits and were led at the plate by Andy Siegenfeld, Ted Cardasis, and Earl Conti. The Indians picked up their runs in bunches, scoring four times in the first inning and four in the third. Bob Petrone picked up the win while striking out eight Owls. Tom Mangone took the loss. Indians shortstop Bob Piselli made several nice fielding plays that killed off Elk scoring opportunities.

Seigenfeld Makes Mays Like Catch in Indians Win

August 12 – The National League champion Indians defeated the Service Club Rams, 5-3, for their third straight win in the city Little League playoffs. The Indians scored four runs in the first inning to put the game away and withstood a late inning rally by the Rams.

The deciding factor in the well played game was a 'miracle' catch by Indians' outfielder Andy Seigenfeld. He raced to the fence and snared a ball labeled for a home run by Jim Lewis. Fans in the stands were thinking of Willie Mays when Seigenfeld made his catch. Less than a year earlier, Mays made a memorable defensive play during Game 1 of the 1954 World Series between the New York Giants and Cleveland Indians at the Polo Grounds in New York. Vic Wertz of the Indians crushed a pitch approximately 420 feet to deep center field. In many stadiums the hit would have been a home run and given the Indians a 5-2 lead. However, this was the spacious Polo Grounds, and Mays who was playing in shallow center field, made an on-the-run, over-the-shoulder catch on the warning track to make the out.

With support like Seigenfeld's, the Little League Indians helped Bob Piselli chalk up the win. He gave up four hits, struck out eight and walked only two batters. The Rams did little damage until the fifth inning when they scored their first run. Then in the bottom of the sixth it appeared as if they might salvage a win when they scored two more runs but Piselli stopped the rally. John DiMenna took the loss for the Rams. He also had two hits, scored a run, and drove in two runs.

In another game, Tom Ruffalo shut out the Elks, 4-0 in an abbreviated game that was called after four innings because of darkness. Ruffalo ran his strikeout total to 23 for two games as he tossed a one-hitter. Marcel Olifers paced the Owls with two doubles, while Ruffalo and John Riganati each added a double. This was the final game of the season for both teams.

Indians Are Little Loop Champions, Scalp Comets In Series Finale, 18-0

The Republican Club Indians climaxed the 1955 Mount Vernon Little League drama at Baker Field yesterday by handing the Comets an 18 to 0 defeat to clinch the city championship. The Indians won both the first and second rounds in the National League in regular season play, while compiling an impressive 15 and 4 record and then added four playoff wins. Manager Steve Acunto's charges may have cruised to the title in yesterday's fracas but six years of preparation went into the makings of the one sided win. The Indians and Acunto have been a part of the Little loop since opening day.

Anthony Tobacco picked the finale as his turn to shine and hurled a brilliant one hitter. Vonnie Wickins beat out an infield roller to scuff Tobacco's fine performance. Along the way Tobacco fanned seven Comets and walked six. Wickins was nicked with the loss, giving up 11 hits, striking out two and walking seven. The Comets gave a good account of themselves despite what appears to be an apparent rout.

The Indians scored a single marker in the opening inning and it looked as if that was going to have to stand up as Tobacco and Wickins zeroed the sides in the second but the fuses were lit on the Indian dynamite stocks and the game exploded in the third.

Ralph Guiliano singled, Tobacco and Earl Conti walked and Ted "Thumper" Caridasis boomed a grand slam homer over the center field fence.

Caridasis' circuit opened the gates and a herd of runs stampeded across before the Comets ended the uprising. Bob Petrone, Andy Siegenfeld and Joe DiMaggio singled, Tobacco came up again and walked, Conti doubled and Caridasis finally ended the inning by flying out. When it was all over the Indians were riding a comfortable 9 to 0 lead.

The run spread was doubled in the fourth when the winners scored nine times. singles by Dino DiFillipo, Petrone, Guiliano and Tobacco and seven Comet free passes.

Tobacco had a tremendous lead to work on but the small scale fastballer was toiling to preserve his shutout. He gave up the spoiler safety to Wickins in the second and walked Phil Napoliatano and then retired the next three hitters. He stranded three in the fourth and two in the final frame.

Manager Acunto congratulated his players on capturing the coveted and quite elusive title and also had a word of praise for coaches Anthony Romanino and John Caridasis and the loyal Indian rooters who hung around long enough to see the Indians win a city championship.

```
                         R. H.
Comets   ------000 00— 0  1
Indians  ------108 9x—18 11
```
WINNING PITCHER — Anthony Tobacco. LOSING PITCHER — Barney Wickins.

Indians (Republican Club), 1955 Little League Champions: 1, Dino DiFillipo; 2, Ray Santora; 3, John DiGiacomo; 4, John Petrillo; 5, Ralph Guiliano; 6, Andy Siegenfeld; 7, Bob Petrone; 8, Ted Cardasis; 9, Tony Tobacco; 10, Bob Piselli; 11, Earl Conti; 12, Lance Woods; 13, Coach John Cardasis; 14, Manager Steve Acunto.

Managers and coaches check the players list as part of the drafting auction.

1955 – City Leagues Consolidate

Managers Select 82 Boys For Little League's Teams

AMERICAN LEAGUE

ORIOLES — Steve Corrado, Henry Howitt, Jim Russell, Ed Sanders, Vince Stenerson, Rick Tourin.

PEACOCKS — Bill Bendlin, Phil Buglione, Mickey Klebanow, Sandy Ramros, Bill Spada.

EAGLES — Jim Bennett, Jim Chesson, Henry Messner, Bill O'Hara, Ed Schultz, Tony Solomon.

OWLS — Jim Brucale, Larry DiMargo, Jim Finch, George Stasko, Ted Thompson.

EASTERN LEAGUE

JESTERS — Eric Bennett, Don Flemming, John Trimachi.

RAMS — Bill Lindfors, Bob Cozza, Bob Gilhooley, Mike Funke, Ted Shannon, John Lewis, George Piccirilli.

LIONS — Don Honeik, Ted Johnson, Andy Karl, Jr., George Rampel.

WILDCATS — Ralph Castaldo, Jim Cummings, Mike Burdi, Tony Faganani, Bill Gazzetta, Tony Rogliano.

NATIONAL LEAGUE

PIRATES — Tony Colarusso, George Bochow, Jack Jordan, Tom Patterson, Mike Viggiano.

INDIANS — John D'Griocomo, Ralph Guiliano, John Petrillo, Bob Piselli, Ray Santo, Lance Wood.

SHAMROCKS — Armistead Bulloch, Vince Falco, Len Goldstein, Bob O'Reilly, Roy Pitchal, August Wines.

PANTHERS — Frank D'Andrea, Tom Greges, John Lynn, Bob Raus, Pete Sizemore.

WESTERN LEAGUE

BULLDOGS — Bob Bourge, Pete Lane, Ed Magner, Ralph Morcel, John Sealy.

CUBS — Pete Coschigano, Armand D'Oyen, Don Grippo, Dick Liscio, Jim Thornbury, Tony Wickens.

COMETS — Barry Berkule, Greg Weber.

TIGERS — Joe Fasano, John O'Reilly, Frank Spero, John Spark.

1954 World Series champion Pirates lead parade before the '55 season opener.

Mount Vernon Mayor Joseph P. Vaccarella takes to the mound on opening day of the 1955 Little League season.

More than 1,200 marchers, including all Little League teams, participate in a 1955 parade honoring the great American pastime baseball.

Ted Cardasis of the Indians trots home after hitting a grand slam home run against the Comets that helped his club win the 1955 city championship.

The Indians Anthony Tobacco scores in Little League playoff game against the Rams. Ram catcher Bob Snyder awaits the throw.

Rams first baseman Andy Bush stretches for throw in retiring Marcel Olifers of the Owls in their Little League playoff game.

1955 Gramatan Men's Shop: 1, Don Ross; 2, Richard Moccio; 3, Nick Giordano; 4, Tom Mangone; 5, Manager Austin Manghin; 6, John Antonelli; 7, Phil Buglione; 8, Coach Phil Buglione; 9, Joe Wasserman; 10, Billy Spada; 11, Batboy Buglione; 12, Richard Merigliano; 13, Mickey Klebanow.

1955 Community Oil (Comets): 1, Greg Weber; 2, Joey Urana; 3, Albert Ragdona; 4, Larry Ferruzzi; 5, Harold Peterson; 6, Rick Miller; 7, Fred Peterson; 8, Clarence Lee; 9, Coach Bob Cassin; 10, Vonnie Wickens; 11, Bruce Fabricant; 12, Bob Delmonico; 13, Mike Simon; 14, Phil Napolitano; 15, Manager Steve Wisner.

1955 Tigers: 1, Rudy Beltramello; 2, Manager Mr. Henderson; 3, Dave Cromwell; 4, Bob Mayer; 5, Roger Wackermann; 6, Jimmy Robinson; 7, Paul Wackermann.

13
1956 – Sponsors Support Program

While Mount Vernon's biggest Little League season opened in 1956 at Hutchinson and Baker Fields with 300 youngsters scheduled to participate, Major League Baseball was experiencing the end of an era when New York's inter-city rivalries the New York Yankees and Brooklyn Dodgers would meet in the World Series for the very last time.

Youngsters playing Little League ball in '56 would not realize until many years later how incredible the eight year time span from 1949 to 1956 was for New York baseball teams. In those years, 14 of the possible 16 teams in the World Series were either the Dodgers, Yankees or Giants. All eight World Series champions resided in New York. That couldn't happen again because of the move west by the New York Giants and Brooklyn Dodgers following the conclusion of the 1957 season.

The 1956 baseball season had many highlights which ended with the New York Yankees win over the rival Brooklyn Dodgers in the World Series. The greatest moment of the season was the one and only perfect game pitched in World Series history by Don Larsen. We watched and listened as Mickey Mantle would hit monster home runs on his way to winning the Triple Crown with a .353 batting average, 52 home runs, and 130 RBI's. Jackie Robinson retired in 1956 rather than accept a trade by the Dodgers to the Giants.

Outside of baseball, the federal minimum wage was increased to $1 an hour, the Interstate Highway System was born, Dwight D. Eisenhower was re-elected president, the cruise ship Andrea Doria sank, the Hungarian Revolution occurred, Grace Kelly Married Prince Rainier, the Dow Jones Industrial Average topped 500 points, and Elvis entered the charts for the first time with "Heartbreak Hotel". Yahtzee, Busch Beer, the snooze alarm clock, Certs breath mints, Jif Peanut Butter, the computer hard disk, and the first videotape recorder made their debuts.

In June, Marilyn Monroe and Arthur Miller were married in the Westchester County Courthouse in White Plains. Late in the year, Floyd Patterson, who at one time lived in Mount Vernon, won the world heavyweight title by knocking out Archie Moore. In 1956 the number of local Little League programs topped 4,000 for the first time.

In early spring, city dignitaries were on hand for the opening of the Little League season at Baker Field. They included Mayor Joseph Vaccarella and Chief Inspector William Bantz. Music was furnished by the Traphagen Junior High School band. Parading to that music was the Westchester Nautical Cadets and Color Guard. Steve Acunto who was chairman of the Little League parade and Mrs. Bertha Martin representing the Mothers' Auxiliary put the event together.

For the first time, Little League teams would not be known by their nicknames. Beginning in 1956, all teams were known by their sponsors' names. Five leagues were in operation with four teams slated to play in each division.

The managerial merry-go-round was in full operation as new skippers took the helm of various ball clubs. The managers for 1956 were:

WESTERN: Community Oil Co. – Steve Wisner (Comets); Uclico – Ray Hendrickson (Tigers); Elco Corp. – Ross Epstein (Cubs).

AMERICAN: Embassy TV – Al DePessimer (Eagles); Tom Godfreys – Frank DeMargo (Owls); Gramatan Men's Shop – Austin Manghin (Peacocks); and Fava Post – Faust Cardillo (Orioles).

NATIONAL: Republican Club Eagles – Steve Acunto (Indians); Braslow Builders – Jack Bourne (Shamrocks); Local 338 – Al Coleman (Panthers); and Perry Soda -Joe Tripodi (Pirates).

EASTERN: County Pants – Eric Favilla (Elks); Mount Vernon Flower Shop – Dick Reynolds (Americans); Democratic Club – Ellwood Smith (Bears); and Nada Fence – Fiore DeMarzo (Aces).

SERVICE CLUB – Lions Club – Sol Dunsay (Lions); Rotary Club – Edward Martin (Rams); Optimist Club -Ernie Altiere (Wildcats); and Kiwanis Club – Dick Yarrobino (Jesters).

In a new approach to scheduling, the Western League games were played throughout the year at Hutchinson Field. All other league play took place on the Baker Field diamonds.

Larry Townsend Like Bob Feller Throws Opening Day No-Hitter

There have been many great pitchers throughout time, but Hall of Famer Bob Feller and Mount Vernon Little League ace Larry Townsend can say they pitched a no-hitter on Opening Day.

On Opening Day in 1940, Feller held the Chicago White Sox hitless as the Indians went on to win the game 1-0. That chilly Chicago day in 1940 was the first Opening Day no-hitter in baseball history, and to this day remains the only no-hit performance to open the season.

Feller was just 21-years-old in April of 1940 and in his fourth season with the Indians. He went on to go 27-11 in 1940, with a 2.61 ERA, and 263 strikeouts. He also made the All Star team and finished second in AL MVP voting behind Detroit slugger Hank Greenberg.

Townsend threw his no-hitter in 1956. Decked out in a resplendent new uniform, The Orioles' Townsend sat down 13 Peacocks on strikes and even hit a home run to lead his team to a 14-0 victory. Teammate Dave Smith hit a grand slam in the fifth inning and his other teammate Larry Casarella hit a round tripper.

Throughout the early season Townsend and Steve Corrado were the mainstays of the Fava Post pitching staff. Corrado was undefeated while racking up four wins including a no-hitter. Townsend won five games while dropping only one. Two of his victories were no-hitters.

The defending champion Community Oil team in the Western League started the season with an 8-3 win over Uclico. The losers were limited to one hit on a collaborative effort by Carl Meyer and Red Peterson. Vonnie Wickens homered for the winners while teammate Greg Weber excelled in the field.

Pitcher Darryl Kowal rapped a homer and triple to lead the Jesters to a 14-8 victory over the Wildcats in a Service League game.

Roy Pizzarello beat Ross Epstein in a pitching duel, 4-2, with Langdon Shop edging Elco Lamp in a Western League battle. Len Glaser doubled with the bases loaded in the first inning and pitcher John Riganati tripled in two runs in the fifth inning as the Owls beat the Eagles, 7-6. In an extra inning game, Mike Funke's eighth-inning home run enabled the Rams to edge out the Lions, 7-6.

Williams, Townsend Homer Twice

Tom Williams made like his namesake Ted and blasted two home runs for the Democrats who easily beat Nada Fence, 11-2. One of Williams' homers was a grand slam. Teammates Jack Bromley and John Ambrose also homered to help winning pitcher Ed Smith who struck out 11.

Larry Townsend's home runs came against Godfreys in Fava Post's 16-9 win. The busy Saturday schedule also saw Gramatan Men's Shop rally to score six runs in the fifth inning as they beat Embassy TV, 11-9. The Pirates lost two National League games over the weekend. An eight-run fifth inning gave the Panthers a 12-4 triumph and later the Shamrocks beat them, 6-5.

Wickens Throws No-Hitter

Pitching a no-hitter is special. Throwing a no-hitter while giving up eight runs is even more difficult. That is what Vonnie Wickens did as Community Oil defeated Elco Lamps, 12-8. Wickens survived a six-run first inning when Elco scored on quite a few Wickens walks.

John Weis won a tight pitcher's as Embassy TV beat Fava Post, 1-0. Weis threw a one-hitter. Carl Viggiano meanwhile fanned 11 and drove in a pair of runs with two singles to lead the Pirates to an 8-5 win over the Indians.

Tom Godfrey Sporting Goods Damaged By Fire

On early Sunday morning June 25, a three-alarm fire wrecked a Mount Vernon athletic landmark, Tom Godfrey Sporting Goods, where many Little League youngsters bought their first baseball gloves.

Three firemen required hospital treatment for smoke poisoning. Several others were treated at the scene as thick smoke filled buildings and cloaked the area. Firemen said the blaze started in the "Mr. Hamburg" restaurant at 3 Fourth Avenue and spread to Tom Godfrey's next door. Firemen battled the flame and smoke for more than an hour and one-half.

Braslows Remain Undefeated

Six games were completed over the weekend including Braslow Builders 9-1 win over Perry's Pirates in National Division play. The victory ran Braslow's undefeated streak to five. Rocco Ciciola, George Ivers and Bob Bullock were the big hitters for the winners, combining for six singles, a double and a triple. Jack Jordan singled in Carl Viggiano for the only Pirate run while Paul Vetrano picked up the win, striking out 11 and walking three.

Community Oil racked up a 5-1 Western Division victory over Langdon Men's Shop on a 16-strikeout pitching performance by Vonnie Wickens. He only gave up two hits but walked seven. Phil Napolitano tripled with two on board in the third inning for the winners. Roy Pizzarello fanned ten but gave up seven hits in taking the loss.

In the American Division, Fava Post's Larry Townsend continued his outstanding pitching in a throwing a two-hitter for a 4-1 victory over Embassy TV. Townsend also homered in the first inning with a teammate on board. Losing pitcher John Weis also homered.

The Lions blasted Rotary, 12-6 in a Service Division win. Ted Johnson did it all. Besides striking out 14 he hit a triple for the winners. Jim Lewis' batting wasn't enough for the losers despite his two doubles and a triple.

Eastern Division's Nada Fence beat County Pants, 13-3, as Lou Geralde went all the way in picking up the win. He also had a three-hit day including a home run and two singles. His battery mate Ray Jones also got three hits.

In another Eastern Division game, the Democratic Club beat the Flower Shop, 7-4, despite Paul Williams' homer and single for the losers. Pete DeAquani picked up the win.

Langdon Shop Wins Pair Over the Weekend

July 20 – Langdon Shop won two games to move into first place in the Western Division. On Saturday, Nino Fiore shut out Uclico, 11-0, as Roy Pizzarello helped out with a two-run homer. The next day, Pizzarello got three of his team's four hits and also was the winning pitcher, striking out 13, while beating Community Oil, 7-6.

Butch Bullock of Braslows singled in Bob O'Reilly in the sixth inning for a 2-1 win over Perry's Pirates. The Pirates rebounded the next day to beat the Republican Club, 6-3. Joe Tripodi and Carl Viggiano had four hits for the winners.

Mount Vernon Flower Shop beat the Democrats by five runs, 13-8. Jim Pagliaroli tripled and doubled for the winners. Ricky Tourin and Bill Pelliccio hit and scored in Fava Post's four-run fifth inning that gave the winner's a 7-5 victory over Embassy TV.

Corrado Tosses 2d No-Hitter as Embassy Wins Title

Steve Corrado pitched his second no-hit, no-run game of the season to lead Fava Post to the American League championship over Embassy TV, 7-0. Larry Townsend helped his teammate's cause by getting four hits including a home run.

Not to be outdone, Red Peterson's pitching and Vonnie Wickens hitting helped Community Oil even its playoff best of three series at one apiece after beating Langdon Shop, 10-1. Peterson had a no-hitter through four innings but then gave up a triple to Roy Pizzarello. Peterson only allowed three hits and did not walk a single batter while striking out ten. Vonnie Wickens hit a grand slam and triple. Teammate Phil Napolitano had three doubles.

Mount Vernon Flower Shop evened its series with the Democratic Club with a 12-1 win. Jim Pagliaroli had three hits and Chris Rezza went two for four including a home run. Winning pitcher

Paul Williams gave up four hits.

Rotary Club of the Service League made a playoff unnecessary by downing the Kiwanis Jesters, 4-1, to win the league's second round. They also won the first round. Don Fiegoli picked up the win and helped his cause with a double and triple.

Democrats Win Eastern League Championship

July 22 – Tom Williams had a home run and two doubles, Johnny Ambrose belted two triples, and Jack Bromley went four for four as the Democratic Club won the final playoff game for the Eastern League championship in beating the Flower Shop, 8-5. Pete D'Aquanni pitched five-hit ball for the win.

Western, Service Stars Are Little League Winners

July 23 – The Western League All-Stars defeated the American League Stars in the first round of play when Larry Townsend wild pitched the winning run home. In the other contest, the Service League All-Stars easily defeated the Eastern League All-Stars, 9-0, behind the fine three hit shutout pitching of Jim Lewis.

Before Townsend wild-pitched the winning run home, Carl Meyer walked, Joe Fasano singled Meyer to second and Nino Fiore got a bunt single to load the bases. Vonnie Wickens, the next batter, bunted also but Meyer was called out at the plate. Roy Pizzarello came to bat and then Townsend uncorked his wild pitch which brought Fasano home with the winning run.

Steve Corrado started for the Americans and was relieved by Townsend in the fifth inning. They allowed but three hits. Meanwhile, Roy Pizzarello was pitching equally as well. He struck out 13 and walked five. He faltered in the third inning when he walked Mike Chesom and gave up back to back singles to Bill O'Hara and Dave Smith that scored two runs.

Townsend's wild pitch wasn't as bad as that thrown by Jack Chesbro of the New York Highlanders (later known as the Yankees) in 1904 when he had one of the finest years in the history of pitching, starting 51 games and finishing 48 while winning 41. On the last day of the season, though, in a game against the Boston Pilgrims, he threw a wild pitch in the top of the ninth inning, allowing the winning run to score from third base and causing the Highlanders to lose the pennant to Boston.

In the other Little League contest, the Service Stars scored in every inning with the game's big hit clouted by Bob Bisordi who homered. Dan Fiegoli added a triple to the nine hit total for the winners.

National Stars Defeat Eastern All-Stars

July 26 – The National Little League All-Star team's power made the difference in the second round for the District 2 championship as they won 8-4 over the Eastern League squad.

Bob Petrone hit a three run homer off losing pitcher Red Peterson. Joe Tripodi played well in the field and at bat where he went four-for-four. George Ivers hit a homer while going two-for-four.

Jack O'Shaugnessy was the winning pitcher. He gave up seven hits and held the powerful trio of Vonnie Wickens, Roy Pizzarello and Phil Napolitano to two of those seven hits.

Community Oil Takes Western League Title

July 31 – Community Oil won the championship of the Western League of the Little League with a 14-2 victory over Langdon Shop. Eleven walks by Langdon pitcher Roy Pizzarello spelled the difference.

The winners wrapped up the victory in the first inning when Pizzarello walked four in a row before Carl Meyers and Fred Peterson hit back-to-back doubles. Red Peterson also walked as did Rick Miller. By the end of the inning six runs crossed the plate. Three more Community Oil runners scored in the third inning as a result of five more walks. Bob Walsh replaced Pizzarello and gave up five hits. Five runs came in when Fred Peterson singled, Larry Ferruzzi singled, and Meyers doubled for the second time. Community Oil's winning pitcher Vonnie Wickens allowed only three hits.

National All-Stars Win LL District Title

The National League All-Stars won the District 3 championship from the Service League All-Stars, 2-1. The base running of Joe Tripodi highlighted the game. The score was tied, 1-1, at the end of the regulation six innings. Tripodi walked in the top of the seventh. He quickly stole second base. Then he stole third base. Tripodi sized up Service League pitcher Ted Johnson and took off for home and did it again.

There have been at least 50 instances when a major league player stole second, third, and home during the same inning. Hall of Famers Ty Cobb and Honus Wagner share the record with four apiece.

Tripodi, meanwhile, figured in the scoring of the National's first run also. Carl Viggiano walked and was out at second when Tripodi grounded into a fielder's choice. Tripodi came home on Bob Petrone's single. Service All-Stars scored first when Joe Zuzzolo singled to left and stole second. Dan Fiegoli lined a single over second to bring Zuzzolo across with the only Service run of the game.

Ted Johnson, the losing pitcher, gave up only three hits and struck out 15. However, he walked 10 and these were costly since the walks set up both National runs. Paul Vetrano gave up five hits and struck out nine. He walked only one batter.

The win was the first step on what could prove to be a long ladder for Steve Acunto's squad. This was the first year that a Mount Vernon team won a district title since Little League started play in 1950. Acunto was assisted on the coaching lines by Jack Bourne, manager of the National League titlist Shamrocks and John Cardasis.

Rams Defeat Oilers, 6-2 in Opening World Series Round Robin

August 8 – The Service Division's Rotary Rams opened the round robin series for the Mount Vernon Little League Championship with a 6-2 win over Community Oil.

Jim Lewis, the winning pitcher, gave up four of his eight hits in the first inning on singles to Rickie Miller, Vonnie Wickens, Phil Napolitano and Carl Meyer that gave Steve Wisner's team a 2-0 lead.

Rotary came back in the fourth when they scored five runs on a double by Lewis, singles by

Bob Snyder and George Piccirilli, three walks, and error and fielder's choice. Lewis picked up the win striking out 12 and only walking one batter. Peterson took the loss.

Rotary Notch Second Win In City Tournament

August 10 – Bob Snyder's hitting gave Ed Martin's Rotary Club its second Little League win without a setback, 4-1, over Fava Post.

Snyder went three-for-three with the big hitting coming in the third inning. Rick Cozza walked and Snyder tripled that scored Cozza with the first run of the game. Snyder then scored on a fielder's choice. Rotary added another run in the fourth and one more in the fifth inning.

Fava had its final surge nipped by a relay featuring winning pitcher Dan Fiegoli. Larry Townsend reached base on an error and came home on Larry Casarella's triple. Townsend was thrown out at home by Fiegoli when he tried to stretch the triple into a home run.

Carl Meyer limited the Democrats of the Eastern League to three hits as Community Oil romped to a 12-1 win. Vonnie Wickens led the 11-hit attack with three doubles. An eight run fifth inning made this game a rout. Four of the eight runs were unearned when an outfielder let the ball get through for a four base, bases loaded error.

Ed Smith doubled after Jack Williams walked for the only run the Democrats scored in the fourth inning.

Rotary Club Routs Democratic Club, 20-2

August 16 – Ed Martin's Rotary Club of the Service Little League won its third game of the playoffs for the city championship when it routed the Democratic Club of the Eastern League, 20-2.

Jim Lewis picked up the win in limiting the Democrats to two hits, a double by Ambrose and single by Jack Bromley. Both hits were in the fourth inning when the Democrats scored their only two runs. Lewis struck out 13 and issued four walks.

Rotary had 15 hits including a pair of doubles by Lewis. Al Nelson tripled. Bob Snyder had four singles.

Steve Wisner's Community Oil team of the Western Division eliminated Braslow Builders of the National League from a chance at the championship by winning 10-9. With Mike DeSantis on third, Phil Napolitano hit into a fielder's choice scoring DeSantis with the winning run.

Community Oil's Vonnie Wickens hit a two run homer. Red Peterson picked up the win and George Ivers the loss.

Service Rotarians Take City Little League Title

Rotary Rams of the Service League won the Mount Vernon Little League championship yesterday at Baker Field with a 5-3 triumph over Braslow Builders of the National circuit.

The Rams had to win to finish with a 4-0 playoff sweep for Fava Post of the American Division crushed Eastern League's Democratic Club, 17-0, as Steve Corrado hurled no-hit ball for the game's five-inning duration. Darkness prevented a sixth inning.

Jim Lewis capped a four-run first-frame for the Service Rotarians by driving in two markers with a double.

The Nationals retaliated with two runs in the top of the second but the champions-to-be got out of it as Phil Capuane started a double play with two on. Service picked up one in the home half of the stanza and National's dying gasp was provided by Armstead Bullock's homer in the sixth. Len Goldstein starred on defense for the Nats.

Winning pitcher Dan Fiegoh issued three hits, fanned five and walked three. Paul Vetrano, the losing chucker, gave up five safe swats, struck out eight but issued nine bases on balls.

Corrado was over-powering with 12 strikeouts and only two free tickets. Five home runs paced the Americans' assault. Larry Casarella parked two four-baggers and teammates Larry Townsend, Bill Pellichio and Vic Magnotta clouted singletons.

The Eastern entry however, claimed victory in their previous contest with the Nationals after charging the latter had used an ineligible player.

The scoring:

ab	r	h	National		Service	ab	r	h
3	0	0	Cicola, 1b		Capuana, 2b	2	1	0
3	0	0	Ivers, ss		Snyder, c	3	2	1
1	0	0	Vetrano, p		Lewis, ss	2	1	1
3	1	1	Pullock, cf		Fiegoli, p	2	1	1
3	1	1	Thelk, c		Gilhooley, 3b	2	0	1
2	1	0	Goldstein, rf		Nelson, 1b	2	0	0
3	0	0	Winer, lf		Plaut, cf	2	0	0
1	0	0	Nardone, 3b		Ceaserio, rf	2	0	0
1	0	0	Fennell, 2b		Marotta, lf	1	0	1
					Piocirlli, rf	0	0	0
					Cozza, lf	0	0	0
20	3	3	Totals			20	5	5

SCORE BY INNINGS

National ____ 020 001—3
Service ____ 410 00x—5

ab	r	h	American		Eastern	ab	r	h
2	3	1	Turin, lf		Ambrose, 3b	3	0	0
3	2	1	Corrado, p		Deemer, cf	1	0	0
3	4	2	Smith, c		Williams, c	2	0	0
4	3	3	Townse'd, 1b		Bromley, p-1b	2	0	0
4	2	3	Casarella, ss		Greene, ss	2	0	0
4	1	3	Pelliccio, 3b		DeVito, lf	1	0	0
4	0	0	Sanders, 2b		Armentano, 2b	2	0	0
4	2	2	Magnotta, rf		D'Aqu'ni, 1b-p	1	0	0
2	0	0	Howitt, cf		DeGreco, rf	1	0	0
2	0	0	Brown, cf		Horowitz, cf	1	0	0
0	0	0	Grogan, lf					
32	17	15	Totals			16	0	0

SCORE BY INNINGS

American ____ 526 40—17
Eastern ____ 000 00—0

Here Are Successful Little League Boys

Here are the names of the successful candidates in the Little League tryouts held Saturday, with the leagues and teams involved.

The American League:

Peacocks: Steve Alvin, Danny Cerrone, Ralph Licursi, Niel Peterkin.

Eagles: Greg Martin, Pat Martimucci, John Hoffman, Mike Kaffee, Gerry Putt.

Orioles: Arthur Bagg, Ernie Leberati, Dick Bleeker, Bob Brown, Tom Grogan.

Owls: John Ryan, Jonathan Kopit, Tony Calcogne, Mark Lerner, Victor Seff.

The Western League:

Tigers: John Dietz, William Wright, Larry Boone, Byron Hancott, Francis Paine.

Bullfrogs: Carmine Busciano, Paul Torresi, Ed Lennon, Bob Walsh, Joe Bastic, Ron Laverde.

Comets: Mike DeSantis, Warren Whitaker, Carly Meyer, Ernest Bleeker, Vincent Kain, Kevin Robertson.

Cubs: Anthony Coschigono, Ronnie St. Clair, Paul Manganelli.

The Service Club League:

Optimist: John Michalak, Bob Lynn, Edward Bant, Henry Polk Jim Gaffe, Anthony Castaldo, Bill Schwartz.

Rams: Norman Marrow, Joel Nacht, Tom Ryan, Dave Alderson, Bob Blockart, Ronald Marotta, Dan Fiegoli.

Jesters: John DeNunzio, Darryl Kawal, Steve Martin, Charles Gross.

Lions: Charles Pegrataro, Anderson Clipper, Dick Cole, Dennis Bodenchur and James Parsise.

The Eastern League:

Bears: Tom Williams, Frank Armentano, Jack Bromley, Dom DeGrego, Joe DeVito.

Americans: Marvin Brown, Ed Sparks, Chris Reo, Paul Williams, Simon Siegal, Frank Lolito.

Elks: George Sirinono, Paul Klieve, Ken Matthews, John Hugel, Ken Freed

Aces: Ken Tufo, Dennis McNamara, Steve Guiliano, Ken Klieve, Tony Pagnotta, Bill Jones.

The National League:

Indians: Richard Colarusso, Henry Blanch, Larry Liebson, Fred Eckhauser, Raymond Stamler, Stuart Tobin, Robert Paone.

Panthers: Vaughan Bridges, Willie Warren, John McFarland Jr., Francois Cascone.

Pirates: Marty Pollack, John Luisi, George Jones, Wayne Rems, Raymond Britts, James Vitarello.

Shamrocks: John Gamble, Rocco Ciciola, Dennis Capalbo, Earle Vaughan Jr., Edward Walther, Robert Alba.

1956 – Sponsors Support Program

1956 Little League Rosters Set

WESTERN: Community Oil Co.—Steve Wisner (Comets); Uclico—Ray Hendrickson (Tigers); Longdogs; and Elco Lamp—Ross Epstein (Cubs).

AMERICAN: Embassy T. V.—Al DePessimer (Eagles); Tom Godfreys - Frank DeMargo (Owls); Gramatan Men's Shop—Austin Manghin (Peacocks); and Fava Post — Faust Cardillo (Orioles).

NATIONAL: Republican Club Eagles—Steve Acunto (Indians); Braslow Builders — Jack Bourne (Shamrocks); Local 338 — Al Coleman (Panthers); and Perry Soda — Joe Tripodi (Pirates).

EASTERN: County Pants — Eric Favilla (Elks); Mount Vernon Flower Shop—Dick Reynolds (Americans); Democratic Club—Ellwood Smith (Bears); and Nada Fence - Fiore DeMarzo (Aces).

SERVICE CLUB: Lions Club—Sol Dunsay (Lions); Rotary Club Eddie Martin (Rams); Optimist Club — Ernie Altieri (Wildcats); and Kiwanis Club - Dick Yarrobino (Jesters).

Western League tilts are scheduled for Hutchinson's No. field. All other loop play is to take place on the Baker diamonds.

Here are the complete team rosters:

LANGDON SHOP: Ed Magner, Nino Fiore, Bob Bourque, Roy Pizzarello, Ralph Marcel, Ed Reynolds, Art Ebert, Dick Spindler, Bob Walsh, Peter Lane, Carmine Basciano, Paul Torrisi, Ed Lennon, Joe Bastic and Ronie LaVerde.

LIONS: Andy Karl, Dick Honeck, Ted Johnson, John Koennecke, Cary Fields, Jack Cummings, Ron Blake, Guy Rampel, Billy Dunsay, Jimmy Persice, Denny Bodenchuk, Andy Clipper, Charlie Pignitaro, Ritchie Cole and Ray Sussman.

KIWANIS: Don Massucci, Don Fleming, Eric Dennett, Bob Fagnanni, Steve Martin, John DiNunzio, Darryl Kowal, Joe Circuranzo, Bob Bisordi, John Limato, Augie Alegi, Pat Carbone, Roy Blumenfeld and Charlie Gross.

OPTIMIST: Joe Zuzzolo, Henry Carideo, Jim Domato, John Tursi, Billy Gazzetta, Ed Bantz, Mike Burdi, Tony Castaldo, Jim Goff, Bob Lynn, Hank Polk, Peter Altieri, Al Rogliano, John Michalak and Billy Schwartz.

UCLICO: Pat Manto, Roger Wackerman, Jim Staric, Joe Fasano, Mike Rizzotti, Jim Robinson, Rudy Beltramello, Frank Paine, Byron Howcott, Larry Boone, Paul Wackerman, Bob Mayer, Bill Wright, John Dietz and Gary Spero.

NADA FENCE: Gary Gregorio, Matt McQuade, Ray Santoro, Lou Geralde, John Needham, Tony Fernandes, Chris Kirland, Ken Klein, Jim Cotton, Mike Viggiano, Steve Juliano, Denny McNamara, Tony Pagnotta, Ken Tufo and Charlie Banor.

ELCO LAMP: Peter Coschigano, Lou Sella, Ross Epstein, Armando D'Oyen, Paul Maganelli, Ed DeBlasio, Ronnie St. Claire, Ray Wiccens, George Pignaro, John Thornberry, Bob Liscio, Tony Cochigano, Dan Grippo and Ken Santore.

EMBASSY T.V.: Bill O'Hara, Joe Chesson, Andy Soloman, John Wies, Frank Castoldi, Tom Carroll, Gerard Patti, Eddie Schultz, Mike Kaffee, Pat Martinucci, John Hoffman, Jim Bennet, Harold Messner, Jim Rodgers and John Martin.

GRAMATAN: Dick Merigliano, Bill Bendlin, John Antonelli, John Liebespach, Mickey Klebenow, Phil Buglione, Bill Spada, Alvin Stephans, Sandy Ramras, Neil Peterkin, Bob Semanick, Dan Cerrone, Jim Baia, Joe Wasserman and Dick Licursi.

COMMUNITY OIL: Joe Urana, Rickey Miller, Vonnie Wickers, Phil Napolitiano, Cary Meyer, Jeff Gebberth, Guy Weber, Fred Peterson, Larry Ferruzzi, Harold Peterson, Warren Whittack, Mike DeSantis, Kevin Robertson, Vince Kane and Ernie Bleeker.

REPUBLICAN CLUB EAGLES: Lance Woods, Ralph Guliano, Lou Russo, Fred Eckhauser, John DiGiacomo, Bob Paone, Dick Collarusso, Bobby Petrone, Jim Ferrara, Henry Blanche, Ray Stamler, Bob Liebson, Stu Tobin, John Dina and Fred Constantino.

LOCAL 338: Jack O'Shaughnessy, Denny Kivolic, Mike Boccardi, John Lynn, Paris Sigemcone, Frank D'Andrea, Dick Raus, Bill Heller, Vaughn Bridges, Bill Johnson, Frank Cascone, Willie Warren, John McFarland, Tom Greges and Mickey Boryla.

BRASLOW: Lou Nordone, Butch Bullock, George Ivers, Paul Vetrano, Rocco Ciciola, Dick Thelk, Gus Wines, George Fennell, Len Goldstein, Bob O'Reilly, John Gamble, Earle Vaughan, Bob Alba, Ed Walther, Denny Capalbo.

PERRY SODA: George Bachow, Bob Merola, Joey Tripodi, Carl Viggiano, Jim Veterello, Jack Jordan, George McLean, Ed Anderson, Wayne Renis, John Mahan, Ray Britts and John Luisi.

FAVA POST: Ed Sanders, Steve Corrado, Dave Smith, Larry Townsend, Larry Casarella, Bill Pelliccio, Harvey Howitt, Vic Magnotta, Jim Russell, Ricky Tourin, Tom Grogan, Dick Bleeker, Ernie Liberati, Bob Brown and Arthur Bragg.

ROTARY: Bob Snyder, Jim Lewis, Bob Gilhooley, Dan Fiegoli, Mike Funke, Bob Flockhart, Al Nelson, Rick Cozza, George Piccirilli, Bill Lindfors, Richie Cozza, Norman Marrow, Joe Nacht, Dave Alderson, Tom Ryan and Ron Marotta.

MT. VERNON FLOWER: Jim Pagliaroli, Vince Grippi, Chris Rezza, Bill Zambrano, Ben Minard, Stan Henderson, Larry Gaito, Bob Bosse, Bill Henderson and Paul Williams.

DEMOCRATIC CLUB: John Ambrose, Tom Williams, Ed Smith, Jack Bromley, Mike Deemer, Warren Tartaglia, Lee Greene, Bob Aschenasy, Peter DeAquani, Mike Mastrangelo, Paul DeGreco, Joe DeVito, Barry DeFeo and Frank Amentano.

* No rosters received from two teams.

It was a banner day for the 1956 season opener.

Twelve-year-old Roy Pizzarello sported a .667 batting average with half his 30 hits going for extra bases during the season.

Joe Tripodi crosses home plate in the National All Stars District 3 championship game. Service League catcher Bob Bisordi awaits the throw.

1956 – Sponsors Support Program

Armstead Bullock of Mount Vernon's Nationals takes a swing in the first inning against Eastchester Americans pitcher.

1956 Topps Cleaners (Tigers): 1, Manager Mr. Henderson; 2, Rudy Beltramello; 3, Mike Rizzotti; 4, Dave Cromwell; 5, Jimmy Stark; 6, Jimmy Robinson; 7, Bob Mayer; 8, Paul Wackermann; 9, Roger Wackermann.

14

1957 – Local 338 Wins Title

1957 was quite a year. In a closely fought series, the Milwaukee Braves beat the favored Yankees in a seven game World Series. The difference was Braves pitcher Lew Burdette who won three games. A space race also was underway when the Soviets sent the first man-made satellite into outer space called Sputnik 1. On Broadway, West Side Story opened at the Winter Garden Theater.

That spring, as hundred of boys oiled their baseball gloves to get ready for Little League tryouts, Commissioner Andy Karl was talking about the importance of developing the competitive spirit of youngsters.

"Youngsters this year have a far greater advantage than we did," he said. "Organized, well-conducted leagues are popping up. Youngsters are foolish who do not take advantage of the opportunity. Competitive spirit can't be picked up over night. It must be developed."

Out of the 340 boys who signed up for the Little League in 1957, 116 would be placed on 20 league teams. For the first time, the league moved to north Mount Vernon and Baker Field for the first of its three Saturday workouts in early April. Some 275 boys turned out for tryouts.

Despite a washout of one of the three scheduled tryouts, a draft was held on April 21. Managers of all 20 Mount Vernon Little League teams did the bidding in an auction held at the 43 Orchard Street clubhouse in the Fleetwood section of Mount Vernon. All youngsters who did not make team rosters were automatically placed on Minor League teams.

Five Little League clubs in 1957 adopted new sponsors. They were Engine 6 (previously Community Oil), Goffi Brothers (Elko Lamp), Mount Vernon Life Insurance (Fava Post), Sundown Restaurant (Godfrey's), and Truck 3 (Topp's).

Corrado, Wickens Fan 16, 13 as Season Kicks Off

May 4 – The Little League season opened with a parade around Baker Field and then Steve Corrado and Vonnie Wickens went to work. Corrado struck out 16 of the 18 he retired as Mount

Vernon Life scored four runs in the first inning to beat Embassy TV, 7-3. Bobby Brown homered for the insurance men while Ed Schultz homered for Embassy.

Vonnie Wickens set down Langdon Shop on three hits while striking out 13 in an Engine 6 victory. Joe Urana's triple sparked a four-run outburst in the first inning and George Guarnio added two singles in the win.

How good were their performances. Remember Camilo Pascual. He was a Cuban pitcher who spent 19 seasons in the majors with the Washington Senators, Minnesota Twins, Cincinnati Reds, Los Angeles Dodgers and Cleveland Indians. From 1961-1963, he was the American League's leader in strikeouts. Yet, the high point of Pascual's career occurred on Opening Day 1960. That day, he pitched a complete game and gave up just one run on three hits with three walks and an astounding 15 strikeouts. His Washington Senators defeated the Boston Red Sox 10-1.

Also on opening day, The Elks Club came up with five runs in the eighth and second extra inning to edge out the Democratic Club, 11-8. The losers had rallied to tie with four runs in the sixth when Jack Bromley tripled with the bases loaded. The Elks Paul Williams one-hit the Democrats for five innings. Vince Grippi had a big day pounding out a homer, two doubles, and a single for the winners.

Paul Manganelli of Goffi Brothers threw a two-hitter at Truck 3 in winning 8-4. The Republican Club pushed across a score in the top of the sixth inning to come from behind in a 3-2 win over Perry Soda. Fred Eckhauser outpitched George Jones. The Lions Club scored four times to top Rotary Club, 9-6, behind Ronnie Blake. Lenny Stevens went 3-for-3, including a double to lead the winners. Losing pitcher Bob Snyder and Phil Capuana got two hits apiece in the loss. The Optimist Club scored eight runs in the last two innings to pull away from Kiwanis Club, 13-4. "AG" Rogliano had two hits while limiting Kiwanis to four in picking up the victory. Pete Altieri homered and Jim Goffi and Bob Spana had perfect days at the plate for the Optimists. Goffi had two triples and two singles while Spana rapped a triple and two singles. Jim Seiler of the winners and Rich Cuneo of the losers had a pair of hits.

Elks Have 23 Hits in Romp

May 11 – The Elks were a hitting machine in rapping out 23 hits in a 17-10 victory over Nada. Third baseman Bob Miller led the attack with two homers and a single. The Elks were on pace to break the Major League record for most hits in a game. The Cleveland Indians in 1932 had 33 hits in an 18 inning game against the Philadelphia Athletics. The most hits in a 9-inning game were 31 in 1992 by Milwaukee against the Toronto Blue Jays.

In Service Division play the Optimists beat the Rotary, 8-4 with John Polk picking up the win. Engine Six sent 28 runners across the plate in trampling Goffi Brothers 28-2. Vonnie Wickens coasted to victory.

Local 338 Trounces Perry Soda, 7-2

May 16 – Local 338 pitcher Mickey Boyle held Perry Soda to two hits in a 7-2 win. He struck out eight and walked five. Bill Johnson and Carl Shilio led the hitting for the winners while Ed Anderson did the same for Perry Soda. The win kept Local 338 in first place with a 3-0 mark.

Braslow Builders Tie For First Place

May 18 – Braslow Builders moved into a tie for first place in the National Division as they defeated Local 338, 5-1. Jack O'Shaughnessy, the losing pitcher, struck out 14 batters while the winner George Ivers fanned 11. John Vaughn led the Braslow hitting attack with two hits, a single and double.

The Republican Club blanked Perry Soda, 2-0, behind the hitting of Jim Ferrara. In a Service League game, Kiwanis nipped Rotary, 9-8. Each team hit a home run, Kowal for the winners, and Snyder for Rotary. Ronnie Blake batted and pitched the Lions Club to an 8-1 victory over the Optimist Club. The win put the Lions into undisputed possession of first place. Blake got three of his team's hits, a single, double, and triple. Behind the pitching of Harvey Howitt, Mount Vernon Life easily beat the Sundown Owls, 11-5. Art Bridges went three for three for the winners while Ken Glaser homered twice for the Owls.

Pagliaroli Leads Elks in Win Over Nada Fence

May 27 – Shortstop Jim Pagliaroli's two doubles helped The Elks whip Nada Fence, 6-2, in an Eastern Division match-up. Elks hurler Paul Williams allowed only two hits. The winners scored three runs in the first inning and coasted the rest of the way. Matthew McQuade and Ken Tufo spoiled Williams' no-hit bid when they both singled. Tony Fernandez took the loss.

The Democrats defeated County Pants in a high-scoring game, 15-11. Both clubs got five runs in the first inning, with the winners sending across another five in the third frame. Braham Horowitz, with a double and single, paced the Democrats attack.

Braslow Builders, behind Paul Vetrano's two-hit pitching, blanked Perry Soda, 3-0. The winners scored twice in the second and once in the third, with Richie Thelk's homer pacing the Braslow batters. Wayne Rines took the loss.

The Local 338 club belted its way to a 12-6 decision over the Republicans. Mickey Boyle, the last of three Local 338 pitchers, had two doubles for the winners. Two of his teammates were also pretty potent at the plate. Richard Raus had a triple, double, and single. George Paone and Anthony Calarusso had two hits apiece for the losers.

By winning their respective games, Braslow Builders and Local 338 moved into a tie for first-place in the National Division with each compiling a 4-1 record. The Republicans are third at 2-3, while winless Perry Soda is 0-5.

Optimists Score in Every Inning for Win

June 3 – The Optimists pushed across at least one run in all six innings to edge Kiwanis, 9-8. Hurler Al Rogliano survived some shaky pitching and picked up the win. Don Mascucci took the loss. In another close game, Bob Gillhooley gave up only two hits while striking out 11 as Rotary edged the Lions, 5-4. Jack O'Shaughnessy picked up the win as Local 338 defeated Perry Soda, 6-2.

Braslow Builders Win Puts Club in Division Lead

June 5 – Braslow Builders rallied in the last of the sixth inning with three runs to defeat Local

338, 5-4. The win enabled Braslow to take over first place in the National Division. Paul Vetrano outpitched Mickey Boyle for the victory. Roy Bretts threw a complete game victory for Perry Soda. He defeated the Republicans 6-5. The winners scored three runs in the first inning.

Braham Horowitz and Tony Fernandez each struck out nine batters but Horowitz came away with the victory as the Democrats beat Nada Fence, 5-4. Fernandez allowed the winners only two hits, one a double by Joe DeVito. Horowitz game up four singles. In an Eastern Division contest, the Elks found County Pants easy game, as they romped, 13-5.

Vonnie Wickens and George Ivers Toss No-Hitters

June 15 – Two no-hitters highlighted Little League baseball at Baker Field as George Ivers pitching enabled Braslow Builders to blank Local 338, 5-0. The win gave Braslow the first-round title in the National Division. Braslow and Local 338 had a playoff for the crown after completing the first round with identical records. Paul Vetrano's two-run home run sealed the victory.

Not to be outdone on the mound was Vonnie Wickens of Engine 6 whose no-hitter clinched the Western Division first-round title. He fanned 14 batters in his club's 11-1 rout of Langdon Shop. He walked seven. Langdon scored their lone run in the first inning. Wickens contributed two of his team's 13 hits. Harold Peterson and Joey Urana also had two hits while George Guarino got three hits.

In a Service Division play-off for first-round honors, the Lions, who scored all of their runs in the first two innings, held on to edge Rotary, 8-6. Each club had seven hits with shortstop John Breen's single and triple doing the most damage for the winners. Catcher Bob Gilhooley had two hits for Rotary. Andy Karl, Jr. picked up the win. Bob Snyder took the loss. Two double plays by the winners helped halt potential Rotary rallies.

Kiwanis Nip Rotary, 11-10

June 19 – Both Kiwanis and Rotary banged out eight hits with Kiwanis getting the most out of theirs. Kiwanis beat Rotary 11-10 in a Service Division game. D. Kowal picked up the win fanning 14 batters. He also had two doubles and a single. Capuana and Snyder were the Rotary pitchers. Besides Kowal who had three hits, S. Martin also had three. (*note: stories about these games and other games in newspaper reports do not reveal first name of players*)

County Pants had an easy time beating the Democrats in an Eastern Division game, 10-2. Bowerman was the winning pitcher. Catcher McCubbin and centerfielder Revesic each had two of their club's eight hits. Rotary used three pitchers, Braham Horwitz, Peter Daquanni and Buddy Deverman. Horwitz, who moved to shortstop after leaving the mound in the second inning, had two of his team's five hits, one of them a triple.

The Elks had an easy time of it defeating Nada Fence, 15-5. Third baseman Bob Miller of the Elks paced the 18-hit attack. He tripled, singled and had two doubles. He drove in seven runs. Paul Williams, Jim Paglioli and Vincent Grippe also hit well for the Elks. Grippe was the winning pitcher and Tony Fernandez picked up the loss.

Wickens Gets Second No-Hitter

June 20 – Vonnie Wickens did it again. He recorded his second no-hitter of the season as he paced his Engine 6 teammates to an 11-1 win over Goffi Brothers in a Western League game. He struck out 13 along the way.

Besides his pitching, Wickens banged out two of Engine 6's 11 hits. Second baseman Joey Urana and first baseman Harold Peterson had three hits apiece. Paul Manganelli took the lost.

In another Western Division game, Langdon Shop easily beat Truck 3, 15-6. Robert Bourque was the winning pitcher with Robinson getting tagged with the loss. Langdon Shop scored three runs in the second, two in the third and put the game away with a 10-run outburst in the fifth. R. Smith hit a grand-slam home run in the big fifth inning.

Engine 6 Wins Title in Western Loop

July 6 – Engine 6 walloped Langdon Shop, 17-9, to win the Western Division second round title. Paul Peterson picked up the win. The firemen got off to an early lead, scoring four runs in the first inning. Mike DeSantis accounted for three of the runs, hitting a home run with two aboard. Engine 6 came back with seven in the second, one in the third, four in the fourth, and one in the fifth. Engine 6's second round record stands at 7-0, with two games left to play. The firemen took the first round title with an 8-2 mark.

While Engine 6 was winning its second round title, Embassy TV won its American Division game on the final pitch of the game. With two outs, a man on first and a three and two count on pinch hitter Joe Verleza, Verleza hit a home run to beat Mount Vernon Life.

Three Stolen Bases Gives Elks The Win

July 9 – Left-fielder Scott of the Elks saved the best for last. With the score tied 5-5 with Nada Fence in the bottom of the last inning, the sixth, Scott reached first on a walk and stole the next three bases to score the winning run. The winners scored off of Nada pitchers Jones and Tony Fernandez. Paul Williams picked up the win for the Elks. In another Eastern Division game, the Democrats downed County Pants, 6-1. Democrats catcher Williams homered in the third-inning with three abroad. Jack Bromley pitched a complete game for the Democrats and collected two of his team's nine hits.

Lions Score 15 Runs in Two Innings

July 16 – The Lions Club scored 15 runs in two innings and romped to an easy 20-5 victory over the Rotary Club. Ronnie Blake and Homer Macon starred for the league leaders. Blake went the distance for the win, allowing just five hits and striking out 12. Macon blasted a grand-slam home run. Not satisfied with a seven run lead during the game, the Lions added eight more runs in the top of the fourth inning. The Lions ended the second round of play with a 7-2 record. They also won the first round with a 5-4 mark.

In the bottom of the sixth inning, Embassy TV came from behind to defeat Gramatan Men's Shop, 6-5, for first place in the American Division. The win clinched first place for the second round play. The Men's Shop jumped to a three run lead when Dan Cerrone homered in the first and Neil Peterkin tripled in the second. Embassy TV took advantage of Bob Semanick's wildness in the third inning and scored two runs. The winners chopped away for two more runs in the fifth as Jim Bennett and Jim Rogers homered. Coming to bat in the bottom of the sixth inning, losing 5-4, Embassy TV combined two walks and a triple by John Moccio to win the game.

Elks Score in Every Inning to Win League Championship

July 19 – The Elks scored in every inning in beating the Democrats, 9-1, to capture the Eastern League championship. John Pagliaroli won, giving up only one run in the first inning. Bob Miller homered twice for the Elks. Right fielder Scott also homered while Vince Grippi tripled.

Gramatan Men's Shop moved a step closer to clinching the American Division crown by trouncing Embassy TV. The Men's Shop was the first round winner and Embassy took the second round.

Blake Hurls 5-Hitter as Lions Win in Round-Robin Tilt

July 22 – Ronnie Blake went the distance as his Lions Club teammates scored runs in every inning for an easy 22-6 win over the Elks in the first round of the Little League round-robin championship playoffs. Blake gave up five hits and struck out 12. He also went three for five at bat including two home runs over the center field fence.

Interestingly, major league pitchers have connected for two homers in a game on 54 occasions. Several did it more than once, most notably Wes Ferrell, who did it on five occasions. Don Newcombe did it three times, and Red Ruffing, Lew Burdette, Jack Harshman, Dick Donovan, Pedro Ramos, Tony Cloninger, and Rick Wise did it twice.

Tony Cloninger hit two homers in a game on June 16, 1966. Only two weeks later, on July 3, he again hit two homers in a game and they were both grand slams. He also had a single and knocked in 9 runs, a record for a pitcher.

In the Lions victory, they scored four runs in the first inning off Jim Pagliaroli with three coming resulting from McFarlane's three-run homer. Len Stevens also homered. Buckalter homered for the losers.

O'Shaughnessy Shines At Bat, On Hill for Local 338

July 22 – Jack O'Shaughnessy homered twice in an 11-run fourth inning and then struck out 11 batters as the National League champion Local 338 got off to a quick start in the post-season playoffs by trouncing American League titleholder Gramatan Men's Shop, 23-4, at Baker Field.

In addition to O'Shaughnessy's two homers, both with men on base, Carl Schillo's four-bagger and Mickey Boyle's doubled figured in the big fourth inning. The winners blasted two Gramatan pitchers for 20 hits. It began in the opening inning when Local 338 scored five runs. Walks to right fielder Bill Johnson and catcher Richie Raus, together with a single by second baseman Dennis Hurlie, loaded the bases. Several errors combined with Schillo's walk and O'Shaughnessy's two-run double brought five runs across the plate.

Local 338 added four more runs in the second inning. Hurlie walked. Raus doubled down the third base line, with the two scoring when the Gramatan infielder threw Schillo's grounder away. A two-run homer by left-fielder Pete Nardone added to the score.

Gramatan Men's Shop scored four in the top of the fourth inning. Richie Merigliano opened with a double and scored when he stole third base and the throw went into left field. A brief flurry of wildness by O'Shaughnessy, together with center fielder Mickey Klebanow's two-run single, helped Gramatan score. It was one of Klebanow's two hits.

Leading the Local 338 hit parade were Schillio and Nardone with four hits apiece while O'Shaughnessy and Raus got three hits each.

Elks Defeat Engine 6 in Delayed Game

July 25 – The Elks, Eastern Division champs, and Engine 6, Western Division titleholders, were tied at 4-4, when darkness forced a halt to the Little League round-robin contest where two losses disqualified a team from further round-robin play. The teams were tied with the 10th inning slated to get underway the next night. The Elks won that game.

Mickey Boyle Throws One-Hitter in Playoff Win

July 25 – Local 338 lefthander Mickey Boyle hurled a one-hitter against the Lions Club. Boyle gave up a home run to Homer Macon in the top of the second inning, but he threw hitless ball the rest of the way not giving up a run. Boyle struck out 14 while allowing only five walks.

Local 338 scored quickly off Lions Club pitcher Andy Karl in the first inning with two runs. They took advantage of Karl's wildness, combining three walks, an infield error and a sacrifice fly. Local 338 came back with three more runs in the bottom of the third. After Richie Raus walked, Boyle singled. A walk to Carl Schillio loaded the bases. Jack O'Shaughnessy doubled to left centerfield to drive in two runs. Schillio scored from third on a wild pitch. Local 338 added three more runs in the fourth capped off by a Boyle home run.

Outstanding fielding plays marked the game. Richie Raus, Local 338 catcher, made a falling catch of a foul pop fly behind the plate. Both teams came up with a double play. The victory was the second in a row for Local 338, while the Lions, who won its first playoff game earlier, now had a 1-1 record.

Lions Club Eliminate Engine 6 as Blake Stars

July 25 – Ronnie Blake hurled a five-hitter for the Lions Club in a 10-3 win that eliminated Engine 6 from the 1957 Little League round-robin playoffs. Earlier in the week he went the route in a win over the Elks.

Engine 6 was hampered when starting catcher Fred Peterson was unable to play because of an injured leg. Joe Urana, who took over the catching chores, was hit in the hand by a foul tip in the first inning and left the game. After giving up two in the first inning, Blake settled down. The lefthander gave up five hits while striking out 10 and walking just one.

Engine 6 scored in the first inning with two runs on back to back singles by Hal Peterson and Vonnie Wickens. Urana then reached first on an infield error which scored Wickens. The Lions came back in the bottom of the first with three runs to take the lead. Jim Persise walked and an infield error let Len Stevens reach first. A wild pitch put them on second and third. More sloppy play followed with Richie Cole scoring on a passed ball. The Lions added another run in the second on three walks and two passed balls. Two runs in the fourth on a pair of walks and another passed ball combined with Cole's double to centerfield upped the score to 6-2.

If you are wondering who gave up the most stolen bases ever by a catcher in a game it is Branch Rickey. On June 28, 1907 Rickey, then a rookie with the New York Highlanders (Yankees) was the starting catcher despite a sore arm. So the man who would break the major league color line in 1947 when Jackie Robinson became a big leaguer, set a record in 1907 which still stands when he allowed 13 stolen bases.

The Lions added four more runs in the fifth inning. McFarlane walked, stole second, and raced to third on two passed balls. Dennis Bodenchuk followed Andy Karl's walk, with a single to right field. Persise and Stevens scored.

Vonnie Wickens, who went the distance on the mound for Engine 6, gave up only four hits while striking out 13. The defeat eliminated Engine 6 from the playoffs.

O'Shaughnessy Fans 16 as Local 338 Whips The Elks

July 30 – In a Little League game a pitcher only has to face 18 batters in six innings. Jack O'Shaughnessy struck out 16 and gave up one hit as Local 338 easily beat the Elks Club in the semi-finals of the Little League championship round-robin playoffs.

The young right-handed fastball pitcher went into the bottom of the fifth before giving up his first and only hit in a 19-0 trouncing. He struck out the side in the second, fourth, fifth and sixth innings.

O'Shaughnessy's teammates pounded out 13 hits off two Elks pitchers. They scored in every inning but the fifth. Local 338 got to Elks starter Vin Grippi in the first inning when they scored two runs. Bill Johnson was on first on an infield error. Dennis Hurlie forced him at second and raced to second on a bad throw to first. Dick Raus doubled over second to drive in Hurlie. Mickey Boyle singled Raus home. Local 338 scored another five runs in the fourth led by singles by Hurlie and Bill Johnson and a triple to right field by Carl Schillio. In the sixth inning, Local 338 batted around and scored nine more runs.

Local 338 Captures Little League Champions

Boyle Hurls Two-Hitter, O'Shaughnessy Stars

Finishing in a blaze of glory, Local 338 defeated the Lions club, 9-4, to become the 1957 Little League champions of Mount Vernon last night.

Paced by the two-hit pitching and long homer by Mickey Boyle and the power-packed bat of Jack O'Shaughnessy, the champs came from behind in the third and scored in every inning till the end.

Boyle, who started on the mound for the milkmen and went the route, displayed a streak of wildness in the opening frame as he gave up three runs. Walks to the first four Lions to face him, a wild pitch, another base on balls and another wild pitch caused the damage.

Local 338 came back in their half of the second with one run to keep them in the ballgame. Jack O'Shaughnessy walked and s t o l e second. After he had scampered to third on a wild pitch, he scored when Vaughn Bridge's infield grounder was thrown wild to first.

The champs tied the game in the top of the third as Dick Raus walked and Mickey Boyle belted a tremendous homer over the fence in centerfield. Boyle gave up one run in the bottom of the inning, but his teammates bounced back to tie the game again in their half of the fourth. The big blow of the inning was Bill Johnsons' smash off the pitcher's glove into centerfield. Andy Karl, who deflected the liner from the mound, had to leave the game.

Boyle held the Lions scoreless the rest of the way, picking up speed and regaining his control as the game progressed. Local 338 added one more run in the fifth to go ahead, 5-4, and to sew up the game.

The fifth inning run came off the bat of Jack O'Shaughnessy, who clouted a long-bagger over the rightfield fence. Not satisfied with a mere one run lead, Local 338 added the finishing touches with a big four-run sixth.

In that frame, Tucker and Hurlie walked. After Raus forced Tucker, Boyle advanced the runners as he fouled out behind first. Carl Schillio's high fly to the outfield was misjudged, scoring Hurlie and Raus. Up stepped Jack O'Shaughnessy. Again he swung into one and laced it deep over the fence, this time to left field.

Local 338, besides coming up with timely hitting and good pitching, played heads up defensive ball. In the bottom of the fifth, with men on first and second, the champs came up with an odd but beautiful doubleplay. In an attempted force, the second baseman bobbled the ball. Homer Macon, who was on first, tried to go to third on the miscue but a perfect peg nailed him. Meanwhile, Ken Miller, who was on second when the play began, streaked for the plate. A bullet like throw from third to home and a fine tag doubled Miller sliding into the plate.

Though Local 338, who played fine ball throughout the R o u n d-Robin playoffs, not losing a ballgame deserved the title, much must be said for the Lions. In order to reach the final game, they defeated some tough teams and played professional-like ball.

With the zest of youth, b o t h teams played like men. It was a fight to the end and the Lions went down swinging.

AB	R	H	Local 338	Lions Club	AB	R	H
3	1	2	Johnson,rf	Persise,2b	3	1	0
0	0	0	Tucker,rf	Stevens,p	2	1	0
2	1	1	Hurlie,2b	Cole,p	3	2	0
2	2	0	Raus,c	Blake,1b	2	0	0
3	1	1	Boyle,p	McFarlane,ss	3	0	0
4	1	0	Schillio,ss	McConney,3b	0	0	0
3	3	2	O'Sh'n'sy,1b	Miller,rf	2	0	2
4	0	1	Nardone,lf	Macon,lf	2	0	0
2	0	0	Bridges,cf	Karl,p	1	0	0
0	0	0	McF'lane,cf	Rampell,cf	0	0	0
3	0	0	Leone,3b	Myers,ss	1	0	0
				Bodenchuk,c	3	0	0
26	9	7			22	4	2

SCORE BY INNINGS
Local 338 .... 012 114 9
Lions Club 301 000 4

Little League Selects 116, Minor Loop Gains Balance

Five clubs have adopted new sponsors. They are Engine 6 (previously Community Oil), Goffi Brothers (Elko Lamp), Mount Vernon Life Insurance (Fava Post), Sundown Rest (Godfrey's), and Truck 3 (Topp's).

Teams and their selections are:

Braslow Builders: Bruce Brodbeck, Mike Buglione, Mark Gould, Fred Griffin and Paul Pallett.

County Pants: James Bolger, Peter Bowerman, Charles Jones, Robert Klein, Joseph McCubbin, Michael Paladino and Paul Remesic.

Democratic Club: Mark Brenner, Paul D'Aquanni, George Deverman, Charles Formes, Martin Kramer and Paul Reedy.

Elks Club: Frank DeVino, William Gauhs, Stephen Keely and James Kenny.

Embassy TV: Thomas DeBellis, John Moccio, Roy Morris, John Oswald and Joseph Verlezza.

Engine 6: Joseph Barrella, Kenneth Ferruzzi, George Guarino, Robert Nelly, Paul Peterson, Michael Stiller and James Tuccillo.

Goffi Bros.: Robert Basciano, Jeffrey Cantor, Robert Grossman, Michael Marks and Richard Santore.

Gramatan Men's Shop: Joseph Buglione, Nicholas Coschignano, Thomas Fasano, James Mouyeas and Michael Peterson.

Kiwanis Club: Cliff Baumgartner, Vito Capece, Richard Cuneo, Michael Goldberg, Mark Kleiman, Joe Marcotte and John Merchant.

Langdon Shop: Philip Arena, Fred Blount, Raymond DeBenedictis, Vincent Fernandes, Philip Leone and Robert Smith.

Lions Club: Richard Alperin, Jonathan Breen, Neal Frankel, Homer Macon, Stephen Reuss and Leonard Stevens.

Local 338: Roger Caro, Gary Grande, Ronnie Leone, Arthur Reuss, Carl Schillo and Alan Tucker.

Mount Vernon Life Insurance: Jim Amandolare, Bruce Carlson, James Corke, Joseph Crescenzo, Cosmo Rabasco, Joseph Salierno and David Wexler.

Nada Fence: David Colton, James Fruselante, Carlo Overton and Anthony Veteri.

Optomist Club: Robert Conley, Vito DeBellis, Paul Domato, Dominic Frisiello, John Richardson, James Seller and James Smith.

Perry Soda: Alfred Goldberg, Oliver Hernandez, Richard Mann, William Nylin, Anthony Tripodi and John Venditto.

Republican Club: Irwin Black, James Cardasis, Thomas Egan, Anthony Parenzino and Anthony Spiridigliozzi.

Rotary Club: Jack Bombace, Richard Caparelli, Robert Hansen, William Hogan, Armel MacDonald, John Student and Dennis Webster.

Sundown Rest: Robert Arena, Anthony Castaldo, John Parenzino, Albert Pirro, James Quinn and Paul Traunecker.

Truck 3: William Fornuff, Douglas Laird, Curtis MacMillan, Kenneth McConney and Ronald Skinner.

15

1958 – The Lions Roar

New names were on the world scene in 1958. Nikita Khrushchev became Russia's new prime minister and in Cuba, rebel leader Fidel Castro sent out the call for all soldiers to desert the military and join him. Baseball Hall of Famers Wade Boggs and Ricky Henderson were born. Meanwhile, around Mount Vernon everyone was singing the Italian song "Volare" which won the first Grammy Award ever awarded. We also were eating Cocoa Puffs and Cocoa Krispies and Sweet n' Low which were on grocery store shelves for the first time that year. And who could forget that new favorite toy the Hula Hoop which was invented by Wham-O.

Remember sitting on the curb and talking about Yogi Berra and Roy Campanella. Oh those arguments. Who was the better catcher? Tragedy struck in late January when Roy Campanella suffered a broken neck in an early morning auto accident on Long Island. There was more sadness in '58 when the Dodgers and Giants unpacked their bags after moving west to California and were playing baseball there.

That spring a group of businesses in Mount Vernon got behind Little League baseball.

By April 1 applications for Little League had to be obtained at specific locations: Tom Godfreys Sporting Goods at 3 Fourth Avenue; Embassy TV on Gramatan Avenue; Tripodi Foods on West Sidney Avenue; Andy Karl's Plumbing at 282 East Third Street, and at the Recreation Commission office at City Hall.

The vast majority of Little Leaguers were youngsters who stayed home for the entire summer and did not go to summer camp. A study of the team rosters through most of the 1950s revealed that there were few boys playing Little League ball who lived in the northern or northeast section of the city. Many went away to summer camp.

Little League took notice of that in 1958 and instituted a unique rule. In order to qualify for Little League, a boy was allowed a two-week vacation period. If any boy had the intention of going to camp for more than two weeks, he was urged not to apply. The League also emphasized that all applicants had to be residents of Mount Vernon.

Tryouts were held at Baker Field on April 12. The following Saturday a player draft was held at league headquarters on Orchard Street. Andy Karl, chairman of the board of directors, and Larry Tracy, Little League commissioner, conducted the draft. Players were selected to fill rosters on 20 teams and were urged to contact their managers for practice schedules. Seven days later the league held its annual Tag Day when Mount Vernon residents were asked to contribute funds to help defray Little League costs. The city swarmed with about 480 Little, Minor, and Pony Leaguers requesting funds from residents.

While league teams were sponsored by local merchants and civic organizations, sponsorship fees were insufficient to carry on the summer programs and the Tag Day was needed. Ralph Merola, Mount Vernon Pony League commissioner, was chairman of Tag Day and his captains were Al Coleman, John Lyons, Bill Siemers and Faust Cardillo. Acting Mayor George Bantz even issued a proclamation:

Whereas the Little, Minor and Pony Leagues have benefited Mount Vernon youth through their activities, and Whereas the leagues have helped teach good sportsmanship, obedience and to face competition, and Whereas many adults, both through time, efforts and financial aid have worked with and for the youth of this community through the three leagues, and Whereas many youngsters have graduated from Little, Minor and Pony Leagues and have gone on to star in high school, college and other athletic endeavors, and Whereas the Little, Minor and Pony Leagues are attempting to acquire the cooperation of adults and teenagers of Mount Vernon and to build an interest in their activities, May 3, 1958 has been proclaimed Little, Minor and Pony League Day.

Karl Hurls 2-Hit Win as Little League Debuts

With his father, Little League Commissioner Andy Karl sitting in the stands along with 500 fans, Andy Karl Jr. pitched the Lions to an opening day victory with a two-hit 4-1 win over the Rams. Karl struck out 13 Rams while losing pitcher Joe Capuano struck out 15 but allowed four runs on six hits. Capuano got the Rams only two hits and scored its lone run.

The first two Lions runs came in the fourth inning when Richard Paloscio hit a 2-0 pitch to deep right field that drove in both runs. Bill Miller singled off the Rams second baseman for his third hit to score Paloscio and Jim Persise. Miller had a perfect day at the plate, hitting a single, triple and double.

In other action, Local 338 pitcher Bill Johnson held Braslow hitless after the second inning and assisted his team in posting a 16-4 win. The Braslow team reached Johnson early and scored four runs through the second inning. But in the bottom of the second, Vaughan Bridges and John McFarland drove in five runs to give the Lions a 5-4 lead. Bridges, McFarland and Johnson continued their hitting in the fourth inning and drove in 10 runs.

A five run first inning. ten run second inning, and four more runs in the sixth inning helped Northeastern Life easily beat Goffi Brothers 19-7. Bob Brown picked up the win and also drove in four runs. Bob Liscio started for the losers and belted a triple and home run in his two turns at bat.

Paul Williams of the Elks pitched a three-hit 4-0 shutout over the Democrats. John Donnellon started for the Democrats but gave up three runs in the first inning on four hits, one a three-run homer run by Dwight Bell. Richard Bromley replaced Donnellon and only allowed one run on two hits over the final four innings.

After playing scoreless ball for nearly three innings, Engine No. 3 scored a run in the third inning and added seven more in the fourth and four more in the fifth that led to a 12-6 victory over Engine No. 6 in a battle of the firemen. Tom Glover went the distance and picked up the win, allowing four runs on three hits. He struck out nine and walked five. Pete Peterson took the loss.

A single to center field by Republican Steve Sperling drove in Rich DeLawder with the tie-breaking run to give the Republicans a 7-6 win over Perry Soda in a seven inning game. John DiGiacomo started for the Republicans and hit a triple and a double. He left the mound after six innings when the score was tied at six apiece. Jim Cardasis got the nod and finished the game.

Richardson Hurls No-Hitter in Optimist Win

Johnny Richardson pitched the Optimist Club to an 8-0 no-hit victory over the Rotary Club. Richardson struck out 15 walked four. Dennis Macauley got two hits for Optimist and drove in four runs.

Roy Wickens threw a one-hitter against Gramatan Men's Shop to give the Goffi Bros. Little Leaguers a 6-1 win at Baker Field. Wickens had no-hitter going into the final inning when he gave up the hit.

Local 338 held on to beat the Republican Club 10-5 as the Republicans got four runs in the last two innings. John McFarland went the distance, giving up five hits. He also doubled. Dennis Hurlie, Gary Grande and Pete Nardone led the hitting attack for Local 338.

Victor Seff pitched the Sundown Lounge to a 3-2 triumph over Northeastern Life. The Lions Club blanked Kiwanis, 14-4 as Lions first baseman Bill Miller homered in the fifth inning. It was his fourth extra base hit in his first eight at bats.

Engine 5 remained undefeated in the Western Division by winning its second game, a 6-3 victory over Engine 6. Engine 6 scored three runs in the first inning on Pete Peterson's home run. Johnny Hoffman of Engine 5 did the same in the fourth inning. He added a triple in the fifth. Harold Messner picked up the win striking out nine in the first three innings.

Guarino and Sullivan Pace Engine 6 To Win

Engine 6, led by center fielder George Guarino's three hits and John Sullivan's three-hit pitching, edged out Engine 5, 4-2. In the first inning, Guarino's single drove home Bob Nelly with the first run. Right fielder J. Mauriello got two of the losers three hits, one a sixth-inning homer. Sullivan gave up three walks while striking out 10.

Nada Fence pounded out 16 hits, including Jim Frushiante's three-run homer in the fourth inning, to beat Langdon Shop, 18-3 in Eastern Division competition. Second baseman John Maffucci got three hits for the winners while Ray Santoro got the win. Ed Magner tripled for the losers.

DeVito, Bromley Home Runs Help Democrats Top Elks

Two homers by Joey DeVito and one by Jack Bromley helped the Democrats cruise to a 12-7 victory over the Elks. Braham Horwitz pitched one hit ball for five innings for the Democrats before he was hit by a pitch and left the game. The Elks rallied for six runs in the bottom of the sixth but it wasn't enough to catch the Democrats. Marvin Brown and Dwight Bell homered in that big inning.

Bromley came on in relief in the sixth for the Democrats. With two out and the bases loaded he allowed a double but struck out the next batter to end the game.

Andy Karl picked up his third win of the season as the Lions Club won its sixth game of the year with a 6-5 victory over the Optimists. Karl gave up five runs on nine hits. John Richardson took the loss giving up six runs on 10 hits.

In the first inning, Richie Cole drove in the Lions first run when he singled down the right field line to score Jimmy Persise. The Optimists took a 3-1 lead in their half of the first inning as Vito DeBellis, who opened the game with a line single, came home as Karl threw wildly in an attempt to nail Henry Polk who bunted. Al Robliano tripled in Polk and John Richardson flied to right as Robliano scored.

The Lions scored four runs in their half of the second inning to put them back into the lead. Dennis Bodenchuk led off the fifth inning for the Lions with a double to right center. He scored on Rampel's hit.

Karl's No-Hitter Clinches 1st Place for Lions

Andy Karl pitched only four innings but didn't allow a hit as his Lions Club walloped the Kiwanis Club 14-0 to clinch first place honors in the first round of Service Division play. Karl's no-hitter went into the record books. A year later Mike McCormick of the San Francisco Giants held the Philadelphia Phillies hitless through five innings before the rains came and the game became impossible to continue.

The Lions scored six runs in the first inning, five in the second and three in the third. Karl helped his own pitching gem with a triple, homer and four RBIs. Teammate Roy Sussman connected for a triple, homer and three RBI's and Dennis Bodenchuk had three singles.

In a tighter game, the Republican Club scored three in the fifth inning to nip Local 338, 4-2. Jim Cardasis picked up the win while allowing only three hits. Perry Soda beat Braslow Builders, 8-5, in another rain-shortened game with Dick Mann picking up the win.

Jack Bromley Pitches Democrats to 6-3 Win

Jack Bromley gave up three runs on five hits but managed to beat Nada Fence as his Democrats won 6-3. Kenny Klein picked up the loss, allowing six runs on six hits. The win clinched a playoff berth for the Democrats. Braham Horwitz was the big slugger for the winners with a three-run home run in the first inning.

Dwight Bell hit a base clearing triple to lead the Elks to a 14-6 triumph over Langdon Shop. Marvin Brown held Langdon to six runs on only one hit. In the second inning, the Elks had four straight singles and a walk followed by a Bell triple. Another homer by Dave Buchalter with three teammates aboard ended the Elks scoring.

Engine 3 won its seventh straight game with a 10-1 victory over Engine 6. Joe McClublin led the hitting parade for Engine 3.

Coshigano's Triple Helps Rout Sundowns

Anthony Coshigano of Goffi Brothers hit a fifth inning base clearing triple to lead his team to an 11-7 win over the Sundowns. Pitcher Roy Wickens benefited from Coshigano's hitting and helped his own cause with a single, double and triple.

Langdon Shop pitcher Robert Smith struck out 13 Democrat batters and gave up only one run on one hit as Langdon easily won 15-1. Jack Bromley got the only hit for the Democrats, a first inning home run. Fred Blount and Ray DeBenedictis both went three for four for the winners.

Rich Colarusso of Nada Fence shut out the Elks, 9-0, on one hit. Dennis McNamara went three for three at the plate including a home run for the winners. Braslow Builders pitcher fanned 16 Republican batters in posting a 4-1 no hit victory.

Jackie Mahon of Perry Soda blasted a grand slam home run in a 10-7 win over Local 338. Richie Brooker picked up the win allowing seven runs on six hits. Despite the loss, Local 338 still won the first round of Little League play with a 6-3 record.

Engine 3's winning streak reached eight with a 16-3 triumph over Engine 5. The game only went four innings and was called because of darkness. Charlie Jones, who relieved Tom Glover, picked up his first Little League victory, allowing one hit while striking out four and walking two in three innings of work.

Northeastern Life beat Gramatan Men's Shop, 7-5, with Bobby Brown picking up the win. Artie Bragg tripled for the winners with the bases loaded in the fourth inning to give his squad an edge. Nick Martucci doubled and singled for the winners.

Paul Peterson pitched Engine 6 to a 9-6 victory over Engine 5. The winners rallied with a five run fifth inning to put the game away.

Clayton's Homer Gives Kiwanis a Win

Kiwanis center fielder James Clayton homered with two teammates aboard in the final inning that sealed a 7-4 win over the Rotary Club. Stephen Martin racked up his first pitching victory while striking out 13. Third baseman Al Bombace homered for the Rotary.

Braham Horwitz did it all at the plate and on the mound for his Democrat Club in beating the Langdon Shop. Horwitz went two for two with a home run and triple. He also threw a six hitter while fanning ten batters.

Nada Fence catcher Tony Pagnotto doubled home the winning run in the last inning to beat the Elks, 3-2. The Elks led 2-0 going into the bottom of the final frame. Jim Frusciante singled over second for Nada Fence. Tony Cimmino followed with a single that sent Frusciante to third. Bob Colorusso then doubled home both runners to tie the score at 2-2. Colorusso scored the winning run on Pagnotto's double and also picked up the win, allowing two runs on two hits, while striking out 10. Paul Williams took the loss.

Richie Cole of the Lions won his fourth game of the season defeating the Elks, 4-3. Cole gave up three runs on five hits. Tony Castaldo was charged with the loss.

Richardson Spins 3-Hitter To Blank Rotary, 7-0

Johnny Richardson won his fifth game in six starts for the Optimist as he threw a 7-0 three-hit shutout against the Rotary Club. Richardson's shutout was saved twice by sparkling defensive plays by Peter Altieri and Tony Castaldo. Both also went two for three at bat. Jack Bombace took the loss, allowing seven runs on 11 hits. The Optimist broke a scoreless deadlock with two runs in the second inning and added five more in the bottom of the fifth.

Ronnie St. Clair paced the Goffi Brothers to an 8-3 win over Sundown A.C. A towering home run by Roy Wickens started off the scoring.

The Republican Club won its third game in a row behind the pitching of Rich Colarusso, a 6-4 triumph over Perry Soda. He also struck out eight. Bob Paone led the hitting attack going three for four.

Local 338 banged out 17 hits to crush Braslow Builders, 14-1. John McFarland picked up the win while Earl Baughn took the loss. The Gramatan Men's Shop posted a 9-2 victory over Northeastern Life Insurance with Bob Semmanick going all the way for the win. He also went two for three to help his own cause.

450 Attend Little, Minor All-Star Game

The Polio Fund benefited as more than 450 people attended the All-Star game between the Minor and Little Leagues that was won by the senior circuit, 22-1.

The Little League All-Star roster was comprised of Billy Wright, Bob Brown, Francis Blount, Phil Buglione, Ray Santore, George Guarino, Al Rogliano, Roy Wickens, Bob Merola, Jimmy Kenny, Bob Petrillo, Tim Williams, Dennis Hurlie, Jimmy Cardasis, Richie Cole, Jim Hoffman, Earl Vaughan and Victor Seff.

Little League Sandlot Highlights

With the end of the regular season fast approaching, Local 338 needed just one more win to cop the National League pennant. Manager Al Coleman expected his squad to wrap it up over the weekend. Local 338 won the flag in 1957. Much of the credit for training the Local 338 squad went to Chet Hurlie, father of Dennis, a player. Ronnie Goss and Jerry Luft also helped manager Coleman.

In the Service Club League, the Lions were hitting better than anyone expected they would. According Manager Sol Dunsay, the team's batting average was .360 with six players hitting well over the .300 mark. The Lions opposition was hitting .240 and had only one home run. Richie Cole and Andy Karl, the two top pitchers, each threw a one hitter. In his last start, Karl tossed a shutout in a win against the Kiwanis Club while striking out 17.

Victor Seff pitched five out of the six wins for the Sundown A.C. that won the first round. The club picked up John Giacone from the Minor League to play first base.

The winners of the first round in the Eastern League, the Democrats were in second place. If they hoped to win they would have to do it without the services of Braham Horwitz, the club's shortstop. Like many youngsters in the city, Horwitz went to camp for the remainder of the summer. He was the squads top pitcher with a 5-1 record. Peter Meehan replaced him at the top of the pitching staff.

Billy Wright, shortstop for Truck No. 3, played outstanding ball in the first half of the season. Runner-up in the first round of the National League, the Republican Club was 4-3 in the second round. Jimmy Cardasis had a 6-1 record to lead the club.

The Elks left-hand hitting first baseman, Jimmy Kenny, was hitting well over .400. Catcher

Dwight Bell hit seven home runs.

Raymond Santoro was one of the reasons why Nada Fence was in the thick of the pennant fight. The 12-year-old righthander had a 7-1 record. The club also relied on John Maffucci at second base and Jim Frusciante in left field.

In a Service Club slugfest, the Optimists outscored the Lions 17-14 in a game that temporarily decided first place in the division. Tony Castaldo started for the Optimists and was relieved by Al Rolliano who picked up the win. Richie Cole, who took the loss, was relieved by Dennis Bodenchuk. Both clubs had 32 hits between them. Kenny Miller homered for the Lions and Peter Altieri homered for the winners. Vito DeBellis went four for five for the Optimists. As a club, the Optimists averaged 12 hits per game.

Nada Fence Blank The Elks, 1-0

Bob Colorusso doubled in the fourth inning and then Dennis McNamara singled him home to hand Nada Fence a 1-0 win over the Elks. Ray Santoro meanwhile threw a no-hitter, picking up his eighth win in nine starts. He fanned 13. On the short-end of the well pitched game was Marvin Brown who gave up four hits while striking out nine.

It took the Democrats only three and one half innings to score 22 runs as they whipped the Langdon Shop 22-7 in a shortened game called because of darkness. Jack Bromley, the winning pitcher, had a perfect day at bat chalking up five hits.

Singleton Blanks Northeastern and Hits Grand Slam

In his first year in the Little League, Ken Singleton shutout Northeastern Insurance and hit a grand slam homer in the first inning to lead his Gramatan Men's Shop to an 11-0 win over Northeastern Insurance. In all likelihood this was Singleton's first win in the Little League. Getting his name in the trivia record book was Carl Thimm who took the loss. Neil Peterkin was the big gun for the winners, going three for three.

Engine 6 Wins on Four-Hitter

Paul Peterson pitched a one run four-hitter for Engine 6 as they beat Engine Truck 3, 6-1. With James Tuccillo, Peterson, and John Sullivan providing the hitting, the winners took a one run lead in the first inning. They added another run in the second and that was enough. Also tapping out hits for Engine 6 were Kevin Robertson, Mike Stiller, George Guarino and James Sliney. Peterson struck out 12 and gave up only two walks. John Wright was the losing pitcher.

Perry Soda came up with two runs in the top of the last inning and held Local 338 to one run in the bottom of that frame to post a 2-1 win. George Bochow, in relief of Richie Brooker, was the winning hurler. Richie Mann's hit in the last inning drove home Bobby Merola with the first run. Losing pitcher Bill Johnson led Local 338 with two hits and drove in the club's only run.

Rich Colorusso won his third game of the season for the Republican Club as they downed Braslow Builders, 3-1. He struck out seven. Jimmy Cardasis led the hitting attack for the winners. Steve Sperling's single to centerfield in the sixth inning broke a 1-1 ball game.

Engine 3 Rout Democrats, 7-3, in Playoffs

Engine 3 scored seven runs on six hits to defeat the Democrats, 7-3, in a round robin playoff game. The Democrats held a 1-0 lead in the third inning but Engine 3 came back with four runs in the fourth frame and held on to win. Ken Fried doubled and singled for the winners. Paul Renesic was the winning pitcher, his second win of the playoffs. He struck out five and didn't walk a batter. Tom Williams was hit with the loss.

Democrats Cop Eastern Division Pennant

The Democrats won the Eastern Division Little League pennant with a come from behind 4-3 victory over Nada Fence.

Trailing 3-2 going into the final inning, Artie Koch singled. Joey DeVito followed with a triple down the left field line to score Koch with the tying run. After Jim Egan struck out, Marty Kramer slashed a drive down the first base line which deflected off the first baseman's glove and allowed DeVito to score the winning run. Jay Polansky and Tom Williams chipped in with triples for the Democrats while Bob Colarusso homered for the losers. Jack Bromley picked up the win and Jim Frusciante got the loss. Both of them homered.

Carl Schillio's triple with the bases loaded in the third inning paced Local 338's win over the Republican Club, 5-4 in another playoff game. Bill Johnson was the winning pitcher, allowing four runs on eight hits. Jim Cardasis was charged with the loss. Pete Baust went three for three at the plate for the winners. Carl Schillio went two for three for the losers while Bob Paone and John DiGiacomo both tripled.

The Goffi Brothers squeezed over one run in the bottom of the seventh inning to down Northeastern Life, 9-8, in an extra inning game. Anthony Coshigano was the winning pitcher. Bob Brown took the loss. Albert Annunziata scored the winning run on an error by the catcher. Lenny Teasedale homered for the winners with one on in the third inning.

Sundown Lounge Wins American League Flag

The Sundown Lounge won the American Division championship when they downed the Gramatan Men's Shop, 2-1, The champs scored all the runs in the top of the second inning when Victor Seff singled to lead off. John Ryan tried to sacrifice and was safe at first on a error. Joe D'Esso then singled in Seff and Ryan. The losers picked up their lone run in the bottom of the third when Bobby Semanick singled home Bill Merigliano. Eddie Lukanik was the winning pitcher, striking out 13 while Kenny Pieterki was the loser. Both pitchers allowed but two hits.

Perry Soda, Lions Win in Round-Robin

Perry Soda eked out one run in the bottom of the eighth inning to nip Sundown Lounge, 6-5, while Andy Karl hurled a no-hitter for the Lions Club as they defeated Engine 3, 8-1.

For Perry Soda, Richie Mann doubled home Jackie Mahan with the winning run. George Bochow picked up the win, allowing five runs on nine hits. He struck out 10 and walked only one. Bochow put his team ahead in the bottom of the fourth with a two run home run. Bob Kukinak was the losing pitcher.

Karl struck out 14 batters in his easy victory. He along with Richie Cole, Dennis Bodenchuk, Roy Sussman, and Bill McConney paced the winners. Each had doubles. Guy Rampel also homered for the Lions.

Lions Smash Perry Soda, 10-2, in Playoff Win

The Lions Club had a cakewalk in its 10-2 playoff victory over Perry Soda. The winners had 12 hits while the losers were held to three. Richie Cole picked up the win, fanning nine. Richard Brooker was charged with the loss.

Perry Soda scored first in the bottom of the third inning when Anthony Tripodi was hit by a pitch. Bob Merola then walked. Ed Anderson lined a double to center field driving in two runs. The Lions came back in the top of the fourth inning when Dennis Bodenchuk led off with a homer run over the left field fence. Roy Sussman followed with a single and Billy McConney doubled to right, sending Sussman to third. Richard Paloscio singled up the middle to score Sussman. The Lions picked up another run when Andy Karl walked. Following a strikeout, Kenny Miller was safe on a bad throw by the shortstop which allowed McConney to score.

In the top of the seventh innings the Lions added to their lead. Paloscio doubled to right. Persise got to first and Paloscio scored when the second baseman threw wildly to first. Andy Karl walked. Kenny Miller tripled to score both runs and then he stole home. Rampel hit a line drive home run over the left center field fence. After Ed Anderson came in to relieve Dick Mahan, Sussman laced a knee high pitch to center field for the final run of the game.

Lions Capture Little League
Enginemen Stopped, 10-3 On Rich Cole's 4 Hitter

The Lions copped the Little League City Championship crown last night by defeating the Engine No. 3 nine, 10-3 before more than 500 spectators at Baker Field.

Young Richie Cole tossed fourth and the final victory for the City Champs, his second in the Round Robin playoff series. He allowed four hits. Tommy Glover was charged with the defeat, allowing 10 runs on 13 hits.

The Lions began their 10 run scoring spree in the first inning. Jimmy Persise tried to bunt leading off but was thrown out, Glover to Skip Bolger at first. Andy Karl socked the first of his three consecutive doubles to left field, and when Ken Fried missed the throw in to second continued home to score run number one. Cole singled to left and stole second and then third. Kenny Miller walked and stole second to put two men in scoring position but Guy Rampel and Dennis Bodenchuk fanned to end the inning and threat.

Ken Fried led off for the Enginemen but grounded out, McConney to Miller. Skip Bolger doubled to center field but Charlie Jones hit back to the box and Cole held the runner on second and then threw Jones out at first. Bill Petilli hit back to the box for the final bout.

In the second inning, Roy Sussman led off for the Lions with a hot single past third. He then stole second and third. Blanch threw into left field trying to nab Sussman and he scored on the miscue. Billy McConney walked, Richard Paloscio struck out and Jimmy Persise walked to put two on. Karl belted another double, this time to left to score McConney. Cole tripled down the left field line scoring Persise and Karl. Miller popped out to short and Cole scored on a wild pitch. Rampel kept the rally going with a neat single through short and reached second on a steal. Bodenchuk lined a single into left field but Rampel was cut down trying to score the run.

The Enginemen failed to score in the bottom of the second and succeeded in holding the Lions to one hit and no runs in the top of the third.

In the bottom of the third the Enginemen finally came to life for two runs. Blanch led off with a hit that went wide of first. Miller went over to cover, came up with the ball and flipped to Persise covering first.

In the mixup at first Blanch was called safe. Persise suffered a bruised left leg but remained in the game. Glover fanned for the first out and Fried hit the first pitch down the left field foul line and over the fence for a home run scoring mate Blanch ahead of him. Skip Bolger flied out to Karl in center for out number two and Jones fanned for the third.

Karl led off with a double for the Lions to start the top of the fourth. He then stole second while Cole walked and stole second moving Karl to third. Miller doubled to center to score the two runners. Miller then stole home. Rampel grounded out Jones to Paladino at first and Bodenchuk singled.

The Enginemen tried to pull the hidden ball trick on Bodenchuk but Glover balked when he stepped off the mound without the ball, advancing the runner to second. Sussman flied to Bowerman and Bodenchuk was cut down trying to steal third ending the inning.

In the bottom of the fourth the Enginemen scored a final run as George Sirignano homered.

Winning pitcher Cole added the tenth and final run of the Little League season when he swung on a zero and two count and blasted a homer high over the center field fence.

In winning, Cole gave up three runs on four hits. He walked three and struck out eight. Glover struck out four and walked four.

LIONS	AB	R	H	ENGINE NO. 3	AB	R	H
Persise 2b	2	1	0	Fried 2b	2	1	1
Holmes 1b	1	0	0	Bolger 1b	2	0	1
Karl cf	4	3	3	Paladino 2b	1	0	0
Cole p	3	3	3	Jones 3b	3	0	0
Miller 1b	3	1	1	Petilli lf	2	0	0
Rampel lf	4	0	2	S'nano cf	2	1	1
B'chuk c	4	0	2	Remesic ss	3	0	0
Sussman rf	3	1	2	B'mn rf	2	0	0
McC'y ss	2	1	0	Mitchel ss	1	0	0
Paloscio 3b	3	0	0	Blanch c	2	1	1
				Glover p	2	0	0
Totals	29	10	13	Totals	22	3	4

Score by Innings
LIONS 150 301
ENGINE NO. 3 .... 002 100

Little League Holds Draft, Team Rosters Completed

BRASLOW BUILDERS—Michael Campareale, Peter Francese, Vincent Lebonitte, Edward Lennon, Robert Maher and Michael Rizzo.

DEMS—John Donnellon, Richard Delewder, James Egan, Arthur R. Koch, Peter Osta and Warren Replansky.

ELKS—Steven Felder, Guido Napolitano, Philip Rizzotti and Thomas Rizzotti.

ENGINE 3—Dennis Burke, Curtis Blanch, Thomas W. DeVito, Thomas Glover and William Petilli Jr.

ENGINE 5—Gene Fialkoff, Richard Brett, Joseph Mauriello, Craig Paff, Donald Rasher, Leon Robinson and James Wellock

ENGINE 6 — Daniel T. Glum, Richard Kahan, Henry Janssen, Ralph Potente, James Silney, John Sullivan Jr. and Robert Wenk.

GOFFI BROS. — Albert M. An'nunziata Jr., Joseph Coschigano, and Leonard Teasdale.

GRAMATAN MEN'S SHOP — Louis DiMenza, Richard Prattella, Robert Schneider, Peter Senatore, and Kenneth Singleton.

KIWANIS — James R. Clayton, Danny Goldberg, Robert Faulkner Jeffrey Matthews, Donald Radogna and Rodney Samlls.

LANGDON SHOP—Joseph Abbamont, Sandy Berardi, Paul Garcia, James Drummond, John Griffith and Alfred Squeo Jr.

LIONS CLUB—Stuart B. Cherney James Dallhoff, Salvatore Nardozzi, Richard Paloscio and Bill Schauz.

LOCAL 338—David Lee Bridges, Frank O. Gould, Jonathan Herson, Douglas Hurlie, Richard Nardone and Lee Steven Oshman.

MOUNT VERNON LIFE—Paul Belinkii, George Casabona, Nicholas Martucci, Arthur Shuster and Karl Thimm.

NADA-FENCE—Anthony Cimmino, Nicholas D'Andrea Jr., John Maffuccci and John Purpura.

OPTIMISTS—Robert Bretts, Dennis L. McCauley and Robert Simels

PERRY SODA—Dennis Ciallela, Paul Cuomo, Anthony Perone and Alan Yasser.

ROTARY—Robert Beckerich, Joseph Gagliardi, Andrew LaGrotte, Frank Marallo and Terry Romanoff.

REPUBLICANS—Stephen Henry Acunto, Peter Baust, Andy Crandall, Craig Ghessi, Adolphus Grant, Scott Kass and William Nylin Jr.

SUNDOWN LOUNGE — Henry Beinert, Joseph DeEsso, John Ferrara, Leonard Pepe, Michael J. Diehl, Christopher Serraro and Kenneth Walsh.

TRUCK 3—Keith Conlon, Ernest Dubriske, Richard Greenbaum, Richard Hensel, Richard Janniello, and Seth Patcher.

1958 – The Lions Roar

1958 Perry Soda: 1, Manager Joe Tripodi; 2, Dennis Ciallela; 3, George Bochow; 4, Coach Ed Anderson; 5, Joe Norelli; 6, Anthony Pirone; 7, Eddie Anderson; 8, Paul Cuomo.

16

1959 – Ken Singleton Played Here

The Barbie doll was introduced worldwide in 1959. "Some Like It Hot" with Marilyn Monroe and Jack Lemmon premiered. Bill Sharman hit an NBA record 56 consecutive foul shots. "Kookie, Kookie Lend Me Your Comb" by Kookie Byrnes and Connie Stevens got to # 4 on the charts while Yogi Berra's errorless streak of 148 games ended. And 10 Little League graduates from earlier in the '50s played on A.B. Davis High School's '59 championship Westchester Interscholastic Athletic Association (WIAA) team. Eddie Martin was singled out as Westchester's best right handed pitcher and Tom Ambrosino and Ted Cardasis made All County honorable mention.

Ten years earlier four men got together and decided Mount Vernon could use a Little League program. By 1959 more than 700 boys were playing in the Little, Minor and Pony League program. There were 20 Little League teams; each one had a manager, one or two coaches, and a sponsor. The acorn had turned into a giant oak.

That was a far cry from the league's first year of play in 1950 when nobody wanted to sponsor a team. Mothers of the 60 boys who were chosen to play on the four original teams and the wives of the "founding fathers" held card parties and bake sales to raise money to outfit each youngster with a complete uniform.

For the first two years the Mount Vernon Little League struggled to raise money. By 1959, the league through sponsors, various fund raising campaigns, exhibition games and contributors, operated on about an eight to nine thousand dollar yearly budget.

Steve Acunto was one of the first managers and handled the Indians, one of the original four teams. He was back again in 1959. So were Joe O'Connor, Jeff Borelli, Larry Tracy, and Mrs. Billie O'Connor, secretary of the Board of Directors. All reached the 10 year mark of service in 1959.

The philosophy of those who worked in Little League in 1959 wasn't any different than that of those who were involved in 1950. Everyone felt Little League was a great tool to help mold boys into good citizens. No one got discouraged when they found out that some parents shuffled the youngsters out of the house and into a Little League uniform just for the sake of getting them out of the house.

Every year you could always find the interested parents at a game. They were the ones who lugged folding chairs, thermos bottles, and loud voices to Baker, Longfellow or Hutchinson Field. They filled the air with: "Let's go, Jimmy!" or "Get a hit, Billy!" every summer.

For 300 aspiring Little League players the summer of '59 really began on April 25 when final tryout sessions were held at 10:30 a.m. at Hutchinson Field. Some 400 youngsters turned out the week before for the first tryouts. They were held under the watchful eye of managers and coaches representing the 20 teams. On April 29, *The Daily Argus* announced the names of 111 Little League newcomers. For the 307 boys who were not drafted by a Little League team they found a spot on a Minor League squad. There were three loops with six teams in each one.

On Opening Day, the late Len Boccardi, 1958 Minor Little League commissioner, was honored during ceremonies inaugurating the 1959 season. A few moments of silence in honor of Mr. Boccardi's memory was held by players and coaches at Baker Field where his widow, Mrs. Rose Boccardi threw out the first ball. Boccardi was involved with the Little League since its inception.

After City Council President Irving Kendall and Department of Public Works Commissioner Albert Annunziata threw out the ceremonial first pitches to start the season, Little League youngsters took to the diamond noting several significant changes mandated by Little League's national headquarters.

The pitching distance was increased from 44 to 46 feet since the league's national headquarters found that youngsters were throwing the ball at about 70 mph. That got the ball up to the plate in less time than a major league pitcher who threw 60 feet at 100 mph. By moving the pitcher's mound back two more feet, Little League boys now had just about as much time to swing, proportionately, as the big leaguers had. In another safety precaution, the modern protective batter's helmet was developed that year by Dr. Creighton J. Hale, then director of research for Little League baseball.

Little League was even recognized by the U.S. government in 1959. In May, the House and Senate passed a resolution proclaiming the second week in June as National Little League Baseball Week. This marked the twentieth anniversary of Little League's founding. President Dwight Eisenhower signed the proclamation. By then, there were 25,000 Little League teams in 5,000 leagues playing in 25 countries.

Mount Vernon's Little League even found another baseball diamond to play on in early June. The ball field on the Wartburg property was officially commissioned as the Democrats rapped out a 9-6 victory over the Elks.

Three No Hitters Mark Opening Day

May 9 – In the early baseball season, a favorite expression is that pitchers are ahead of hitters. That sure was the case on opening day. Paul Remasic of Engine 3, Tony Castaldo of The Optimist, and Gregg Martin of Truck 1 all threw no-hitters.

Remasic beat Truck 3 18-0 and struck out 13. He also went four for five at the plate while driving in five runs. Mike Paladino hit a grand slam homer for Truck 3. Castaldo had an easy time of it as The Optimist belted losing pitcher Robert DiCisco of Kiwanis for 11 hits in a 15-1 win. Castaldo struck out 15 and walked three. The Optimists scored four runs in the first inning and three more in both the fourth and fifth innings. Castaldo, Bobby Brett and Bobby Simels blasted homers with Brett also adding a double.

In his first pitching outing, Gregg Martin hurled Truck 1 to a 10-0 win over Engine 6. Paul Peterson was the loser. Gramatan Men's Shop came up with a run in the seventh inning to nip Leonardo Electric, 2-1. Ken Singleton was the winning pitcher. He also banged out four of his club's eight hits. John Ryan took the loss.

North Eastern picked up five runs in the first inning and coasted to a 7-4 win over Goffi Brothers. Karl Thimm, the winning pitcher, fanned 12 batters, while John Thornberry, the losing hurler, struck out five batters.

Mike Camporeale allowed six hits as his Braslow Builders defeated Local 338, 3-2. Richie Silvester and Peter Frances were the big hitters for the winners. Jim Frusciante threw a two-hitter and struck out eight batters for Nada Fence, which whipped Davis Electric, 7-4. Phil Leone was the loser.

George Bochow also pitched a two-hitter as he hurled Perry Soda to a 5-4 win over the Republican Club. Jim Cardasis, the losing hurler, allowed four hits. Each pitcher struck out 12 batters.

Home Runs Galore Over Weekend

May 18 – It was Marathon Saturday at Baker and Hutchinson Field with six games and plenty of home runs.

Gramatan Men's Shop put together 13 hits and six and seven run innings to blast Goffi Brothers, 15-3. Ken Singleton went the distance for the win and helped his own cause with two hits, one a home run. He struck out 14. Tony Coschigano and Jerry Erbaio shared the pitching for the losers with Erbaio getting the loss. Singleton and teammate Vernon Biederman each batted in three runs. Rich Pratella also homered for the winners.

In a battle of the firemen, Engine 6 stopped an Engine 3 rally in the top of the sixth inning to eke out a 4-2 win at Baker Field. With two on and no outs in that inning, Engine 6 came up with a double play to stamp out the threat. Both teams had seven hits. Paul Peterson's triple and single paced the winners and Bob Kline's home run and two doubles leading the losers. Kevin Robertson and Henry Vanssen also had triples for the winners.

In an extra inning victory, Ronnie Leone's double drove in Billy Altenhein with the winning run as Local 338 beat the Republican Club, 3-2. In the second inning, David Bridges' two-run homer gave the winners their first runs. Joseph Coutee and Lee Oshman shared the pitching chores for the winners, with Coutee, who relieved in the seventh, getting the win. Jim Cardasis went six innings for the Republican Club.

Davis Electric had eight hits in an 8-4 win over the Elks. Bobby Garcia was the winning pitcher. Phil Arena came in relief in the fifth inning to halt a bases loaded Elks rally. Ed Magner had two hits for the winner.

Perry Soda held on for an 8-7 win over Braslow Brothers despite a three-run uprising by the losers in the sixth inning. Paul Cuomo and Richie Mann shared the pitching duties for the winners with Mann picking up the victory. In the third inning, Perry Soda scored six runs. Anthony Perrone, A. Yasser and Paul Cuomo each got two hits for the winners.

Behind the two-hit pitching of Bobby Brett and Gregg Martin, Truck 1 beat Truck 3, 6-3. The winners scored three runs in the fifth inning to ice the game. John Moccio of the winners had two hits including a home run.

Leonardo Printing scored three runs in the first inning and held on for a 5-3 win over Northeastern Life. Mark Lerner picked up the win. Barney Giacabello doubled in the first inning for the printers while Lerner tripled in the third. Eric Liberatti homered for the losers.

Buddy Alderson's two-run home run in the last inning gave the Democrats a 6-4 win over Nada Fence. George Bronsky got two hits for the winners. Pete Meehan and Jay Polansky shared the pitching for the Democrats.

In the top of the seventh inning, the Lions came up with four runs to down the Kiwanis Club, 8-6. Jim Dallhoff picked up the win.

Bodenchuk Homers Twice in Lions Win

June 1 – Pitcher Dennis Bodenchuk's two home runs paced the Lions in their 12-0 romp over the Rotary Club. Teammate Bill Schauz also homered as Bodenchuk allowed only one hit in his route-going performance in which he struck out 16 batters.

A big six-run third inning powered Engine 3 to an 11-1 win over Engine 6. Paul Remesic got the win while Pete Peterson was tagged with the loss. Peterson's home run accounted for Engine 6's only score.

Despite a six-run fifth inning, Northeastern Life still came up on the short end of a 9-7 loss to Leonardo Printing. Nick Martucci's grand slam homer was the big blow. Mickey Riehl had a pair of doubles and triple for the winner.

Perry Soda, with pitcher George Bochow blasting a single, double and homer, whipped Braslow Builders, 6-2. Mike Camporeale was the losing pitcher. B. Scaramucci homered for the winners while Frank Gould hit a four-bagger for the losers.

Nada Fence came up with four runs in the final inning to edge the Democrats, 5-4, as Jim Frusciante outpitched Jay Polansky. The Republican Club picked up two wins over the weekend, blasting Local 338, 6-3, and Perry Soda, 17-3. Peter Baust picked up the first win helped by teammate Willy Alejandro's two successive home runs. Jim Cardasis also homered for the winners. In the nightcap, Cardasis won as he struck out 15 batters.

The Democrats walloped the Elks, 16-8, as they came up with five runs in the first inning and eight in the second with Artie Koch's three-run homer and George Bronsky's triple pacing the winners. Marvin Brown won and Frank Bartolotta picked up the loss.

The Optimists on a Role

June 8 – The Optimists won their sixth game in a row without a loss when they came up with a run the bottom of the final inning to edge the Lions, 5-4. They were led by Tony Castaldo on the mound and Vito DeBellis and Dennis McCauley at bat. Both DeBellis and McCauley homered and Castaldo gave up four hits. Losing pitcher Dennis Bodenchuk clouted a homer.

Davis Electric behind Phil Leone's 10-strikeout performance beat the Democrats, 11-6. Centerfielder Fred Blount got three hits for the winner, two of them home runs. Davis Electric also picked up a weekend victory over Nada Fence, 12-6, with John Griffin getting the win and Bobby Garcia collecting three hits.

Robert Duncan's two-run triple in the fifth inning was the key hit in a Local 338, 8-3, win over Perry Soda. John Argentina chimed in with two hits for the winners. Frank Gould was the winning pitcher. Tony Coschigano pitched and batted his Goffi Brothers to a 7-3 win over Leonardo Printers. He hit a first-inning homer while teammates F. Mancuso and J. Cantor had two hits apiece.

Gramatan Men's Shop, aided by a three-run first inning, cakewalked to a 5-1 win over Northeastern Life. Ken Singleton, the winning pitcher, gave up two hits and got two of his team's five hits.

Phil Leone No-Hits Nada Fence

June 15 – Phil Leone didn't give up a hit and hurled Davis Electric to a 6-0 win over Nada Fence in a game that was called after four-and-a-half innings because of rain. First baseman Bobby Garcia got two of the winners five hits.

Leonardo Printing, paced by three runs in the second inning, beat Gramatan Men's Shop, 4-1 behind John Ryan's five-hit pitching. Ken Singleton's home run in the fourth was the loser's only run of the game.

Truck 1 scored five runs in the second inning led to a 7-2 win over Engine 6. Gregg Martin's grand slam was the big blow. Bobby Brett, the winning pitcher, fanned nine batters. Davis Electric had nine hits in beating the Elks, 14-0, with Blount, the winning pitcher, striking out 14 batters.

Braslow Builders edged Local 338, 3-2 with Rizzo picking up the win and Frank Gould the loss. The Republican Club blasted 16 hits in an 18-4 win over Perry Soda with three of the hits being home runs by Alessandro, Gant, and Tony Spiridigliozzi. Jim Cardasis was the winner.

Goffi Brothers won its sixth straight game as John Thornbury struck out 14 batters in leading his club to a 6-2 win over Northeastern Life. Frank Mancuso and Tony Coschigano led the hit parade. The Democrats nipped the Elks, 2-1, as winning pitcher Peter Osta drove in the deciding run with a sacrifice fly. Peter Meehan's triple was a big blow for the winners.

The Wartburg Becomes Little League Diamond

A new Little League diamond on the Wartburg property was commissioned as the Democrats beat the Elks 9-6.

In the bottom of the second inning the Democrats were losing before doubles by Johnny Donnellon and Jay Polansky brought them back from a two run deficit into a 5-2 lead. Polansky was never in any serious trouble as he went the distance for the victory. Marvin Brown took the loss, getting relief help from Frank Bartolotta and Tom Reisman.

At Baker Field, Paul Remesic threw a three-hit shutout as Engine 3 beat Truck 3-0. This was Remesic's seventh win of the season as he struck out nine and walked four.

George Bochow, who struck out 15 batters, was just one out away from a no-hit win for Perry Soda when he gave up a hit in the final frame. He won 6-1. He joined some pretty famous company of pitchers who went down to the final batter before losing a no-hitter like New York Met Tom

Seaver, Chicago Cub Ken Holtzman, and Baltimore Oriole Mike Flanagan. Anthony Perone got three hits for the winner and Richie Mann got two. Bochow tripled with the bases loaded to help his cause.

Steve Acunto Jr. Steals Home To Win Game

July 1 – What did Steve Acunto Jr. and baseball great Ty Cobb have in common? They both stole home. In Acunto's case, he slid under the tag to score the winning run as the Republican Club rallied in the bottom of the seventh inning to beat Perry Soda, 10-9. Ty Cobb holds the records for most steals of home in a season (8) as well as for a career (54). Jackie Robinson was also renowned for the thrilling feat of stealing home, which he famously accomplished in Game 1 of the 1955 World Series, sliding under Yogi Berra's late tag.

For Acunto's Republican Club the score was tied at the end of regulation play and in the top of the seventh inning, George Bochow hit a grand slam home run to put Perry Soda ahead, 9-4. The Republican Club rallied for six runs, winning the game on Acunto's stolen base.

In another Baker Field game, Ken Singleton struck out 10 Leonardo Electric batters while allowing four runs on six hits as Gramatan Men's Shop won 5-4. John Palmer and Chuck DiSalvo went two for two for the winners driving in two runs apiece. The Elks rallied for two runs in the bottom of the sixth inning to give Frank Bartolotta the win.

Anthony Coshigano Takes Game Into Hands for Win

July 7 – Anthony Coshigano did not need much help from his teammates as he pitched and batted the Goffi Brothers to a 7-2 win over Gramatan Men's Shop. He gave up the two runs on two hits. He also blasted a grand slam home run in the third inning to give his team the lead. Kenny Singleton was the losing pitcher.

The Republican Club, with the aid of Steve Acunto's two run triple in the fourth inning, rallied to beat Local 338, 8-5, for its fourth straight win. Jim Cardasis went the route for the win while Frank Gould lost. Catcher Tony Spiridigliozzi doubled and Craig Chezzi tripled for the winners.

Jim Arena pitched the Democrats to a 2-1 win over the Elks, allowing two runs on two walks and a single by Frank Bartolotta. Phil Leone hit a grand slam homer for the winners.

Palmer, Singleton, Pratella Spark Haberdashers Win

July 14 – The trio of John Palmer, Richard Pratella, and Ken Singleton provided the big hits as the Gramatan Men's Shop beat Leonardo Electric, 9-3. They all got two hits apiece. Anthony Coschigano was the winner, striking out 11 while only giving up three hits. A five run fifth inning put Gramatan Men's Shop in the lead.

The heavy-hitting Democrats did likewise in the slugging department as they defeated the Elks, 13-5. Buddy Alderson, Francis Montumerro, Artie Koch and Jay Replansky got the big hits for the Democrats. Fine defensive plays by Richie Mann and Gary Cortellessa helped Perry Soda win a 2-0 shutout of the Republican Club.

Leone Tosses 2-0 Shutout

July 16 – Phil Leone chalked up another win for Davis Electric in pitching a three-hit, 7-0 shutout over the Democrats. Centerfielder Fred Blount hit two home runs to help the cause. Phil Armentano took the loss despite Phil Koch's two hits.

A grand slam by Phil Argentina in the bottom of the fourth inning broke a 6-6 tie ball game and rallied Local 338 to a 14-8 win over Perry Soda. Winning pitcher Frank Gould had three hits and scored three times in four at bats.

Two No-Hitters Highlight Weekend

July – A pair of no-hitters shared the spotlight at Baker Field as George Bochow's effort paced Perry Soda to a 5-1 win over Braslow Builders and Local 338's Frank Gould sparked his club to a 10-0 whitewash of the Republican Club.

Bochow struck out 11 batters while his teammate Dennis Cialla hit a home run and drove in four runs. Right fielder Joe Norelli's great catch in the top of the fifth, with the Builders having the bases loaded, saved the no-hitter.

Besides pitching a no-hitter, Gould had quite a day at bat. He came up with two home runs, a pair of singles, and six runs batted in. Gould during the season tossed another no-hitter in beating Perry Soda, 6-2. Again he was something else at bat getting two hits including a three-run home run.

Truck 1, with a four-run second inning, beat Engine 3, 7-4. Bobby Brett, the winning pitcher, struck out 10 batters. Gregg Martin and Tony DeBellis each had two hits for the winner. Davis Electric had 14 hits in beating the Democrats, 17-5. Phil Leone gave up seven hits in the win. Ed Manger homered for the winners while teammate Fred Blount added three hits, one of them a triple.

Singleton Strikes Out 15 as Gramatans Win 9-0

July 23 – The talented arm of young Ken Singleton was on display again for the Gramatan Men's Shop as he struck out 15 batters while allowing only one hit in a 9-0 win over Northeastern Life. Singleton faced 19 batters over the six innings and walked but two of them. Triples by Pete Santore, Rich Pratella and Singleton resulted in all the runs needed. Santore and John Palmer had doubles in their three for three efforts.

Nada Fence routed the Elks, 24-0, as John Maffucci only allowed two hits while his team's nine base hits resulted in all the runs. Second baseman Pat Warner went three for four.

Mark Klieman's triple, double and single resulted in seven RBIs for Kiwanis as they beat the Rotary Club, 19-5. Jamie Gelardo drove in three of those runs with a single while Ralph DeGisco and Donald Bennett also tripled.

Gramatans Romp, 22-1; Win AL Flag

July 23 – The Gramatan Men's Shop won the second round title of the American division with a convincing 22-1 victory over Leonardo Electric. Vernon Biederman belted two home runs, one a grand slam and drove in 10 runs in his three for three effort at the plate. Pete Santore went four for four, all singles, and scored four times. Nick Coschigano was the winning pitcher, going four innings and allowing one run before being relieved by Chuck DiSalvo. Jim Moyas homered for the winners.

In other action, Perry Soda beat Local 338, 7-6, to give the soda men the second round National division title. George Bochow was the winning pitcher while John McFarland took the loss.

Optimist, 338 Wins Even Two LL Playoffs

July 29 – The Optimists beat the Lions, 9-2, to even the two-out-three series in the Service League at one game apiece, while Local 338 came from behind to nip Perry Soda, 6-5, and tie up the National League race at one-game each.

In another playoff game, Davis Electric topped Nada Fence, 11-9.

Optimist hurler Dom Frisiello allowed only four hits while striking out seven. First baseman Charles Rogers and left fielder Dennis McCauley each collected two hits off losing hurler Bill Dallhoff, who gave up seven hits. One of McCauley's hits was a homer with Frisiello also belting a four-bagger. Frank Gould's bases-loaded single drove in Lee Oshman with Local 338's winning score in the sixth inning.

In the Local 338 game against Perry Soda, the soda men started the scoring with three runs in the second inning and two in the third, but the winners came back with one run in the fourth, three in the fifth and two in the sixth. Third baseman Ronnie Leone drove in four runs with a pair of home runs. Local 338 collected only five hits off losing hurlers Dick Mann, Dennis Cialla and John Scaramuzzo, whereas Oshman, the Local 338 pitcher, was pounded for 12 hits. Oshman allowed only two earned runs.

Davis Electric earned its 11-9 win over Nada Fence as a result of a six-run outburst in the second inning. The winners pounded losers Steve Giuliano and John Tetro for nine hits, while the losers got to Pat Griffin and Fred Blount for seven hits. Phil Arena's triple in the second inning drove in three runs for the winners. Teammate Ed Magner also tripled.

Playoffs Begin For Series Berths

July 27 – The 10th annual scramble for the Mount Vernon Little League Championship drew nearer to a close as teams in four of the five divisions met in the first of three scheduled elimination games. Engine 3 won both rounds in the Fire Department division and were not required to participate in a playoff series.

The Lions took a 3-2 victory over the Optimists in the Service Club loop, while Nada Fence scored a 5-2 win over Davis Electric in the Western division. Perry Soda scored an exciting 1-0 win over Local 338 in the National division. In the American division, Gramatan Men's Shop routed Goffi Brothers, 10-1.

Kenny Singleton for the Gramatan Men's Shop struck out 13 and allowed one run on one hit. A nine-run fifth inning sparked by Peter Senatore's grand slam, broke a 1-1 tie ball game. Senatore also got a double and triple and drove in five runs. Teammate James Mouyeous tripled with three men on base in the big fifth inning.

The defending City Champs, the Lions, scored one run in the top of the fifth inning to beat the Optimists. With one out and the score tied at 2-2, Andy Karl, the winning pitcher, singled to left field to put the tie-breaking run on base. With two out Dennis Bodenchuk stroked his third hit of the game, a single to left field to bring Karl home from third. Karl allowed two runs on three hits. He scored all three runs for his team on a single, double and triple by Bodenchuk. Jim Castaldo, who struck out 14, was the losing pitcher.

In another contest, Nada Fence had an early lead, held it for four innings and then withstood a belated rally to gain a 5-2 win over Davis Electric. Jim Frusciante picked up the win, allowing two runs on two hits. Phil Leone was the loser although he struck out nine and walked only two. He gave up six hits. Home runs by Frusciante and Warner gave Nada Fence an early lead. Larry Tetro, first baseman for the winning club, made an unassisted double-play to close out one inning single-handedly.

Dennis Cialla, Perry Soda shortstop, tripled with one away in the top of the ninth inning and scored the winning run seconds later on a wild pitch for a stunning 1-0 win over Local 338. George Bochow was the winning hurler striking out 20 of the 29 batters he faced. He allowed two hits and walked four. His opponent, Frank Gould lost a tough one, fanning 14, walking four, and allowing the fatal wild pitch.

Local 338 came close to scoring the first run of the game in the second inning when a perfect throw from left fielder, John Perrone, cut down John Argentina at the plate. Bochow ended the game with a flourish, striking out the last seven batters.

Gramatans, Local 338, Optimists Take Division Titles

July 31 – Three Little League division titles were decided at Baker Field.

In the deciding games, Gramatan Men's Shop routed Goffi Brothers, 15-0, to capture the American League crown; Local 338 nipped Perry Soda, 6-4, to win the title in the National League, and the Optimists ripped the Lions, 12-0, to take the Service League crown.

The Men's Shop, paced by a 14-hit attack and one-hit pitching by Ken Singleton, scored in every inning, capping off their attack with seven runs in the fifth inning. Singleton struck out 12 batters. He also went 4-for-4, while teammates Pete Senatore, Joe Buglione and John Palmer had two hits apiece. Tony Coschigano was the losing pitcher.

In beating Perry Soda 6-4, Ronnie Leone and Frank Gould shared the pitching for Local 338. The winners pounded out eight hits, with Leone, Gould and Bridges getting two hits apiece. George Bochow and Yorio were the Perry Soda pitchers. Bochow blasted a two-run homer in the third inning. Richard Nordone connected for a three-run triple for the winners in the second inning.

The Optimists pounded out 13 hits behind the three-hit pitching of Anthony Castaldo. Bob Simels, Vito DeBellis, Dennis Macauley, Sid Rogers and Bob Bretts each got two hits for the winner. Andy Karl took the loss for the Lions. He had two hits.

Gramatans, Local 338 Win Little Loop Tilts

August 3 – Local 338 and Gramatan Men's Shop won as the final round of games for the Little League championship moved into the completion stages.

Ken Singleton held off a final inning charge to give Gramatan a 7-6 triumph over the Optimist Club and Local 338 came from behind to rout Nada Fence, 7-3. Singleton gave up six runs before he cut short the last inning rally. He had a shutout going until then. He fanned seven and walked four. Tony Castaldo was the losing pitcher with Charlie Rogers finishing up in relief.

Frank Gould struck out 14 batters as Local 338 beat Nada Fence, 7-3. He walked but two and allowed three runs on three hits. Despite striking out 11, Jimmy Frusciante picked up the loss.

Optimists, Local 338 Win Round-Robin

August 5 – The Little League round-robin resumed with the Optimist Club winning 8-7 over Engine 3 and Local 338 beating Gramatan Men's Shop, 8-3.

The Optimists went in the final inning trailing by two runs, 7-5, before they pulled it out. With one away, Howie Greenberg walked Norman Morrow, the Engine 3 pitcher. Bobby Simels doubled and then Vito DeBellis singled to load the bases. Tony Castaldo walked scoring Simels. Charles Rogers followed with a double to score Greenberg but Castaldo was called out on a close play at the plate. Bobby Bretts was called in to relieve and retired the Engine 3 side in their last at bat. Rogers and Bretts got seven of the Optimists 13 hits. Bobby Fried of Engine 3 homered.

Nick Coshigano may have fanned 11 Local 338 batters while Frank Gould struck out only seven Gramatan Men's Shop players, but Gould came away with an 8-3 triumph over Gramatan. With the score tied at one apiece in the first inning, catcher John Argentina of Local 338 doubled with the bases loaded to put his club in the lead. Ronnie Leone and Gould had seven hits between them. Ken Singleton got two of Gramatan Men's Shops five hits.

Gramatan Men's Shop, Engine 3 Win Semi-Final Games

August 7 – In two semi-final Little League games, Gramatan Men's Shop beat the Optimist Club, 11-1, and Engine 3 romped to a 16-0 shutout over Local 338.

Kenny Singleton gave up just five hits while his Gramatan Men's Shop teammates scored 11 runs off 13 hits. He struck out six and walked three. Don Frisiello took the loss.

Gramatan Men's Shop was coasting by the time they reached the third inning when they scored another four runs. Singleton was also doing most of the hitting for his club, belting two doubles and a single to drive in five runs. Second baseman Nick Coschigano drove in two runs on a pair of singles.

In the top of the sixth inning the winners scored five more runs. In the bottom of the frame, on successive hits by Howie Greenberg, Vito DeBellis and Bill Batiste, the Optimists scored four runs.

In the other semi-final game, Engine 3 pitcher Paul Remesic threw a one-hitter as his club easily defeated Local 338. Engine 3 left fielder Robert Klein and teammate Ken Mathieu each hit a triple and both went two-for-two at the plate. It was a hit parade all game for Engine 3 with Remesic, Mike Paladino, Norman Morrow and Tim Blanche each getting two hits apiece.

Gramatan Men's Shop and Local 338 in LL World Series

August 10 – Gramatan Men's Shop defeated the Optimist Club, 11-4 and Engine 3 shutout

Local 338 in the semi-finals of the 1959 Mount Vernon Little League championship.

Kenny Singleton gave up five hits in the six inning game, while his Gramatan teammates scored 11 runs off 13 hits. He struck out six and walked three. Don Frisiello picked up the loss for the Optimist Club.

Leading with one run in the first inning and adding another in the second, Gramatan Men's Shop was coasting and piled on another four runs in the third inning. Singleton provided the hitting, belting two doubles and a single to drive in five runs. Teammate Nick Coschigano followed in the RBI department with two. Chuck DiSalvo and Pete Santore both had two hits for the winners.

The Optimist got on the board in the bottom of the sixth inning on successive hits by Howie Greenberg, Vito DeBellis and Bill Batiste. Four runs scored.

In the other semi-final game, Engine 3 pitcher Paul Remesic allowed just one hit, a double. He struck out seven and walked but one. Engine 3 left fielder Robert Klein and teammate Ken Mathieu both tripled. Teammates Mike Paladino, Norm Morrow, Tim Blanche, and Remesic got two hits apiece. Bernie Oshman picked up the loss, allowing 13 hits.

1959 – Ken Singleton Played Here

Engine 3 Wins LL Crown

Jones Hurls 4-Hit, 12-0 Victory Over Gramatan

Charlie Jones, an 11-year-old righthander who gave up just four hits last night, socked a two-run homer to launch his team, Engine 3, into the scoring column in the second inning, and then went on to pace them to a 12-0 shutout victory over Gramatan Men's Shop for the Mount Vernon Little League Championship at Baker Field.

Jones, who saw only limited mound action this past season, grew stronger with every pitch he threw. He struck out four and walked one, retiring the opposition in order in the first, fourth and fifth innings.

Some 350 parents, brothers, sisters and relatives were on hand for the final game of the Little League season and saw Engine 3, winners of both rounds in the Fire Department division, convert 15 hits into 12 runs.

Engine 3, managed by Eric Favilla and coached by Frank Falco, won seven straight in the first round, then lost two, taking the round in a playoff game. In the second round they won nine straight, lost one game to the Optimists in the round robin, and came on strong to nab the title.

With two out in the bottom of the second inning, Paul Remesic, ace pitcher for Engine 3 and 14-game winner, drew a base on balls. Jones followed in the order and promptly blasted one over the fence in center field to start the Firemen rolling on all cylinders.

Skip Bolger, Engine 3 first baseman, tripled to lead off the third inning and scored on teammate Norm Marrow's triple. After two were out, Marrow scored on Ken Fried's single.

The fourth inning was where the Gramatan team lost all hope of survival as the Firemen scored seven runs on four hits, four walks and a hit batsman.

To lead it off, Ken Matheio and Mike Paladino walked. Bolger got hit with a pitch to load the bases. Matheio should have scored from third on Marrow's sacrifice fly to deep center field but signals got crossed somehow and he remained on third, scoring seconds later along with Paladino and Bolger on Tom Blanche's triple.

Bob Klein struck out to put two away and Ken Fried drove home Blanche with a solid double to right field. Remesic walked and scored along with Fried on Jones' second hit of the game, a double to deep left.

In his second time up that inning, Mathieo doubled. He stayed on base as Paladino was walked for the second time and Bolger flied to the outfield.

In the bottom of the fifth inning, Marrow got his second hit of the game, a homer over the center fielder's head.

Nick Coshigano was the starter and loser for the Gramatan club, getting relief from Chuck DiSalvo in the final innings.

Gramatan's catcher, Jim Mouyeos, got the best hit of the game for the losing club, a double in the second inning. Ken Singleton, Coshigano and Rich Pratella got the remaining three hits for the losers.

Next season, according to Engine 3 manager Favilla, Jones, dubbed "The Sleeper" and Klein will handle the bulk of the team's pitching assignments.

After the game, the managers, coaches and parents of the players celebrated their joint victory.

GRAMATAN	AB	R	H	ENGINE 3	AB	R	H
DiM'na cf	3	0	0	Kane rf	0	0	0
Sentora 1b	1	0	0	Moore rf	1	0	0
B'llone ss	2	0	0	P'dino rf	1	1	0
S'leton 2b	3	0	1	Bolger 1b	3	2	1
Palmer rf	2	0	0	Marrow cf	4	2	2
Mouyeos c	2	0	1	Blanche c	4	1	3
DiSalvo 3b	2	0	0	Sackle lf	0	0	0
C'snano p	2	0	1	Klein lf	3	0	1
Pratella lf	2	0	1	Lovrett 2b	0	0	0
				Fried 2b	4	1	3
				R'esic 3b	2	2	1
				Jones p	3	2	2
				Mathieo ss	2	1	2
Totals	19	0	4	Totals	27	12	15

111 Youngsters Gain Berths In Little Loop

The names of the newly drafted players and the teams to which they have been assigned are as follows:

NADA FENCE: Edward Knight, Dominick Mascolino, Patrick Warner, Larry Tetro, Richard Bentham, Louis DeFillippo, Fred Valentino and Anthony Bruno.

GOFFI BROTHERS: Kevin Murray, Vincent Aquilino, Roy Kinkead and Darrick Warner.

DEMOCRATS: George Bronsky, Anthony Penna, Francis Montemorro and William Alderson.

NORTHEASTERN LIFE: David Goldsmith, Donald Salierno, Craig R. Carlson and Dennis LaBarbera.

ELKS: David Staminger, George Valavan, Thomas Mouyeas, Jay Reisman, David Minet and John Silva.

DAVIS ELECTRIC: James Wallace, Robert Flannagan, Bobby Pucci, Martin Hartog, Frank Lanzilote and Frank Williamson.

LIONS: Steven Holmes, John Sackie, Eugene Costa, Harry Krimkowitz and Ned Levitas.

ROTARY: Barry Leaville, Glen Miller, William Cobb and William Cassanol.

OPTIMIST CLUB: Sydney Rodgers, Charles Rodgers, Frank Palazzo Jr., Howie Greenberg, Caesar Armanio, William Batiste Jr. and Michael Rao.

KIWANIS: Edward Sallade, Robert Colarusso, James Gelardo,

ENGINE NO. 3: Peter Weiser, Michael Kain, Alec Leggat, Raymond Sackie and Raymond Moore.

ENGINE NO. 6: Dennis Donahue, Robert Dura, Madrid Rabina and Harry Soderlund.

LENARDO PRINTING: Thomas Riehl, Barney Giacobello, Anthony Troiano, Paul Visser, George Schultz Jr.; and Frank Longshore.

GRAMATAN'S MENS SHOP: G. Richard Goetchius, Charles DeSalvo, Matthew Ferrari and David Muir.

LOCAL 338: Fred Burak, Joseph Cootee, Lee Oshman, Michael LaPorte, John Argentina, Abe Ramsey, Richard King and Anthony Servino.

BRASLOW: William Sheehan, Vincent Tiso, Mario Sclafani, Frank Annunziata, Nicholas Rao and Robert Almeida.

REPUBLICANS: Wilfred Alejandro, Hugh Anderes, Andrew Lukanik, E. George Shute, Ralph Frusciante Jr. and Frank Salierno.

PERRY SODA: John Scaramuzzo, Frank Yorio, Joseph Mack, Kevin Kelly, John Gleason, Chester Merola and Joseph Felix.

TRUCK NO. 2: Stephen Ferrara, David Fleming, Denis Carroll, Lawrence Schleicher and Richard Vogel.

TRUCK NO. 1: William Sullivan,

17
Conversation with Ken Singleton

Ken Singleton has been a New York Yankees analyst for the YES Network since 2002. Born in Manhattan and raised in nearby Mount Vernon, Singleton played both baseball and basketball in high school. After receiving a basketball scholarship to Hofstra University and playing baseball as well for one year, Singleton was drafted by the Mets in 1967.

In April 1972, he was traded to the Expos and, in 1974, he was traded to the Orioles. His .438 on base percentage (in 1977), 118 walks (in 1975) and 35 switch-hit home runs (in 1979) are all still Orioles single season records. He retired after the 1984 season as a three-time All-Star with a 1983 World Championship ring.

Singleton is one of only six players in Major League Baseball history to hit 35 or more switch hit homers in a season. During his career, Singleton was named to the American League All- Star Team in 1977, '79 and '81. He was named Most Valuable Oriole in 1975, '77 and '79. Singleton received the Roberto Clemente Award from Major League Baseball – the highest off-the-field honor in baseball – in 1982.

He also was honored with the "Denzel Lifetime Achievement Award in Sports" at the Boys & Girls Club of Mount Vernon's 100th Anniversary Gala in 2012.

I remember playing for Gramatan Men's Shop in 1959. I also remember trying out for Little League at Baker Field where there were about four or five fields there. Mount Vernon High School is located there now. I was taking ground balls at third base and I remember throwing to first a few times. I noticed a lot of the coaches said I had a pretty good arm. Later I remember when John Branca, Ralph's brother, told Ralph, 'I have a kid in this camp, and if he keeps going he's going to be pretty good.' That was me.

I eventually was taken by Coach Phil Buglione for his Gramatan Men's Shop team. I pitched and when I didn't pitch I played third base. Mr. Buglione was a very nice man. He had two sons on the team. He didn't live far from me in Mount Vernon.

Mount Vernon was special place to grow up. I rode my bicycle everywhere and have fond memories. As a kid, my Aunt Helen wanted me to play the piano but after a couple of weeks she told me, tell your mother you want to play baseball for a living. I said, she already knows. I wasn't a great piano player.

As I said, I had to ride my bike all the way over to the other side of town to Little League games. That was about a two mile ride. At the end of practices or games Mr. Buglione would put my bike in the trunk of his car and take me back home near Graham School where I lived.

I remember being on some pretty good teams playing for the Gramatan Men's Shop, as well as playing on All Star teams that traveled. We once went to Trenton, New Jersey to play. We also went to Ossining for a tournament.

In those days the kids who threw the hardest were the pitchers. I was a pitcher. I remember throwing five one hitters and then finally throwing a no hitter. I also could hit. I think my last year when I was eligible, when I was 12 years old, I hit .636 for the season.

All I can remember was the one year of Little League. I remember our Gramatan Men's Shop uniforms. We had white jerseys with red hat and socks. I also played PAL ball.

My dad really introduced me to baseball. He was a big Dodgers fan and I can remember watching games on our black and white TV when I was four and five years old. In New York there were three teams at the time. Most of the time we watched the Dodgers primarily because of Jackie Robinson. The Dodgers were a very good team. I remember switching television channels to watch the Yankees and Giants. There was always baseball on.

I lived on Seneca Avenue in Mount Vernon. When I was about four years old I lived in New York City. My dad and I would have catches at a playground across the street where there was a school yard. He would pitch to me and I would hit. Even at a young age I could hit the ball. My dad, Joe, would chase it every single time. He would come back. As long as I wanted to hit, he would chase the ball.

The other kids I played with were a little older and they didn't believe I was four or five years old. To me baseball was a lot of fun.

It may have looked easy. But when I got into professional ball I realized it wasn't so easy. It was more of a job than people would think even though I loved playing. It definitely took some work to be proficient at it.

Growing up we played stick ball at Graham School. I also played at Memorial Field and Hutchinson Field where we would have pickup games with my friends. We would ride our bikes down to the fields and then ride them back up the hill on Sanford Boulevard. We'd stop at the Carvel stand at the corner of Sanford Boulevard and Columbus Avenue. I remember milk shakes were a quarter.

I'm not really sure about the story of our house on Seneca Avenue and the Branca family. My dad did buy the house from the Branca family. I'm not sure if it was Ralph who lived there or Ralph's father. At the time, I was only six or seven years old. I do remember walking into the house the first time. Ralph wasn't there. It must have been his dad. I can remember walking through the house and having a very good feeling about it, not knowing if my parents were going to buy the house which they did. They worked very hard to pay for it over the years.

I began switch hitting in the playground. My favorite team was the Giants and when I played stickball with my friends I would go through the Giants lineup. Whenever Willie Mays was hitting I would bat right handed and whenever Willie McCovey would be up I would hit left handed.

When I was playing American Legion ball and earlier when I played in the Little League I would only hit right handed. Then one day I was playing in the Bronx Federation League and I was fooling around before the game. I must have been 15 or 16 years old. I was taking batting practice and I was hitting left handed and hitting well. So my coach said, "Why don't you hit lefty during the game since we're facing a right handed pitcher today?" I hit two home runs that day. From that point on ever since I was 15 I started switch hitting all the time. It was a tremendous advantage. I got to play all the time.

I asked Ken whether he thinks Little League has changed since he played in it in the late 1950s. He said, when I was playing my parents were working and they didn't get to see me play very often. They were busy working paying for the house that they bought. That was ok. They were hard working people.

When they retired they got to see me play all the time. They went to the big league games. The payoff was at the very end for them. The thing that parents nowadays have to learn is that baseball of all the sports is the hardest one for youngsters to learn.

You're afraid of the ball. It is hard to hit it. It's hard to catch it. It's hard to be accurate when you throw it. I think parents don't like to see their kids fail. Just to be a good hitter you fail 70 percent of the time. I don't think parents are willing to accept that compared to other sports like soccer in particular.

Last year I had an off day and I rented a car and drove up to Mount Vernon. I drove around and went to all the fields where we used to play. They were in bad shape. It kind of hurt me. Memorial Field was weeded over. The high school baseball field didn't look in particularly good shape. These are the places where I grew up as a baseball player and wanted to be a major league baseball player. I couldn't see any kid wanting to do it on the those fields and the condition they were in. Hopefully they can remedy this. I hope they rebuild Memorial Stadium. I learned a lot of good lessons from baseball.

18
Conversation with Ralph Branca

Ask yourself who is the most famous athlete ever to come out of Mount Vernon. Ask yourself which Mount Vernonite has been written about more than any other person. The answer is a fellow who hasn't appeared on a professional athletic field for nearly sixty years. Even today, his name always appears regularly in the sports pages. He is Ralph Branca.

Yes, he is best known for throwing the pitch that resulted in Bobby Thomson's "Shot Heard 'Round the World," the historic home run that capped an incredible comeback and won the pennant for the New York Giants in 1951. Branca was on the losing end of what many consider to be not only baseball's but sports most thrilling moment. That notoriety belies Branca's profoundly successful life and career. The event has been shrouded in controversy in recent years as it has come to light that the Giants in all likelihood schemed to steal the Dodgers signals through an elaborate system featuring a telescope, wiring and buzzers.

"A Moment in Time" is Branca's new book, written with David Ritz and published by Scribner, that details the remarkable story of a man who could have been destroyed by a supreme professional embarrassment, but wasn't. I highly recommend the book if you want read about a rare first-person perspective on the golden era of baseball, about growing up on Mount Vernon sandlots, about attending Mount Vernon schools, and about hearing of many local families you were familiar with.

Anyone who has played organized baseball in Mount Vernon owes a great deal to Ralph Branca and his brother John for the many contributions they made to the success of the city's sports programs and to the well being of its citizens. Ralph became a member of Little League's executive committee in 1950 and appeared at Little League games with his Dodgers teammates. For many years he helped promote and raise funds for Little League and attend season-ending functions. His brother John called ball and strikes behind home plate at Mount Vernon Little League's first game. He later went on to coach baseball at Edison Tech High School from 1952 to 1961. He also coached varsity football there and for 19 years was commissioner of recreation in the city where he provided services and activities for senior citizens, the handicapped and mentally retarded citizens.

The Brancas came from a large close knit family. Ralph grew up with much older brothers Julius and Ed, his slightly older brother John, and younger brothers, Paul and Al. As a youngster, Ralph's mom had 17 children. She lost two infants to diphtheria. Two sisters died when Ralph was a youngster growing up at 522 South Ninth Avenue, right off of Sandford Boulevard. He grew up in a neighborhood with friends and neighbors who included the Casuccis, the Veteris, the Amarusos, the Merolas, the Lichtenfelds, the Ligouris, the Tartaglias, the Cerrones, the Tuckers, the Levinsons, and Woodsons.

As a school kid, Ralph worked at Kaplan's Kosher Meat Market. He even worked for my father, who was a partner in a wholesale dry cleaning plant located right next door to his home on South Ninth Avenue. His brother John was a quarterback at A.B. Davis and Ralph was his end. In Ralph's junior year and John's senior year, they were both pitching stars. John made the New York Journal-American All-Star team and didn't lose a game all season. He was 12-0 and Ralph was 2-0. Ralph even threw batting practice for the Brooklyn Dodgers at Ebbets Field in the summer of 1942 when he was a junior in high school.

He made his major league debut against the Giants at the Polo Grounds on June 12, 1944. At the end of the season, he went home and started an amateur basketball team that played at the Mount Vernon armory. That year he helped buy his parents a better home at 409 Seneca Avenue. In an incredibly odd twist of fate, it was the same house that Ken Singleton would grow up in years later.

When Branca was 20 in 1946 he was the youngest player ever to start a postseason game, a record that still stands. That was when he pitched in the Dodgers-Cardinals playoff game to decide the National League championship.

The following year, 1947, was Ralph's best. He won 21 games. He joined a select company of such Hall of Famers as Lefty Gomez, Bob Feller, Babe Ruth and Christy Matthewson, because he was a 21-game winner at the age of 21. He also led the league in starts with 36. He had the third-best ERA, 2.67. He was second in the league in strikeouts. He pitched in 280 innings. He never missed a single start. His salary was $6,500 and he still took the bus and two subways to work at Ebbets Field from his home in Mount Vernon. He appeared in three All-Star games and was the starting pitcher in game one of the '47 World Series at the age of 21. He played professional ball for 13 seasons, from 1944 to 1956, during which he won 88 games and lost 68. He pitched for the Dodgers, Detroit Tigers and New York Yankees.

Despite Branca's great 1947 season, it still isn't remembered today as Ralph's year. There was a far bigger story. In 1947, Jackie Robinson made an impact on America's baseball, history, culture and society. He became the first black big leaguer.

In "Moment in Time" Branca said, "I was a witness to history. And I was also deeply fortunate to be able to befriend a man of extraordinary ability, intelligence, and guts. I loved Jackie and was privileged to call him a teammate and friend. No other man could have represented his people with greater dignity, stamina and skill. He was a great athlete, that's for sure. But it was Jackie's qualities as a leader, his moral courage and unwillingness to compromise his high principles, that guarantee him an indelible chapter in the history of our country."

In 1956, after striking out Willie Mays and Bill Sarni, he went back to the Dodgers dugout and would never pitch in a major league game again. After Ralph retired, his love for the game and his concern for the players' welfare was as strong as ever. It tells you what kind of fellow he is. He got involved with BAT, the Baseball Assistance Team. He was the first president and then CEO of the organization. He served in that capacity for 17 years. BAT did great work, helping those major and minor league players who had fallen on hard times.

In his new book Ralph talks about the day Thomson hit the home run, "The darkness of that day – October 3, 1951, has been overwhelmed by a life filled with light. Father Rowley was right when, after The Pitch, he said, 'God chose you because He knew you'd be strong enough to bear this cross.'"

Branca went on to say, "To be honest, on this final page of the book, in spite of my abiding Catholic faith, I had planned to be true to the vindictive paisan within me and conclude with this thought: In 1951, the Giants didn't win the pennant; the Giants stole the pennant."

I was only four or five when I watched my older brother Julius Branca play baseball. He and my brother Ed were much older than my brothers John, Paul, Al, and me. Julius was about 15 years older than me. He was a very good player for sandlot ball. Ed probably bought John and me our first mitts. I remember pitching to Julius when I was six years old in the driveway of our yard.

Ed and Julius would take us to see our first major league games. They were Giants fans so we would go to the Polo Grounds about six times a year and Yankee Stadium twice. We wouldn't go to Brooklyn. That was too far.

You call it Hutchinson Field. I and everybody else called it Stinson Field. Old man Stinson must have owned the property and gave it or sold it to the city.

We would walk there from our home on South Ninth Avenue. We would walk by Longfellow School and go over the B&W tracks and end up at Fulton Avenue. Then we had to go in another two to three feet into Stinson Field. There were a couple of fields there. I haven't been there in a long long time.

I remember Howard Field behind the A.B. Davis High School on Gramatan Avenue. We played baseball there. It really was a football field. A football field is only 160 feet wide. So right field had football stands close by. It was nothing to hit a ball into those stands. Center field and left field were ok.

We played at Memorial Field. The recreation commissioner had a baseball program divided by age into midget, junior, intermediate and senior divisions. Midget was 12 and under; junior 14 and under; intermediate 16 and under; and over that was the senior league. We would play at other fields like Longfellow but I remember the championship games were at Memorial Field.

I asked Ralph Branca if he remembered the dry cleaning plant located right next door to his home at 522 South Ninth Avenue. My father was a partner in the plant back in the 1940's. I remember hearing Ralph's name for the first time in 1948 when I was six years old.

I sure do remember that plant, Branca said. Before the plant a guy had a farm there where he grew vegetables. He gave that up and then it was an empty lot. Then the cleaning plant was there. I worked in it. The clothes would come out of these big tumblers and I would pick the clothes out and there was a number on them because they were doing the cleaning for all these little cleaning stores. Every once in a while I would pick out a garment with a zipper and it was really hot. I probably got paid a penny an hour because it was your father.

I worked in the off-season when I was playing ball. During the '50s I worked at Tom Godfrey's sporting goods store in the winters. I almost bought the place. I also taught pitching at Phil Rizzuto's American Baseball Academy at an armory in Manhattan. I also worked in the American Shops, a clothing store in Newark, with Yogi Berra, Rizzuto and Gene Hermanski. They lived in New Jersey and they got me to work there Thursday nights from 5 to 9 and Saturday from 1 to 5. It was great. I made $150 a week.

I haven't been around Little League too much lately but I know way back when in the beginning there was too much emphasis on winning rather than learning the game and loving the game and learning how to participate. Win or lose graciously. I think the emphasis may have slackened a little bit about winning and now it's about learning how to play the game and loving it.

19

Conversation with Richard Wolff

This free-wheeling conversation I had with Rick Wolff should be of interest to any parent or grandparent who has a youngster interested in playing sports. Rick is a nationally-recognized expert in the field of sports psychology and sports parenting. Often quoted by the media about the issues that face today's athletes, he has written and lectured widely on the psychological pressures that accompany America's passion for sports.

He has written hundreds of widely-acclaimed prescriptive columns on sports parenting that ran in Sports Illustrated and has authored or co-authored 18 books, including four in the sports parenting field. He also was the co-founder of the prestigious Center for Sports Parenting, the nation's leading resource on sports parenting issues.

For the past 12 years, Rick has hosted a weekly sports parenting program, "The Sports Edge", on WFAN Radio in Westchester County, New York. He's been a featured expert on Oprah, ESPN, CNN, ABC's "NightLine",

ABC's "20/20", The Today Show, Good Morning America, CBS This Morning, Fox & Friends, Fox Business, CNBC, PBS, A&E, MSNBC, Court TV, Lifetime, Sports Channel, the Madison Square Garden Network, and dozens of other media outlets.

Rick graduated from Scarsdale High School, then graduated magna cum laude in psychology from Harvard University. He resides in Armonk, NY.

Parents over involvement in Little League, I can't give you a precise date when it began, but I would say around the early 1990s. That's when we began to see a real shifting of parents and their involvement in their kids' sports. Up until then it was different. Kids went out and played, but let's not make it sound like it was something out of Norman Rockwell. There was something so refreshing when kids went out every day, didn't have distractions like the internet, and played ball with their friends down the street or in sandlots. The parents really weren't involved. They said go out of the house, play ball until we call you home for dinner.

Those days don't exist anymore. I'll give you some reasons why that has changed. I think a lot has to do first of all, in the 1950s, most future professionals in a sport needed a modest amount of money. You know from your sports history, getting to the big leagues and playing for the Yankees in those days meant in the off season you didn't have enough money to pay the rent, so you had to get a job. Like everybody else, ballplayers had to pay their bills.

The reason I bring this up because you think playing pro sports is just a wonderful thing to do. You get paid for playing a sport. Years ago it wasn't a full time occupation or career because there wasn't enough money in it. There wasn't any television money or corporate sponsorships. It really was a way to extend your adolescence. That's the first thing.

There were college scholarships for sports in those days but most kids weren't aware about getting scholarships for baseball or other sports. The biggest thing you could do then was to play for your high school varsity and get a varsity jacket. That was a huge deal and most kids accepted the fact that that was going to be the peak of their career. Their parents thought the same thing.

Here you have a situation about the joy of playing sports and the pure fun of it. And that was pretty much what the '50s was all about. Then things changed for two reasons.

One is that the amount of money players received accelerated quite rapidly. All of a sudden, parents began to realize, gee whiz, 'my kid is a pretty good athlete' and maybe he or she will get that college scholarship and that will save me a lot of money; or maybe the kid is going to turn pro. Suddenly athletes weren't just making six figure salaries but guaranteed seven figure salaries. Parents started looking at their little athlete as perhaps a real meal ticket to fame and fortune.

The second thing that happened along the way is that we saw more and more of a situation in the early '80s, '90s and 2000s where both parents worked. Now there was a dual income household. In the '50s and early '60s, traditionally the dad was the breadwinner and the mom stayed home and kept an eye on the playground. She knew where the kids were all day. That has disappeared. Now you really can't leave your kid alone on a playground because of concerns of sexual predators.

The next thing you had was a situation where parents were saying, "I'm going to make sure my kid is playing in an organized league where there is real coaching, real involvement, and I can be there as a parent to oversee all of this."

The combination of those factors, the acceleration of the big money with college scholarships along with the sense that both parents were working, resulted in what we have today. There is tremendous over involvement with moms and dads with their kids.

In the '50s and '60s parents came out and watched their kids play. There really wasn't anything at stake then. I'm sure my dad took pride in the fact that I could hit a baseball or catch a pop up or throw a ball across the diamond. There wasn't any sense I could be a star or a pro ball player.

The kids were having fun. It is the same thing when my dad was growing up. For him playing baseball was fun. Nowadays, parents are saying, "'My kid is really a star of his little league team. He is on the fast track to go on and be a pro." The parent says he has to get his act together to make sure his son gets the best equipment, the best private coaches, the best travel teams.

And once you are on that fast lane and spending a lot of money on the expenses and time involved, a parent then thinks if his son gets called out on a bad third strike, I am going to be angry about that. I am going to yell at the umpire because the umpire is getting away with my kid's career.

At other times, a coach may be playing a child at a position that the parent doesn't think is the right position. Parents then voice their displeasure to the coach because he too is interfering with the kid's progress to play for a major league team.

I've spoken about the issue of aluminum bats for years. I think the safety issues of aluminum bats, the issue of overuse of pitchers, throwing curveballs, are all tied in with this overwhelming sense that moms and dads honestly believe that their kid is going to be on the fast track to the big leagues. They don't understand. Parents think that the kid who may be starring in Mount Vernon, which has a great sports tradition, is going to be a star throughout all of Westchester. It is fun to buy into that and play along with that. But we know that it doesn't work out that way.

Most parents who have played serious sports themselves at the high school or college level or even pro level know it is silly to expect that their kid is going to end up as a professional athlete. They know that the odds are stacked against the youngster. The problem comes from the parents who are not familiar with sports at the upper echelon and have never gotten beyond the junior varsity team themselves or sat on the bench. They don't know how competitive it is.

I've been doing this sports parenting advocacy work for well over 20 years now. I do a lot of speaking events around the country. Wherever I go, Dallas, Tampa, San Francisco, whoever the host is wherever I speak, will say to me, "In this town we take our sports very seriously." I am still looking for the town that doesn't take its sports seriously.

Here is the problem. Parents today, it is not that they are evil, it is just the opposite. They are so eager to afford every athletic opportunity for their kid and do everything they possibly can do. They will go to any length to save money to do that even though they see the statistics which reveal that less than five percent of all high school varsity athletes ever make the college team at the division 1, 2, 3 level.

Parents still say, "My kid is the star. My kid will be that one singular exception to the rule and will be the next Michael Jordan or the next Mia Hamm." That is just the way it is. They don't see it because they are blinded by the fact that in this small one town community their youngster is great.

People often will say "Kids today don't understand how much fun we had when we were playing ball. They miss out on that. There was much more pure joy and enthusiasm when we played."

I don't know if that is true or not because how do you compare mind sets? But I will add this. When I talk to kids today, I will ask, "Do you play a variety of sports?" The kids might be 10 or 12 year olds. They will say, "Yes, I play soccer for real but I also play basketball and baseball for fun."

When you grew up in Mount Vernon 30, 40, and 50 years ago and a kid said, "I play soccer for real and play baseball and basketball for fun", you would have said, "I don't understand. What are you talking about?"

Kids start so young these days and get into these organized structured sports that they miss the sense that this is a job. This is an obligation. This is real work playing soccer. But if I want to goof off with my friends, I will fool around playing basketball or baseball. Those are the sports they are allowed to play without practice like soccer. That speaks volumes about how kids approach sports today.

There is a whole realm of issues today that we never got involved with years ago. How many orthopedic surgeons have you heard complain about over-use injuries or competitive use injuries today? Kids are playing one sport, specializing all year round, and before you know it, they are tearing their ACL or knee or are having elbow problems from pitching. We didn't have these issues when we were kids.

Little League makes a big deal about pitch counts. I am thinking, well, I guess that is all right. But I don't remember any of my buddies when I was a kid having arm injuries playing baseball. That just didn't exist.

I am a big critic of Little League because I worry about what their research and motivation is. Little League officials say to this day that aluminum bats are the same as wood bats. I speak to officials of Little League quite often and ask, "Do you really believe that? In your heart of hearts do you think a ball hit off of an aluminum bat has the same speed as a ball hit off of a wood bat?"

I've been told by an official that "I have a couple of boys playing college baseball and I guarantee that is true." I said, "Go out and throw batting practice to your boys and see for yourself that you wouldn't feel safe with an aluminum bat." I think that is a disservice to kids. Do kids have more fun today? I do know this. If you take a bunch of kids today when they are 10 or 11 years old and you put them on a basketball court or a baseball diamond, they are not really equipped to have pick-up games. They don't know how to do it spontaneously. They are not taught that because their parents and umpires are always there.

When I grew up there were things that were just more pure and less competitive in a sense. On a nice spring or summer night, kids would show up after school or after dinner and have a pickup touch football game.

You never knew who was going to show up for the game. Invariably the two older guys would be the captains. They would pick the teams. You never said to somebody even if there was an odd number of players, or one or two of the kids weren't particularly good at football, you never said to those kids, "Ok, you sit out." Everybody got to play in the game.

The most amazing thing is and I mention this all the time at speaking events. I ask parents "What did you do after playing touch football when you were a kid and after 15 or 20 minutes it was apparent that one team had scored four touchdowns and the other team scored none?"

Everybody said, "We would stop the game and reshuffle the sides to make it more competitive."

I then would ask, "Would you do it today with your flag football or soccer programs if one team is dominant?"

They all laughed and said, "No, we wouldn't do it now because we are the parents." It is all about fun. Fun is rarely a priority. It is more about just winning today.

There is a movement underway in Canada right now. They are going back and redesigning all their youth sports including ice hockey, soccer, basketball and baseball. They want all the younger levels "to stop keeping track of scores. Stop keeping track of organized teams."

They want to go back to a more spontaneous kind of approach to youth sports as it was 30 or 40 years ago. It is called "Long Term Development Athletics". It has been going on for several months now. They won't see the results obviously for a few years.

They note that the Canadian soccer program is not very competitive around the world. They looked around and asked, "What do they do in Brazil which is great in soccer? What do they do that we don't do?"

The Canadians found in European and Brazilian soccer programs that the youngsters, who were 6 to 14, did not play on teams that kept score. They also changed team rosters all the time. There it is more about individual development as opposed to who wins the fifth grade soccer championship.

When you have a kid who is physically bigger than the other kids when he is 8, 10, 12 years old, and the kid can physically dominate a game like soccer, baseball or basketball, that youngster is going to get the bulk of the playing time. That kid is going to be featured against the other teams. Everything is going to be focused on his development whereas the other kids don't have a chance to mature and develop skills.

That is what it is all about now. How can you tell whether a youngster is going to be good, bad or indifferent when he or she is 8, 10, 12 years old? But the way our system is set up, we focus on the big kid. But that is silly. It doesn't work that way. The kids who are left in the dust quit playing sports.

20

Best of the Decade

In the early '50s, many of us had the good fortune to fall in love with baseball at the beginning of a great era; the years 1950 to 1959, the greatest decade in baseball history.

Since then baseball has played a role in my life and career in sports marketing. You see, baseball turned me on to reading. I always wanted to be a sportswriter. In 1951, I was given my first book, *Big Time Baseball,* which had stories about all the colorful personalities, records, famous players, blunders and big moments from 1900 to 1950 that endeared baseball to millions.

I practically memorized the book and still have it on a bookshelf. Here is the All-Star Team of All-Time, as picked by a blue ribbon panel of judges back in 1950 – Walter Johnson, pitcher; Bill Dickey, catcher; Lou Gehrig, first base; Rogers Hornsby, second base; Honus Wagner, shortstop; Pie Traynor, third base; Joe DiMaggio, left field; Ty Cobb, center field; Babe Ruth, right field. Who should be on that team today? There is enough controversy here to stir any fan's heart and mind.

That's the major leagues. What about the hundreds of players who took to the Mount Vernon Little League diamonds in the '50s? Who were the best ballplayers during that decade? If you played in the Little League then I'm sure you would be partial to players on your team or your league. But what about youngsters who played four, five and six years after or before you? How good were they?

I spent countless days at the Mount Vernon Public Library reading about every Little League game reported in the *Mount Vernon Daily Argus.* I wanted to find out who were the best players. News coverage was extensive in the league's early years, less so at the end of the decade. The newspaper records don't fib.

So now I come to *Mount Vernon Little League's Best of the Best,* the cream of the crop, the top ten of the decade. They all played in the '50s. When we were young we argued the merits of Mickey Mantle, Willie Mays, and Duke Snider on elementary and junior high school playgrounds. We might have even screamed and cursed. But there weren't any fist fights.

So here is my *Best of the Best – The Top Ten* in alphabetical order. I also list some honorable mentions as well. I might be right on target with all of them or some of them. All of the choices are mine. Are they yours? Who shouldn't be listed? Who did I leave out? Let's hear your picks. We don't have to fight about it. We can just have a good time. So send me your choices at bfabric459@aol.com.

This is why we love baseball for a lifetime.

George Bochow, Jr.

Who would have known when 11-year-old George Bochow was playing Little League ball for Perry Soda in '58 and '59 he would go on to star on the diamond for New York University and get drafted by the San Francisco Giants? There were probably some teammates and coaches who said that George had that "it" thing that separated him from other youngsters.

As a pre-teen he was strong with a great physique even at that young age. On the field he did it all, hitting line drives and legendary home runs. He did equally as well on the mound. He won his first game in a relief role and quickly picked up another win as a starter with a two-run homer to boot. The following season on opening day he threw a two-hitter and struck out 12. In his next win he singled, doubled and homered. Then he came within one out of pitching a no-hitter while striking out 15. Two games later George had his no-hitter. He was on the mound to clinch the second round National Division title.

In the opening elimination game, he pitched nine innings in winning 1-0. He struck out 20 of the 29 batters he faced, allowing only two hits, and ending the game in a flourish striking the last seven batters. His baseball future was ahead of him.

Larry "Goodie" Bradford

There wasn't anything indirect about Larry "Goodie" Bradford's pitching. He would just lean back and then explode that fastball towards a batter. Piling up strikeouts isn't just about throwing hard; it's about attacking hitters with your best stuff and challenging them to hit it. It's about being a fearless competitor on the mound and not being afraid to ruffle some feathers when the time calls for it. That was what Bradford was all about.

He was the ultimate power pitcher in Mount Vernon Little League's early years playing for the Orioles in '51 and '52. He had an overpowering fastball. It wasn't a pleasant experience for many batters to face Bradford.

There probably never was a year like 1952 in Mount Vernon Little League baseball with so many outstanding pitchers. And Bradford stood above the rest. His manager Tom Nelly described Bradford simply "as exceptionally fast". On opening day he threw a no-hitter. Early in the season he tied the single game strikeout mark with 16. In almost 33 innings of work early in the season he allowed but seven hits and had a league-leading 72 strikeouts. By early July he had three no-hitters, a one-hitter, and one two-hitter. "Goodie" was just that good.

Andy Karl Jr.

We all can think back to a time when we were young and played catch with our fathers in the backyard or local baseball field. Very few were lucky enough to have their first catch with fathers who were also Major Leaguers. Andy Karl Jr. learned his lessons well from his dad Anton Andy Karl, one of the founders of Mount Vernon Little League. And yes, he was a star relief pitcher for the Philadelphia Phillies in the 1940s.

Andy Jr. played three years, 1957-59, for The Lions Club. He was one of Little League's most versatile players during the decade. He did it on the mound and at bat. He picked up his first win in '57 and didn't stop winning.

His breakout year was '58 when he hurled two no-hitters and a one-hitter, the first no-hitter clinched first place honors in the first round of Service Division play. He helped his own pitching gem with a triple, homer and four RBIs. Later in the season he no-hit the Kiwanis Club. Playing centerfield, he led the Lions to the '58 Little League City championship as the Lions defeated Engine No. 3, 10-3. He had three consecutive doubles and scored three runs.

Ed Lombardi

He was a big fellow, much taller than most of his teammates and opponents. For three years, from 1952-54, he was a dominant and impactful player for the Pirates who won the city championship in '52 and '54, the only team to win the title twice in the decade.

Ed was a big game pitcher who threw hard. Early in his career he was the second banana on the Pirate staff, right behind Dickie Mergenthaler. They could have been the best pitching tandem on one team during the decade. His coaches handed him the ball even as a young little leaguer. As a ten-year-old, Ed beat the Panthers, 2-0, throwing a one-hitter in the playoffs to clinch the National League pennant. He then started and beat the Orioles in the last game of the World Series. In '53, Ed's fine pitching continued, highlighted by a win to deadlock the World Series against the Orioles, as he bore down to stop the tying run from crossing the plate in the sixth and final inning.

In '54 he led the Pirates to another city championship, frequently striking out ten or more batters in a game. He wasn't an easy out at the plate either. A good long-ball hitter throughout his career, most pitchers didn't take lightly when he came to bat. Quite often he helped his own pitching cause with home runs. He was one of a few Mount Vernon Little League players in the decade who played minor league baseball, spending a year in the Pittsburgh Pirates and San Francisco Giants farm systems.

Eddie Martin

I never saw Eddie Martin pitch for the Shamrocks during his three year Little League career from '51 thru '53. But I sure did in high school at A.B. Davis. I played behind him at second base. It was easy to see how in '59 he was Westchester's best pitcher going 7-0, with three shutouts and a no-hitter while leading Davis to the county's WIAA championship.

Plain and simple Eddie was a pitcher rather than a thrower. He was as smart a pitcher as there was in the league's first decade. He took pride in locating the ball. His style was Greg Maddux-like. He relied on command, composure and guile to outwit hitters throughout his career. He was a very effective groundball pitcher. His control was outstanding. In researching the Little League decade, he was the only pitcher I came across who did not walk a single batter in a game. He did that twice in '52. That control was learned in his backyard where he played games throwing a ball against a wall, trying to figure out which brick to hit. He wasn't like virtually every little league pitcher who reared back and fired. As those pitchers got older, they quickly found out there was always somebody who could hit the fastball.

Throughout his career, Martin kept the ball low and mixed speeds. He was involved in classic duels, those battles of the early 1950s, between himself, and Dickie Mergenthaler of the Pirates. Martin's pitching philosophy was simple. He never tried to hit anybody but he did throw inside. He didn't give anybody anything. He didn't give a good hitter a good pitch. And it worked.

Producing over the long haul, over a number of Little League seasons, is the mark of an outstanding player and Martin did it for three years. In '51, as the youngest player on the Shamrocks, he played right field and singled as his club won the city championship trouncing the Owls, 7-1. In '52 he became the mainstay of the staff, often walking but two batters per game.

In '53 on opening day he beat the Panthers, 5-4, while also hitting a home run and two doubles. His batting for average and power continued throughout the season as he hit quite a few triples and home runs. He made the National League All-Star team in '52 and '53.

Dickie Mergenthaler

Trades happen all the time. Players change uniforms. The biggest mistakes are long remembered like when the Mets gave up a young but wildly talented Nolan Ryan, who became the greatest strikeout pitcher in history.

The most unforgettable and impactful trade during Little League's first decade occurred when the Indians gave up Dickie Mergenthaler and two other players to the Pirates. In 1952 as an 11-year-old Mergenthaler threw a no hitter and two-hitter in his first four starts. Later in the season he no-hit the eventual city champion Pirates. Mergenthaler was the youngest of several pitching standouts in '52.

When Carmine Casucci stepped down as Pirates manager after the '52 season, Joe Tripodi, who was an assistant coach for Steve Acunto's Indians, took over the reins of the Pirates in '53. He brought along Mergenthaler, Tom Ambrosino and Vin Carosella. Mergenthaler picked up where he left off. In '53 Mergenthaler continued his fine pitching as he anchored the Pirates staff piling up victories as he became the National League's leading pitcher. He won quite a few low scoring close ball games. He threw sidearm and had a wicked curve ball. He had decent control but was wild enough to make your feet a little nervous when you faced him.

Fred O'Connor

Difficult as it is to narrow the prospects for the title of best Little League batter of the decade, or the best pitcher as well, determining who should be selected as the most versatile is a lot easier. Freddie O'Connor, who played for the Panthers during the league's first three years, wins hands down.

He was one of the best catchers in the National League during his tenure. As a pitcher, he was a winner, throwing the best curve ball in the league. He was an outstanding shortstop. He ultimately became a third baseman when he played for Mount Saint Michael's undefeated 1958 team and then later for Fordham University.

As a ten-year-old in the '50, he started 70 percent of the games at shortstop and 30 percent behind the plate as the Panthers won the city championship. On opening day the next season he was behind the plate as the starting catcher as he was for 65 pecent of the games. He was a starting pitcher for the rest of them. On July 23, he and Ed Carrozza each pitched three hitless innings while the Panthers blanked the Indians 4-0. While one pitched his half of the no-hitter, the other served as catcher. He caught for the Mount Vernon All-Star team that competed in district playoffs.

In '52, O'Connor divided half his time on the mound and behind the plate. He was one of the league's top hurlers. He no-hit the Shamrocks in seven innings, one more than the regulation Little League game. He threw several one and two-hitters over the course of the season. Here is something interesting. Brent Mayne who spent most of his career with the Kansas City Royals, has the distinction of being the only catcher in the twentieth century to win a game as a pitcher. Freddie O'Connor outdid Mayne by a long shot.

Pitching and defense is one thing. Batting is another. Freddie was one of the league's best hitters, following the advice of almost all the successful Little League coaches at the time. "Don't emphasize the home runs, emphasize contact, choke up on the bat when you have two strikes," they said. Freddie followed the rules to the nth degree.

George Pacchiana

The Orioles were a dominant team in the Little League in '52, '53 and '54, winning the city championship in '53 and ending the season as runner-ups the other two years. They did it mostly by climbing on the back of George Pacchiana who led them in both pitching and hitting.

He was a dominating pitcher who frequently helped his own cause with a big bat. He hit his share of singles. But the long ball was what George was all about. He had numerous extra base hits with quite a few home runs. He started off the '54 season with an opening day win and didn't stop there. All season long he allowed few hits in most of his games while fanning as many as 15 batters on several occasions.

He was the ultimate contributor both on the mound and at the plate. In the 1954 playoff series against the Bulldogs, Pacchiana blasted four home runs had a playoff batting average of .769. He led all batters in both home runs and batting.

Ken Singleton

And then there is Ken Singleton.

Almost from birth, it seemed as if Ken Singleton was destined for a future in major league baseball. Growing up in Mount Vernon, Ken lived in a home once owned by former Brooklyn Dodger Ralph Branca.

He played youth baseball in a Mount Vernon baseball camp run by John Branca, Ralph's older brother. John Branca spent 19 years as the commissioner of recreation in Mount Vernon, and also taught and coached at Edison Vocational High School. He knew talent.

"When he was coaching Little League, my brother told me, 'I have a 12-year-old kid who's going to make the major leagues,'" Ralph Branca said. "That was me," Singleton said.

In 1958, Ken's first year in the Little League, he shutout Northeastern Insurance and hit a grand slam home run in the first inning to lead his Gramatan Men's Shop to an 11-0 win. In all likelihood this was Singleton's first pitching win in the Little League. Getting his name in the record book was Carl Thimm who took the loss.

Ken only got better in his second season in 1959. He won nine games. He lost one. On opening day he was the winning pitcher and also banged out four of his club's eight hits. He frequently won games while going 3-for-3 or 4-for-4 at bat. He had double digit strikeout totals in most of his games. In *A Conversation With Ken Singleton* he said he batted .636 for the season. Who is to argue with that.

After graduating from A.B. Davis High School, he went on to play both baseball and basketball at Hofstra University. The New York Mets made him their #1 selection in January 1967 with a $10,000 signing bonus. And the rest is history.

Vonnie Wickens

The usual pitching suspects are always mentioned when you talk about the best Little League hurlers in the 1950s. One name that is rarely brought up is Vonnie Wickens. He was one of the hardest throwers in the mid '50s.

His record speaks for itself. He boasted a rare combination of longevity and consistency. He played and starred for four years in the league from 1954 thru 1957 for the Comets/Community Oil/Engine 5 teams. He was the Cy Young, the Nolan Ryan of Little League. Both Young and Ryan had long and successful major league careers. Few Little Leaguers played as long and as well as Wickens.

Add all of Wickens' career pitching starts together and you will most likely find he has more victories and strikeouts than any other pitcher in the decade. He was his team's chairman of the board for four seasons. In my book, longevity combined with consistency equals greatness.

I was his teammate for two of those years when we played together on The Comets in '54 and Community Oil in '55. I saw what he was like on the mound. He worked fast. He was an intimidating pitcher. He was wild enough that batters did not like to dig in when they faced him. In '55 his blazing fastball led the Comets to the city's championship game. In '56 he became even a better pitcher tossing in a no-hitter along the way and racking up double digit strikeouts in most games, again leading his team to the Western League championship. He was also the team's top power hitter at the plate throughout most of his career.

In '57 he struck out 13 in an opening day victory. On June 15, his no-hitter clinched Engine 6's Western Division first-round title. He threw another no-hitter a week later. All Vonnie Wickens did for three years was win. You couldn't ask for more.

Honorable Mentions

Jimmy Cardasis, Ted Cardasis, Don Cook, Ralph Merigliano, Tom Nelly, Jack O'Shaughnessy, Roy Pizzarello, Larry Townsend.

21

Alumni Remembrances

We all recall those moments. It wasn't just sitting with your kids at Yankee Stadium, but it's your father with you at the Polo Grounds many years earlier. Baseball does that to you. For all of us, memories are baseball's lifeblood.

When we were kids there was a magical light that glowed around baseball. For a bunch of us, baseball was the very structure that defined our existence. Little League baseball was our passport around Mount Vernon when we were 8, 9, 10, 11 and 12 year olds. Some of our fondest childhood memories came from playing catch with our fathers at Baker or Longfellow fields, or in our own driveways, backyards, and front lawns. We recall logging countless innings of imaginary baseball throwing a tennis ball against a wall, pitching against the Dodger, Yankee, and Giant lineups we read about all summer long in *The Daily Argus* newspaper.

We were captured by the game. I refused to go to New York City with my parents on more than one occasion because the trips interfered with upcoming games. We read newspapers and baseball magazines like *Sport*. We put together baseball scrapbooks with stories and pictures of our heroes like mine, Nellie Fox.

Baseball author Lawrence Ritter once said, "The best part of baseball is the past." I couldn't agree more. Over a lifetime, we have all played the inner game, baseball in the mind. I know I have. It's all about recalling and picturing what once was. Baseball became our constant companion. The fifties were our era. When we weren't playing ball, we were talking about Mantle, Mays, Snider, Robinson. And if you didn't like a New York team there was Robin Roberts, Eddie Matthews, Henry Aaron, Frank Robinson, Al Rosen, Harvey Kuenn, Rocky Colavito and Ernie Banks. We soaked up baseball statistics like a sponge. I follow the game today. I doubt however if I could still name one major league lineup as quickly as I could name all 16 back in 1955. That was our Golden Age.

There were many churches and synagogues in Mount Vernon in the '50s. But baseball was the kind of secular church that reached into every ethnic group and religion of the city and bonded us kids together.

Think about it. For most of us, playing Little League baseball was the biggest sports stage we ever had the opportunity to play on. It was a place, a time, and that small window of our existence where we could be a hero. And it was by Little League baseball that our memories bronzed themselves. Remember the wave of terror when you threw the ball over the first baseman's head. Remember how tears then blurred your eyes when you ran towards your bench. Remember those winters tossing snowballs at trucks on Lincoln and Columbus Avenues or on Sandford Boulevard.

Memory does strange things when it comes to sports, particularly baseball. Even now there is no forgetting the sounds and smells of summer nights standing in line at Baker Field waiting to buy an ice cream or getting into your father's car to drive home after the game. That was yesteryear. Yet today most tracks of our lives aren't examined. I don't remember what I did last weekend or what I ate two nights ago. So what did our obsession with baseball back then leave us with? Some of us do remember. So come back now and hear 28 Mount Vernon Little League alumni from the '50s reminisce about the baseball fabric of their early lives.

Ed Abbatecola

I played in the Mount Vernon Little League the year it came into being under the leadership of Andy Karl, a former big leaguer and local businessman. The tryouts held at Hutchinson Field were a big deal to those aspiring baseball players who wanted the opportunity to participate on teams with uniforms and in games with umpires on groomed fields.

Following the arduous tryouts, I along with the other hopefuls eagerly anticipated the selections that were to be printed in *The Daily Argus*, the local newspaper. I went through the names but mine was not there. Or so I thought! When one of my friends came to share his joy of being selected, he pointed out my name as well.

Until participating in Little League, my baseball activities were mostly confined to the neighborhood. Bicycling to Longfellow School, where the games were held, from the west side of town, gave me and my friend and teammate, Bobby Ragnone, the opportunity to explore another part of the community. Since we were always looking for a quicker and easier route to travel, we saw and learned a great deal about our city.

Besides providing the opportunity to compete and to become a better player, the Little League experience helped cultivate relationships that carried on beyond childhood, some into the present.

A competitive relationship that developed into a working one was with Ralph Merigliano. Ralph pitched for the team that was our toughest opponent. Years later, Ralph and I became colleagues as physical education teachers at Nichols Junior High School. There were others like John Ward, who was in my homeroom as well as a football teammate at A.B. Davis High School. Mickey Rinaldi, who was the only left handed pitcher I faced, reminded me years later of backing me off the plate and striking me out. There were others I also recall, like Tony Montez, Curly Essemplace and William Crockett, who were also graduates of the A.B. Davis High School class of 1956.

Let's not forget those who kept the games moving like umpires John Branca and Zeke Jewell. John entered my life once more when he was Mount Vernon's Recreation Commissioner and I worked for the city as a playground leader and recreation supervisor. Mr. Jewell was a science teacher at A.B. Davis with whom I conversed about academics as well as baseball. His daughter was a classmate of mine. The Little League gave me insight into Mount Vernon and its people as well as the opportunity to play ball and make friends. It was an experience I will always cherish.

Augie Alegi

I faced major league pitching for the first and last time in the early spring of 1951 when I was nine years old. I was trying out for the Little League at Hutchinson Field No. 3 and the batting try out pitcher was Andy Karl, who had pitched for the Phillies, and at one time held the major league record for appearances in one season. He wore his Phillies jersey inside out and kept pumping high hard ones. I was helpless and did not make the Little League that time.

I had actually learned the fundamentals of baseball at Johnny Branca's Baseball School, which he held every year at the small diamond at Memorial Field, near the handball courts. I went to that program every year from about seven through eleven years of age. Everything I knew, or still know, about baseball I learned from John. Later, when he was commissioner of recreation in Mount Vernon, I worked for him as an umpire, basketball referee and playground director.

I was assigned to the minors and my team was the Giants. We played our games at Longfellow Field No. 1 and at the small diamond at Memorial Field. As was true during my entire short lived baseball career, I didn't connect that much, but when I did, I could really hit for distance.

At the next year's tryout, the pitcher was someone's father. I did quite well and made the league. My team was the Jester's and the coach was Mr. Iaribino. We played our games at Longfellow, Hutchinson and Baker Fields. The uniforms were permanent and had to be handed back every year. Ours had a Jester on the chest and you had to buy a "J" at Tom Godfrey's and your mother sewed it on your cap which you got to keep.

The next year the Little League went to sponsors and the Jesters became the Kiwanis and we played in the Service Club Division with the Lions, Optimists, and one other team. While our club was pretty good, we never made the playoffs. I initially played the outfield, but later I played first base. I usually batted fifth in the lineup, good power, not a lot of contact. I played Little League from 1951 through 1955.

I later played Pony League for Fox Realty in Eastchester and for Frank Merola's P.A.L. team in a mid-teen league, where they turned me into a pitcher. Larry Tracy, who was the Little League commissioner, hired me as an umpire and one of the players I called out on strikes was Ken Singleton, later a Met and Oriole star, and current Yankee broadcaster.

Overall, Little League was a great experience. So important at the time and such a fond memory now.

Jane Borelli
(Talking About Her Father Jeff Borelli)

My dad was born June 17, 1906 and grew up in Brooklyn and went to New Utrecht High School where he played third base. After that he played semi-pro ball for a while.

Baseball was always his passion. He saw Lou Gehrig and Babe Ruth play. He and my mother only had a girl. That's me.

Dad must have been in on the ground floor of Little League in Mount Vernon. I was born in 1944 and we lived at 98 Vista Place. There was an iron works down on the corner. All my aunts and uncles lived in Mount Vernon. In 1951, when I was seven years old, we moved to Eastchester/Scarsdale. But dad continued all through the years to coach Little League in Mount Vernon.

I never followed Major League baseball but I went to quite a few Little League games. The boys were around my age and I thought they were cute. My first boyfriend, when I was 12 years old, was Jackie O'Shaughnessy who played on The Panthers.

My dad passed away on November 6, 1998 at the age of 92. We lived together. He and my mom helped raise my kids after I was divorced. We lived in Pleasantville. We bought a new house there.

The morning of his wake, I was standing at the kitchen sink doing dishes, and I looked out the window to an acre of property and right in the middle of the backyard was a baseball just laying in the yard. I am sure a dog must have brought it there. But I never saw it there before. I never saw one there afterwards. I walked out and picked it up. I still have that baseball. It felt like my dad was kind of looking out and it was a comfort and I saved the baseball.

At his funeral there was a baseball and all his grandchildren and nieces and nephews autographed it and put it in his coffin. He was also buried with a Mets key chain. When my daughter and her husband bought an old Victorian farmhouse here in Ossining an elderly man cleaned everything out of the house when he left. I got a call from my daughter and son in law and they told me when they went into the basement on a shelf there was a baseball. They say if you have faith such things aren't coincidences.

Everybody loved dad. He was gentle, kind and adored my mother. All women were on a pedestal to him. He didn't come from money. He worked hard and started as a male secretary and ended up as vice president of a large manufacturing company in Manhattan.

He always felt blessed if somebody needed help. He was always there. He smoked cigars for a while and if he was at a party and somebody was playing the piano and singing that was his favorite thing.

On Saturdays in the summer all the games were on television. If he wasn't going to a game he was watching one on TV. He wasn't much interested in football, just baseball. He could quote batting averages from way back when.

Here in Briarcliff when he was in his 90s, he was still driving into town every day. He would stop in to stores to do his errands and everybody loved him. They called him 'The Mayor'. There is even a bench from the Rotary Club there dedicated to his memory.

My father's birth name is Andrew Borelli. But they called him Andy. But he was also known as Jeff Borelli. The reason for that is that my dad was short of stature. He had a best friend who was very very tall. So they called the two of them 'Mutt and Jeff'. And Jeff stuck. He was known as both Andy Borelli and Jeff Borelli.

Dad would never have taught the boys to be "Good Losers". He did teach them to be "Good Sports". I never remember seeing many hanging heads or tears. I do remember a lot of enthusiasm, energy and smiles. I think Dad's passion for baseball caught fire in those little boys.

Though I was his only child, and a girl, I never for a minute thought that he wished he had

had a boy. I was his princess and most of my earliest years were spent on the baseball fields with him in Mount Vernon. I always felt included. The other coaches and their families were our friends. And dad always made sure we had our special times alone on a regular basis. They were the best of times.

Dad had such love for the game and such love for all "his boys". He was always soft-spoken and patient, an incredible teacher. He helped all the boys feel good about themselves and their abilities. He also taught them how to be graceful losers....as well as champs!

I also want to share with you that after my mom died at the age of 90 in 1996, Dad's heart was broken. What got him through was watching baseball games on television with his little dog at his side. I can remember the little dog crying for Dad to go up to bed and Dad telling him, "Just a little while longer, Coco...just a couple of more innings."

Tony Cioppa

I remember the first time I met my high school teammate Eddie Martin. We were in Little League playing against each other, and my coach put me in to catch. In fact, that was the first time I ever caught in a game. Eddie was on the other team. He comes up to bat and drives the ball between the outfielders and tries to stretch it into a home run.

As he rounds the bases and heads home everybody in the stands starts screaming at me, "Block the plate. Block the plate." He comes into home plate and I step on his leg with my spikes. He starts bleeding profusely.

The next thing I know I look in the stands and my mother and his mother are screaming at each other. They almost came to blows. That's how I met Eddie Martin.

Where did my baseball career begin? I found my first glove down at Hutchinson Field. It was a real shortstop's glove. It was a good one. It was broken in and very flexible. That was the glove I used for a long time. My father used to buy me gloves, but they weren't the same as that first one.

I had an unfortunate incident with the Little League when I first tried out as a nine-year-old. I made the team, the Indians, and my father was happy about that. The coach cut me from the team and replaced me with another kid who was older than me. That was politics. My father got mad and consequently would not let me play in the Little League until I was twelve when I made the Bears.

I could always hit and remember hitting quite a few home runs that year. We were sluggers and we won everything. I played shortstop, and I remember Ernie Motta was around playing in the Little League at that time. That's when I first met him.

I began catching when a coach saw that I had a strong arm. He tried to make me a pitcher but put me behind the plate. I caught the rest of my career.

Alyson Bochow Cohen
(Talking About Her Brother George Bochow)

My father was Dr. George Bochow. He actually grew in Yonkers but moved to Mount Vernon and graduated from Mount Vernon High School in 1922. He moved to Archer Avenue around 1938. Before that he lived on South Fulton in an apartment and prior to that he was in the Army.

My folks had six kids, Darrell, George Jr., Alyson, Michelle, Brian, and Gregory. We all lived at 19 Archer Avenue. We still own the house. My brother Greg lives there now. My mom passed away in 2010 and my dad died in 1980. We are in the process of selling the house now. My father was the quintessential Marcus Welby of that era. He had his office on the first floor of our house. Three times a week, Monday, Wednesday and Friday from 1 to 2 in the afternoon there were office hours downstairs and we had to be very quiet. He also had office hours Tuesday and Thursday evenings.

Besides his own practice, he also was the doctor for the Mount Vernon Police Department, Fire Department, Seebury Memorial Home, and the Little League. I remember young boys playing in the Little League and coming to his office. At Little League games, you could see him there smoking his pipe and holding our dog, Prince, on a leash.

Dad wasn't as much of an athlete as were my brothers. He played ball with them when they were younger, particularly George. We all went to Lincoln School. All three of my brothers played in Little League. They all played for the Perry Soda Pirates.

I would have to say that George and Brian pursued baseball more than Greg did. George went on to play professional baseball in the San Francisco Giants organization. He played in Medford, Oregon. He played with George Foster in the minors. Foster went on to play for the Cincinnati Reds and the New York Mets. Brian played for the Pirates in the minor leagues for a while.

One of George's friends who he went to New York University with was Jay Horowitz who is the public relations director for the Mets. George arranged for us to go into the Mets dugout where we sat next to and talked to Mookie Wilson, Rusty Staub and Frank Howard. That was a fun time.

Don Cook

I'm not 100 per cent sure, but I think the Mount Vernon Little League had its inaugural season around 1950. The League was formed by Andy Karl, the former Boston Braves pitcher. He was supported by another Mount Vernon native who helped promote youth baseball in the area, Ralph Branca, the former Brooklyn Dodger pitcher.

I had just turned 8 years old at the start of the inaugural season. I was told, however reliable I don't know, that I was the youngest player in the original grouping of four teams (Indians, Shamrocks, Eagles and Owls). I played on the Indians my first year. Steve Acunto was our coach.

I played on the Eagles in subsequent years until I graduated to the Pony League. My dad, Charlie Cook was on the Eagles coaching staff. Dad told me I was going to be the team catcher. I never caught anything except a cold up to that point. The team had no catching candidates. He said, "You'll have to be our catcher. There's no one else. Besides, if we're going to risk getting somebody's kid killed behind the plate it might as well be you. That way we don't risk getting someone else's kid hurt."

My fondest memories were playing Little League baseball with my neighborhood friends, Fred O'Connor, John Tripodi, Ralph Merigliano, Ed Martin and George Pachianna. We all lived within three blocks of one another on the East side of town near the Pelham border.

The Mount Vernon Little League experience presented the foundation, as well the opportunity to learn the game properly, an experience that led eventually to a career path in intercollegiate athletics, 20 as a college baseball coach, 47 years combined, as a coach and athletic director.

Had it not been for being in the positive learning environment provided by the Mount Vernon Little League experience, I'm not sure I would have been motivated, or even advised to pursue a career in athletics.

What I remember vividly was how generous Andy Karl was with his time. He devoted endless hours to supervising the early years. He would visit with each team at practices; in fact, he pitched many batting practice sessions.

Fast forwarding the story, Andy helped me with my college pitching staff at Fairfield University in the 1970's. We stayed in touch over the years. His daughter Rose Marie was my classmate in grammar school at St. Catherine's in Pelham. I was her date at her high school prom. Soon after, she entered the convent. I must have made quite an impression!

Those early years made a lasting impression. They represented a critical time for learning the game. More important, the experience gave us the first taste of what it meant to be a teammate, a friend, a caring neighbor, how to be a good sport, and how to give up some of oneself for others. Without that early education, far more important than the baseball we played, we wouldn't have developed the skill sets needed to grow and mature into our teen years.

Frank Cuomo

I experienced a wonderful Little League that was run very efficiently, had excellent managers, and players who were serious about winning and playing good fundamental baseball.

Give credit for the League's success to guys like Bill Real, Larry Tracy, Steve Acunto, Faust Cardillo, Jeff Borelli and my manager Joe Tripodi.

Tripodi managed my team the Pirates for two of my three years with the team. He was a wonderful man. He owned a grocery store in Mount Vernon. Joe was a great teacher and even a better motivator. He possessed a serious demeanor, but he never abused his players. He was a master at getting his team motivated and keeping all the players happy. He substituted liberally and gave every kid the innings that they were required to receive according to official Little League rules.

Joe also treated the team well when we won the championship in 1953. He took us to a pizzeria around 238th Street in the Bronx, and we had a heck of a time celebrating. He also threw end of the year barbecues at Baker Field for the players and their families.

For a kid whose parents struggled financially, going out to eat and picnicking was something that was a big deal, and 60 years later it is a fond memory. The Pirates had a lot of success in my three years with them. We won the championship in '52 and '54. I started as a ten-year-old and each succeeding year improved my game. It was all about confidence and continually improving by playing the game in the playgrounds at Longfellow and Graham.

My father never played catch with me. He was too busy commuting four hours a day to Brooklyn and working as a longshoreman. So, I honed my skills by playing a lot of fast pitch stickball at the Graham playground. Since I spent a lot of my summers at my grandparents home I played a great deal of pick up baseball at Longfellow Field which was across the street from their home.

I remember playing with some outstanding players. Ed Lombardi was our star. He was a big kid, and was our pitching ace and long ball hitter. Eddie eventually signed a contract with the Pirates and spent a year in the minors. Tommy Ambrosino, Joey Tripodi, and Dennis Rocchio were also excellent players on those teams. I was always a good fielder and played third and second base.

I also remember being selected by the Little League to be one of three youngsters who would appear on Happy Felton's Knothole Show at Ebbets Field. I also made the All Star team during my last year in the league. One fond memory I recall was when our manager Tripodi used some motivation which led to my first and only Little League home run. It was 1954 in the championship game against the Orioles.

Before the game Joe thrust a bat into my hands and said, "Use this bat tonight. It's got a lot of hits in it." The bat had a fat barrel and very thin handle. My first time up with two men on I was facing the Oriole ace George Pacchiana, one of the league's best pitchers that year. I swung at a fastball and had no clue where the ball went. As I started running toward first base the crowd roared.

The first base coach told me I hit a home run over the right field fence. I was shocked. I wasn't a home run hitter. Big Ed Lombardi was the guy on the Pirates who hit home runs, not me. The next day *The Daily Argus* wrote that the home run travelled 185 feet! Wow! I was still stunned a day later that I went yard and knocked in the three runs that was all we needed in a 3-1 victory for the championship.

A great benefit to playing Little League ball was meeting so many kids from all over the city. These casual relationships were great and when I entered high school at A. B. Davis I was able to rekindle these relationships with guys like Ted Cardasis, Nick Giordano and Joe Brescia. There is no doubt that the five years I spent playing Little League and Pony League ball in Mount Vernon were some of the happiest days of my life.

Bruce Fabricant

On Sundays my dad and I watched doubleheaders on television. Between innings we would race outside. He would cross Claremont Avenue and stand in front a sloping plot of land and I would be across the street in front of our house. A quick catch would follow. We might have tossed the ball back and forth 20 times before running into the house to hear Mel Allen's description of the Yankee game.

By the time I was nine, my dad thought I was ready for the Little League. I don't remember the tryout but I know I wasn't picked. That dreaded postcard came in the mail telling me that. For me, that only meant I had to try harder and maybe I'd make a team the next year. There was nothing wrong with failure. No one in my family was upset. That's a lot different than today where adults believe kids are so fragile, that the word "lose" and "fail" have practically been removed from a child's vocabulary.

So a year passed. Twelve months later, I was back at Hutchinson Field again on a freezing cold morning. That was the same Hutchinson Field we would call home in high school. I have very few memories about the tryout that I thought would seal my baseball fate forever. There out on the mound pitching to me on a bright sunny day was a huge man. It was Andy Karl and he was wearing a beautiful Boston Red Sox white home jersey with "Red Sox" emblazoned on the blouse. I would soon read about Karl, who was born in Mount Vernon, and played in the big leagues for Boston, Philadelphia Phillies, and Boston Braves from 1943-47.

I must have hit Karl pretty good because the next thing I found out was that I made a team. I was a Comet. Our telephone rang several days later and Mr. Wisner was on the other end. He was my first manager. He was telling my mother that he and his assistant, Mr. Cassin, would be over that night to drop off my uniform. When the doorbell rang there was Mr. Wisner holding my uniform. At that time it was probably the prettiest thing I had ever seen. It was folded as neat as a shirt display at Bloomingdale's Department Store. I was the happiest kid on our block.

Little League was fun. I played two years in '54 and '55. The first year we were called the Comets and the following season we were Community Oil. And we were pretty good, Bobby Delmonico, Vonnie Wickens, Mike Simon, and me. I don't remember much about the actual games. We got to the city finals in '55 and lost. I lost contact with all my teammates after our Little League careers were over except for Bobby. I liked him a lot. In high school, he attended Edison Tech and I was at A.B. Davis. We played baseball against each other. To this day, I regret not talking to Bobby during those games since he played shortstop and I played second base. When an inning ended we would race off the field never looking or saying a word to each other.

Little League ball was special. It was a great learning experience and took quite a few years to realize that. Probably the best thing that Little League competition taught me was how to cope with failure. That's right, how to fail. Little League had tryouts and not everyone made the team. Those who didn't make it had to learn to deal with disappointment. We learned how to cope with failure when we lost a game or made an error. We had to try again, to not blame others more than ourselves. Now our grandkids have to learn the same thing. It is harder for them. Today's parents try to save their youngster's self esteem on and off the ball fields. No one hardly loses today. Awards are handed out just for showing up. It's only postponing the inevitable when a youngster feels the sting of defeat for the first time.

Nino Fiore
(Coached The Bulldogs in the mid 1950s)

I lived on Sheridan Avenue. All I had to do to get to Baker Field was to go right out my back yard and walk on to the field. I managed the Bulldogs with Mr. Pizzarello, who was the father of Roy, a star pitcher on our team.

I got involved coaching because my son, Peter, got involved with Little League first. He came and said, "I want to join Little League but you have to give me your approval." I asked, "What is this Little League?" I didn't know the first thing about it until I went to a meeting and found out what it was all about. Then Peter became a little leaguer. So my younger son, Nino, wanted to join also. That was when Little League expanded and added four teams. That's how I got involved.

I coached for about four or five years and really enjoyed it, leaving my business in the Bronx early to coach the boys. Mr. Pizzarello had to get to practices from his work in New Jersey.

It wasn't difficult managing my son, Nino, who was on the team. I didn't favor him. Those kids who got a chance to play were those who played well. If they didn't do well they still played but not as much. We taught them how to play and how to act on the field as well. That was what I tried to teach them.

Phil Arena was one of our good ballplayers. He was small. He was our shortstop. He was a real fine player and wonderful boy. His father belonged to Leewood Country Club where I belonged. I got the biggest kick from this young fellow, Phil. He was a young man and graduated from Little League. Years later he was talking with the golf pro at Leewood when I came in to the pro shop. Young Phil came over to me and looked at the golf pro and turned around and said to the pro, "This is the man who made me a gentleman." That made me feel good.

Peter Fiore

You can feel baseball humming inside you. The beautiful trajectories, the soft angles, the subtle precision. The smack of the bat hitting the ball, the murmur of the fans. The diamond itself, a work of art, an emerald city. . . and of course, the chance to do amazing things.

I remember moments in games.

In the spring and early summer of 1953 I played third base for the Shamrocks. I was 11. We did a lot of winning, but despite having Eddie Martin, Steve Brindisi, and Freddie Casucci we lost a league playoff to the red uniformed Pirates, with Dick Mergenthaler, Eddie Lombardi, and Tom Ambrosino.

In the middle of that playoff, when it was still close, Joey Tripodi came to bat with a man on third and less than two out. The Pirates loved the chop bunt. I think they invented it. The batter would set up for a bunt and then just before the pitch arrived bring in his hands and try to chop the ball through either the charging first or third baseman. Tripodi was the smallest second baseman in the league, maybe the smallest player in the league. I think he was 10, and liked to bunt. Crouching in the left hand batter's box Tripodi squared as Martin went into his wind-up. I charged until I saw Joey pull his hands together, then retreated, and then had to race back in as Joey's chop bunt turned into a little flare that I caught on my knees.

Cheers from the small crowd at Longfellow Field. The next batter was Dennis Rocchio, the Pirate shortstop, another little guy. Rocchio took Martin's fast ball and lined it over Gary Munsterman's head in center for a triple.

The rest of the game is a blur. In fact I'm not even sure if all these events happened in the same game, or even the same year. They both did occur. The first was definitely in the playoff game of 1953. Dennis Rocchio's triple could have happened the next year when the Shamrocks battled the Pirates down to the last game with the Pirates victors again. It was kind of like playing the same season twice. The Shamrocks got out fast and won the first half of the season, and then the Pirates bounced back to take the second. Memory does some funny things, it almost becomes a dream. You see something and if you don't grab it immediately, you lose it.

My first at bat, my first game at Hutchinson Field on a cold April Saturday, I walk on 4 pitches. We're playing the Panthers. Freddy O'Connor is catching. I can't remember the pitcher but do remember Freddy getting on his knees to get the target low enough. The Shamrocks go up early and the next two times up I walk. Fat Jake is behind the plate, a legendary umpire with a loud strike out call—"Steeeerrriiiik"– and many other dramatic movements. I'd seen him umpiring Recreation League games on Saturday mornings at Baker Field where I lived on Sheridan Avenue. Then I come up in the fifth, the game clearly ours, and on a 3-2 pitch take an inside fastball, and Jake calls out "Steeeeerrriiiik," and as I walk away I hear him say, "You gotta get the bat off your shoulder some of the time, son."

Little League melts into Pony League. Our manager puts me at second, my worst position—

something about the angle of the ground balls—besides he can't even hit infield practice. We lose a lot.

The next year the Regals get Mr. Ferrari, a tiger of a manager, and he switches me to short, and I get to pitch every once in a while. We're maybe a notch above 500, but I make the All-Star team, which Ferrari is managing. One night in July we're practicing on the field behind A.B. Davis. It's a field where the clay is hard as concrete and the infield is strewn with little stones and small pieces of broken glass. I'm trying to beat out Lou Main at short. Main's taller, has a better arm, can hit the long ball, but I'm faster and hustle like hell.

At the end of practice Ferrari's smacking balls at us and we fire over to Lombardi at first, I think. I'm charging everything and submarining my throws to rise up and hit Eddie in the chest. Main is making all the plays too, smoothly and without any rush. And we're both feeling the rush and exuberance of physical activity. Ferrari hits the next ball right at me and I find it hard to get an angle. Then the ball jumps up and hits me squarely between the eyes and knocks me on my back. I don't pass out but I don't want to take any more ground balls that night. Main gets the start.

I always wondered if I were tough enough. I later became a catcher in a fast pitch soft ball league at Michigan State, a team that like the Shamrocks finished second many times. I could never get the final out.

A hot Saturday in early July, one of our last games. I'm pitching against the Godfreys and winning 3-1 in the 7th. The first batter up is George Pacchiana, a great pitcher and one of the best hitters in the league. He fouls off a couple and on a 1-2 pitch I throw the knuckle-curve John Weis from St. Catherine's in Pelham had taught me and George is way out in front. Next is Eddie Abate, another dangerous hitter, maybe even more so than Pacchiana because he always makes contact. Whatever I'm doing I get him to 2-2 and drop in the knuckle-curve which he takes for strike three. One more out.

Eddie Romanino is up. Romanino has a hitch in his swing that distracts as I deliver the pitch and makes me feel helpless, it becomes impossible to focus on the pitch I need to execute. After 2 balls, I just lay the next one down the middle and Eddie hooks it down the left field line for a double. I'm not sure what happened next but it wasn't pretty.

When I think about all this I wonder if what I learned was to sharpen my killer instinct. Play every ball as if it were the last. I've been playing tennis since I was 32. I started playing tournaments at 35. It took a whole year before I won a match. Then three years ago I beat a fellow who'd been #15 in the country in Men's 65 Singles the previous year. I had an opportunity to blow it deep in the second set, slipping on the grass and laying out flat on my stomach, sucking wind. But I got up and on the next point hit an all-out topspin backhand that rose up through my ankles so hard my opponent couldn't move for it. I'm not sure I couldn't have done that without those two playoff losses to the Pirates under my belt.

Dan Fuchs

For whatever reason my buddies and I never were exposed to Little League. It just never really surfaced in the immediate neighborhood around Saints Peter & Paul Church. That doesn't mean we weren't playing ball all the time, because we were at it whenever we had time and the weather cooperated.

We had immense amounts of fun but it was mostly the stickball variety in the large church parking lot or under the Fulton Street/Cross County Parkway overpass with home plate drawn in chalk on the concrete vertical arch. That provided the strike zone (you pitched from the other side of the street) with no need for a catcher.

Either way no real equipment needed, organized as we imaginatively saw fit, and as competitive as it could get, especially with no impartial umpires available. We could be the Yankees vs. the Dodgers for team play or Mantle vs. Drysdale for the individual confrontations. We even argued which was better, Knickerbocker or Schaeffer Beer – as if we knew! Games lasted till someone's mother called out for lunch or dinner.

With my own kids that "time" was long gone and my three sons had long careers in Little League (with me doing some coaching) from T-Ball through Pony League and high school varsity.

Barney Giacobello

For what it's worth, here are a few of my memories off the top of my head.

When I first tried out for Little League, I was pretty good if I do say so myself. I was probably 9 or 10 years old, so the year was '57-'58.

I went to the first tryout and did pretty well. Just before the second tryout a week or two later, I was hospitalized with a brain concussion from a fall at the Pennington Playground (can you see the lawsuit if that happened today).

I was hospitalized for about a week for observation (just like today). One of the team coaches/managers visited me there to tell me he was upset when I didn't show up to the second tryout. He asked around and found out I was in Mount Vernon Hospital so he put me on his team anyway. I don't remember his name. The team was Leonardo Printing.

I remember the coaches used to put the weaker kids either in right field or at second base.

One day our coach looked out and we didn't have a right fielder. He had no idea why, so he called time out and put another kid in right field. About twenty minutes later the right fielder came out of the woods where he had been chasing butterflies.

Knowing the weaker kids were at second and right field, I would try to push the ball that way when I was up at bat. Usually even if I hit it to the second baseman, I would end up with a single. If I got it past him, I would keep running and by the time the right fielder got the ball and figured out where to throw it, I was at least at second base if not trying for third.

I played against Kenny Singleton and we became semi-friends. He was on Gramatan Men's Shop and I was on Leonardo Printing. One day I was watching Kenny pitch (we probably played next), when he hit the batter so hard he broke his arm. The batter was Nicky Coshigano, younger brother of Anthony Coshigano, a self proclaimed tough. A mini riot broke out. Bringing things full circle, when I got the news about making Leonardo Printing, Nicky Coshigano was also in the hospital, I seem to remember also for a head injury.

I remember our coach sometimes taking us to a sub shop down by Oil City across from EJ Korvettes – hot meatball or sausage subs were the best I ever had.

Nick Giordano

We played catch all the time. We had the pick of three ball fields, the Nichols playground, A.B. Davis High School middle field between Nichols and Davis, and the high school.

As I got older, I started playing with Tony Moretti, Pete Pucillo, Tom Girardi, John Girardi, Vinny Rocco, and Basil Ciampi in the neighborhood. We had a softball team that competed against other playground clubs from Hartley Park, Brush Park, and Howard Street. We must have been pretty good since we won the Mount Vernon Recreation Department championship several times.

I remember playing ball from morning until night. My mother would yell out the window and call me home for supper. She had quite a pair of lungs. I could hear her all the way up the street yelling, "Come and eat." She screamed that to get us home.

We played all types of ball. There were handball courts behind Nichols where we played ball. We would take chalk and mark a box on the wall. I'd play against another kid and we'd throw a tennis ball. If it hit the box, it was a strike. We had different markers for a single, double, triple and home run.

I really don't remember trying out for the Little League. I know I was ten years old. When you're ten, your coordination is way behind eleven and twelve-year-olds. So I sat on the bench and watched most of the games. I played for the Peacocks from 1953 through 1955, and Joe Moccio was my coach for one year, and then Mr. Mangone managed another year. Donnie Ross was our catcher, and I pitched and played the outfield. Donnie was an excellent ballplayer. He actually lived in the Bronx over the line from Mount Vernon. Tom Mangone and Tommy Ambrosino were also on the team. When Tommy wasn't batting third or fifth in the lineup, then I would be in those spots. Bottom line, as a 10-year-old, I didn't get a hit and sat on the bench. As an 11-year-old, I played and started in the outfield and also pitched. As a 12-year-old I was an all star.

Frank Gould

Like many of us of little league age, my world was pretty limited. I lived on the south side of Mount Vernon and went to Graham Elementary and then Graham Junior High School. Although I went to Sunday school and played basketball at the "Y," I didn't know many kids from other parts of Mount Vernon.

A couple of my friends played in the little league in 1957, and I loved baseball, so I tried out in 1958. I remember my father taking me to Baker Field for the tryout. There were so many kids. Where did they all come from? We each had a few swings and had a few ground balls hit to us, and that was pretty much it. A few days later, I got a phone call that I was selected to play for Local 338, the Panthers. I was excited to be chosen because I knew that not everyone was, but I remember thinking I still didn't know what it meant or how things worked.

During the first few practices, I found out that the team I was on had won the Mount Vernon Little League championship the previous year and had some star players, most of whom who had moved on to the Pony League.

I also found that there were 20 teams in total, spread across five leagues, or divisions, each with four teams. It also seemed that the concept of sponsors, in my case Local 338, was relatively new, and most people referred to their teams by their mascot name. We played 18 games in the season, divided into a first and second half of 9 games each. In each division, the winner of the first half played the winner of the second half for that division championship, with the winner of each of the five divisions going to the playoffs for the city championship.

My father died in early June of 1958, so my recollection of playing that year is really clouded. I do remember coming back to play after a period of mourning and seeing how supportive the kids were, kids who I had met maybe only two months earlier. And their parents and the coaches were amazing. I am sure the shock for the parent of an 11 year-old dying affected all of them, and their support was incredible.

In 1959, our team won our division title and played for the city championship. My recollections of this time are surprisingly clear (at least I think they are!). I particularly remember my mother being so nervous during one close playoff game that she burned a cigarette hole in her pocket book.

We were in the National League and competed against the Braslow Builders Shamrocks, the Perry Soda Pirates and the Republican Club Indians. I am less clear about the Shamrocks, but I know that Jimmy Cardasis was the best player for the Indians and George Bochow was the star for the Pirates. They were terrific players, even at ages 11 and 12. I loved the rivalry with those teams and with those players, and it felt great to win our division.

In the playoffs, I got to play against and beat my closest friend at that time, Jimmy Frusciante, who played for Nada Fence. Ultimately we lost the championship to Gramatan Men's Shop, whose star player was Ken Singleton, with whom I went to Graham. At the end of that season I was chosen to play on a travelling all-star team, where we lost in a New York state tournament. I remember being shocked that we lost, because we had a lot of really talented players.

In 1960 and 1961, I continued to play in the Pony League, though by then I was going to summer camp and really only played maybe two thirds of a season each year. My mother also decided after eighth grade to send me to Horace Mann for high school, where I went from 1960 thru 1964. One of my biggest disappointments was not having the opportunity to play baseball in high school with so many of the guys I played with and competed against in Little League and Pony League. I played at Horace Mann, but it just didn't have the same feeling and I knew it was not nearly the experience I would have had had I stayed.

Recollecting the details aside, most important was the experience itself and how it expanded my horizons. Graham was a pretty diverse school at that time, but this just felt like a whole new world had opened up.

I had a chance to make new friends, go to different places and have experiences that I otherwise would never have had. Although in retrospect it feels cliché, it really was a melting pot experience where it was all about the game and the camaraderie. In the same way that many ballplayers expressed in "That Perfect Spring" about the 1959 A. B. Davis High School championship baseball team, growing up in Mount Vernon at that time was really very special, and playing in the Little League for me was a big reason why.

Len Henderson

I can remember my father buying me my first baseball mitt. That cost my dad $9.95. That was a lot of money back then. He bought it on Fourth Avenue. I needed a mitt for a left hander.

Therefore I could not use my brother Billy's mitt. I didn't make the Little League team that year and was assigned to a minor league team, the Unicorns.

We practiced around Devonia Avenue near Pennington School in the north side of Mount Vernon. It seemed like a long way from my home on Union Avenue. But it really wasn't that far.

Playing for the Unicorns was a great experience and I met two of my lifelong friends and high school teammates, Teddy Cardasis and Wendell Tyree. The next year we tried out for the Little League, and I ended up on the Indians.

The Indians' coach was a chap named Steve Acunto, one of the foremost boxing instructors in the world. He was in ring demonstrations with the likes of Muhammad Ali, Rocky Marciano, and Willie Pep. He was inducted into the World Boxing Hall of Fame.

The Indians didn't have much fire power in the beginning. That's when I met two later high school teammates Eddie Martin who played with the Shamrocks and Ernie Motta. Ernie was legendary in Little League. Back then, Ernie had a big curve ball. Neil Arena also played with us. He was quite a baseball player. I played left field more than anything else. Sometimes I'd play center.

What an experience Little League was in building friendships and character. I would not give up one day of that experience. I hope that any kid would get to enjoy what that Little League experience is all about.

Braham Horwitz

I played on the Democrats Little League team for three or four years. We had a great ball club, winning a league championship one year. Two good ballplayers were Jack Bromley and Tommy Williams. I remember when Mayor Joe Vaccarella met to congratulate the team.

My best and worst experiences in Little League happened in the same game. I was pitching a no hitter for a full five innings and we were the visiting team. In the top of the sixth inning while at bat I was struck on the bone side of my forearm and ultimately was taken out of the game because my arm started to swell.

Our manager, whose name I have forgotten, put in his younger son to pitch the bottom of the sixth inning. We were winning 12-1, with our opponent scoring an unearned run. The kid pitcher gives up nine runs and we barely win. *The Argus* had a little summary of the game and mentioned the no-hitter in the last paragraph.

One more funny story. My parents thought Baker Field was in the Bronx, although it turned out that was the name of Columbia University's field. Needless to say, we were late for the Little League game and quite embarrassed since we lived only five minutes from the field.

Andrew Karl

My experience with Little League baseball in Mt. Vernon started well before my eligibility to play at age eight. This was due to my father, Anton "Andy" Karl, who was instrumental in the start up of the entire program.

By 1950 my father was only a few years removed from his retirement from major league baseball, and as a native son of Mount Vernon he hoped to have his name recognition help the foundation of the league. In this era too, baseball was still the true national pastime and Little

League was a big deal in town. My father was named the first president of the Little League and remained in that position for about 20 years.

As a toddler during those busy developmental years for the league, I routinely accompanied my dad to games and practices. I got a ton of exposure listening and learning about how the game should be played, while thoroughly enjoying everything about the baseball experience.

Meanwhile my dad continued playing himself, pitching on Sundays at the New York Athletic Club in Pelham, N.Y. Again I was along for the ride. From the time I was three until I was finally old enough to tryout for Little League, I served as 'bat boy', chased down foul balls for the team and loved every minute of being immersed in the game.

My time spent around baseball with my father helped me when my own tryouts began, as I had also become familiar with this process over the years. Unlike kids who showed up for the first time, I knew what to expect and how I would be judged. The annual tryouts were a big deal also because my father would drag out one of his old major league jerseys to wear while pitching all day long to the kids trying out.

It was a thrill to beg him to throw me his famous knuckleball while he warmed up for the tryout sessions. After my first tryout I was thrilled to get a call shortly afterwards from the manager of the Lions. I had been chosen to play for the team, part of the four-team division sponsored by the city's service organizations: Lions, Kiwanis, Rotary and Optimists. It was a real thrill to be selected to play in the Little League at 8 years old without having to first prove myself in the minor league group. It was also scary knowing I would be facing players up to 12 years old.

My recollections are more about the amount of time involved in baseball between the ages of 8 and 12 than about specific games. I lived near Memorial Field and Hutchinson Fields. After school and summer vacations were largely spent at one or the other, playing some form of baseball, depending on how many kids showed up.

We played games on the handball courts at Memorial Field with taped up balls and broken bats nailed back together. We played stickball at Graham School and punch ball with pink Spalding rubber balls at school lunch times and at home after school in the street.

The PAL (Police Athletic League) ran a summer baseball school at Hutchinson Field where everyone played all positions and different skills were emphasized each day. Kids got together during the summer at a makeshift field in the woods along the Hutchinson River near the Pelham border, a great place to play baseball and avoid the heat of the summer sun. And of course we played catch in the street, calling balls and strikes on the pitches as we went through the lineups of the Yankees and Giants, arguing constantly who was the better player, Mantle or Mays! All these experiences were instrumental in developing the skills that showed up on the field at Little League games. My father invariably demanded I 'rest' for a few hours prior to a game and that I get my pre-game meal in well before the 6 pm games. I was forbidden to throw a curve ball as a Little Leaguer, as Dad believed no one of that age had developed enough to withstand the demand on the arm. This theory later proved very beneficial for me. Saturday games could be agony when my team was scheduled for the second game of the afternoon, starting about 3 pm. It seemed game time would never come. The 1 pm games were okay, and I would get there early to start practicing. Another random recollection is that as kids we all knew all the league umpires, who was good and who was bad, always hoping for one of the better ones to be assigned to call our game. These early days of Little League baseball were good times, providing a lot of kids with constructive life lessons and experiences. It was my experience that Little League did quite a bit to help with racial integration, bringing together not only kids on the teams but also parents who showed up to watch their kids. We were teammates, not caring much what color we were, what part of town we all came from, which school or church we attended. All we wanted to do was play baseball!

My father's involvement with baseball was a huge influence in my life. It is fitting to remember and honor him and all the fathers and men who devoted enormous amounts of time developing and keeping Little League alive and growing. Hand in hand with them were all the mothers who worked as part of the Little League Auxiliary, supporting the teams and raising money for equipment, uniforms, and all the costs associated with running the league.

Mickey Klebanow

I played Little League ball in Mount Vernon from 1953-56 and it was a great learning experience. The only bad experience I had was being hit in the helmet (I was gladly wearing one) by Larry Townsend and we joked about this for many years, high school being the last time. Perhaps getting hit in the head was an awakening or a reason for other unmentionable things.

In any event, the most memorable thing that anyone said to me in Little League was by my coach, Mr. Mangone. I was a real hustler in all positions played (other than first and second base) and he said he wished the entire team was made up of the likes of me. What I liked most about playing Little League ball was the multi-cultural aspect of the sport since its makeup represented the city of Mount Vernon.

It was the beginning of many great experiences with our town and, for the most part, its great respect and tolerance for different religions, races, nationalities, economic backgrounds and genders. It proved to me that stereotypes and generalities only applied to a small percentage of those being stereotyped and still do. Playing Little League baseball and growing up in Mount Vernon was a wonderful experience that has followed me for life….and an experience that I am very grateful for.

Eddie Martin
"Before Girls, Cars and Rock 'n Roll"

I can still remember pitching for the Shamrocks in a playoff game against the Pirates in 1953. We had scored in the top of the sixth to tie the game at 1-1. If I could keep the Pirates from scoring I felt we could win in extra innings and earn the right to play the Orioles, the American League champs, for the Mount Vernon Little League Championship.

The Pirates have a runner on first with one out. A slow grounder is hit to the third baseman who throws to first for the out. The runner on first rounds second and heads for third. the first baseman's throw to third is low. The runner heads for home. The third baseman recovers the ball and throws home to the catcher. The play at the plate is close but the umpire spreads his arms and yells "safe". My Little League baseball days are over.

Pony League, Connie Mack League, a high school baseball championship and Westchester All County honors would follow.

But for now, I'm thinking of a warm early summer evening in 1953. The Shamrocks are scheduled to play the Indians at 6 o'clock at Longfellow Field #1. The Owls and the Peacocks have already begun play on Field #2. My parents, along with approximately 50 other fans, are sitting on the stone bleachers along the first base side of the field waiting for the game to begin. Both teams have finished taking infield practice. The field is being groomed. Lou has just parked his hot dog truck behind the bleachers on South Fourth Avenue. The umpires have arrived. I hear Mr. Borelli (our manager) shout out, "Start warming up Eddie, you're pitching tonight."

Bob Mayer

I played in that Little League from 1954-1958, ages 8-12. It probably helped me get the basics down.

I remember pitching at about age 11 and getting an 0-2 count on the Comets best slugger, Vonnie Wickens. My manager comes out to the mound and tells me to walk him. Unfortunately, no one ever taught me how to pitch an intentional pass. The next pitch I lob one up near Wickens shoulder. He creams it for a home run. I think the ball is still traveling!

Davey Cromwell was our best player for a while as he was two years older than me. It took me a while to catch up.

Ernie Motta

I don't remember getting my first baseball glove. But, to tell you the truth, my father had so many old mitts. They were the ones that just covered the hand. He used to give me his hand-me-downs. I started out with one of those.

Summer time meant baseball on our street. We played bunting in the backyard using either a Spalding or a softball. Someone would try to hit it past you and run around the backyard. It was great because it helped us develop the ability to field a short bunt. We did that a lot. Then we graduated to stickball.

I always was a pitcher. That goes back to when I was ten years old. My father put down a rubber plate in the alley way next to our house. That's where he taught me how to pitch.

He was catcher. He encouraged me to try out for the Little League when I was eight years old. The Little League then was a lot different than it is today. I remember in my first year getting up to bat against a pitcher named Goody Bradford. He was twelve years old. He threw a monster fastball. I was shaking.

I had a cousin, Fred Corrado, who was on my team. He was older. In later life, he became president of Planter's Peanuts. Anyway, when I was up at bat, he was screaming at Goody Bradford, "Don't hurt him. Don't hurt him." Meanwhile, I'm shaking. I swung the bat and hit the ball. I was so surprised. Everyone in the stands were yelling, "Run, run." I remember that so vividly.

We were called The Eagles. One fellow we graduated high school with, Bill Bauersfeld, was a teammate. His father coached the team, and my father helped him out coaching.

I don't remember too much about our regular Little League seasons. I played four years of Little League ball, from 8 through 12 years of age. We played on quite a few diamonds like Longfellow School and then later at Brush Park and at Hutchinson Field.

Between Little League games we played stickball right next door to our house, which was right next door to a Baptist church. I remember breaking more than one church window with a batted ball. Sometimes my folks had to pay to fix those windows.

Freddie O'Connor

In 1950 Little League baseball came to Mount Vernon, NY. That was perfect timing for me since I was ten years old that year.

Looking back now, I'm proud that I was part of that first year of Little League ball in the city we called home. And wouldn't you know it, our team, the Panthers, won the city championship that first year. All Little Leaguers remember their first manager. I sure remember mine. Bill Real was something special. Plain and simple he was a teacher of baseball. He taught us the game and we responded. In that inaugural season, Ralph Merigliano was the unquestioned star of the team. He was our best pitcher and also our best hitter. But he couldn't do it alone and relied on our teammates like Mike Bossi, Bill Allman, Bobby Donato, Eddie Carozza and Roger Boccardi. I became friendly with Ralph and our family eventually lived in the same house with the Merigliano's on Beechwood Avenue.

Interestingly, both my mother, Billie, and father, Joe, became deeply involved with Little League in the early 50's. In fact, my dad had quite a run, coaching and managing throughout most of the 50's and 60's. Both parents were members of Little League's Board of Directors. I had the opportunity to follow in their footsteps, coaching and managing in the 70's and 80's and also serving as a member of the league's Board of Directors.

While I was born in New Haven we moved to Mount Vernon when I was three and lived there with the exception of one year until after I was married in 1963. My parents continued to live there until the 70's.

Fast forward and today my wife Mary and I have two children and five grandchildren. Here's an oddity that most Mount Vernon Little League graduates cannot boast about. My son, Kevin, played in the league in the '70s and my grandson, Kenny, plays in it now. We're probably the only father, son, and grandson who can trace their Little League roots back to the beginning in 1950.

I remember it was quite a beginning in 1950 when the League was founded by Andy Karl, Leonard Boccardi, and Mike O'Connell. There is no doubt that Mount Vernon has these three men and the volunteers who helped out to thank for baseball in our town. Back then it seemed all our summers were centered around baseball. The Little League season ran into August. But it wasn't just Little League. There was the Police Athletic League (PAL), stickball and the makeup games in lots all over town. We couldn't get enough baseball.

After our Little League games I recall how our parents would get together at the local restaurants and, of course, we would often tag along. It was in those restaurants and ball fields where many friendships were formed. Many of these friendships have lasted a lifetime.

Early on, we played our Little League games at Longfellow Field. Now, 60 years later, those games are played across the street from Longfellow at Brush Park. And you know the enthusiasm of the players and the fans hasn't changed much at all. The teaching of the game still goes on as does the desire to win.

Like most boys, my baseball started with catches with my father in the yard. When I was six and seven, I started playing with the ten and twelve year olds in a lot across the street from our house on Third Street. But it was in Little League where I really learned the game. I went on to play at Mount Saint Michael in the Bronx with a group of Mount Vernon Little Leaguers, John Tripodi, Tom Nelly, Bob Cusick and Joe Glazer.

That 1958 Mount team was a lot of fun especially since we went 20-0 and won the city championship. I had the good fortune of being selected to the All City team. Joe Torre was one of my teammates on that squad. I then went on to play baseball at Fordham University.

None of this could have happened without the help and guidance I received from the men and women of the Mount Vernon Little League. I am thankful for that help for many reasons. It not only gave me guidance in 1950, but also helped my son in the '70s, and my grandson in 2012. And isn't that what Little League should be all about.

Tony Petrillo

After every game, win or lose, we always had hot dogs and soda with the team. These were great times with great friends.

Being told by Mr. Steve Acunto, our manager, that I could not go swimming on a day that I had to pitch.

One thing I will never forget is a home run that Eddie Martin hit off me. I can still see the ball going over the trees at the ball field.

Bob Puccillo

When I was about eight years old and living on Locust Street there was a lot right across the street from our home. That's where my dad taught me how to pitch.

I remember him telling me that when the season was about to begin I should start off real slowly. Then, after a while, he had me bearing down. He showed me how to throw a curve, fastball, and a drop. So I had three pitches.

My dad wasn't really into sports except when he was a kid himself. He read a book about Bob Feller, the Hall of Fame Cleveland Indians pitcher. I remember the book vaguely which he eventually gave me. I wasn't much of a reader. But it had instructions about how to throw a fastball.

My dad groomed me. He even took a peach basket and had me throw into it to improve my control. Baseball was my favorite sport back then. I tried basketball, but with baseball I could stand on the pitcher's mound and just throw and then enjoy hitting.

I don't know if you remember, but at Hutchinson Field there used to be woman who was in charge of baseball teams. I think this was the Pee Wee League. This was around 1948 when I was eight years old. I remember going down there. She had a book with the names of all the players. She was in charge of everything.

I have memories of playing there at the time. That was even before I played in the Little League. I was a pretty good pitcher and hitter on The Pirates in Little League. I remember there was a school not far from Hutchison Field with two ball fields.

I remember playing a game, and my dad was in the stands directing me with what pitch to throw. He would signal by holding down his fingers, one hand over the other hand like a catcher would do. "One" would be for a fast ball, "two" for a curve, and "three" for a drop.

I'd sneak a look over at him to see what I should throw. My coach never knew what I was doing. I also recall in Little League hitting a ball right behind second base. There was a hole in the ground there. The ball went right into the hole and the fielders couldn't get it out. I ended up on second base with a double.

Ira Scharaga

I got on my bike with my glove in the basket and playing cards in the spokes. I was ready. I took off for my two mile ride to Baker Field, now the site of Mount Vernon High School, and for my date with destiny.

I was on my way to try out for the Mount Vernon Little League in 1951. Once there I recall seeing Andy Karl who was in charge of the tryouts. He was wearing a Boston Red Sox jersey. They gave everyone a number to put on their back. Then they told us to line up in the position we wanted to play. I ran out to second base. That was for me since I was all of 5 feet 5 inches tall and weighed in at 115 pounds.

Tryouts began and I was ready. First it was all about grounders. They hit a few balls to me and I fielded them cleanly. Then it was my turn at bat. I had a chance to hit four pitches and I don't remember what happened. Then the organizers told us that if we were selected we would be notified by mail.

So for the next three days I ran to the mailbox to see if I was chosen. On the fourth day the post card arrived. Right there in black and white it clearly stated that I was selected. I was a Little Leaguer. I was a member of the Shamrocks.

I tossed and turned in my bed the following Friday night. I couldn't sleep but I could not have been happier. I would be meeting my teammates the next day at our first practice. I don't remember what happened at that practice but I do recall our manager, Mr. Borelli, said I would be playing second base and batting second. They also handed out uniforms that day.

I couldn't wait to get home to see how my uniform fit. I remember how white it was and how a green shamrock adorned the left side of the jersey. I also put on the team's green hat and green socks. To this day I will always remember how happy and proud I was putting the uniform on and looking at myself in the mirror. The jersey was a little too big for me and the pants were baggy. I didn't care.

Our opening game was the following Saturday at Longfellow Field located on the other side of town and far away from where I grew up. Strangely enough I remember not being nervous. I was so proud wearing that uniform.

I took two buses to get to Longfellow and hoped that people would look at me wearing it. I felt on top of the world. Our team batted first and when I got up to bat I heard the catcher say, "Ira, you can't hit this guy." I looked around and it was Bruce Leaf who was a year ahead of me in school. I took the first pitch. I said to myself that I could hit this guy. On the next pitch, I hit a bullet right to the shortstop, and that's all I remember. I guess in life you remember what you want to remember. Even today when I think about that time I always smile and see myself in that beautiful white uniform.

Dr. Robert A. Scott©
Brief Reflections on Life and Baseball

I recently participated in my high school reunion. Reminiscing, I recalled when my seventh grade teacher told me that I was sitting in Ralph Branca's seat, the trolley taking me to Memorial Field went past Sidney Poitier's house, and I gave up the clarinet.

I also realized again that comparatively few of my school friends lived on my side, the south side, of Mount Vernon. But, I found classmates I recalled with fondness and events I remembered with clarity, such as standing on the Davis stage advocating Owen Knopping's candidacy for Class President.

Meeting with classmates and taking the bus tour from our White Plains hotel to our former school, and back, underscored a lot for me. We didn't pass Third Avenue and Third Street, where I lived in a house that became the foundation for a parking lot. Nor did we pass Grimes Elementary School, to which I walked, and then walked two miles across town once a week to the First Presbyterian Church for Bible study, and back home, another two miles. I lived so far from school I was allowed to eat lunch at restaurants in the fifth and sixth grades. My mother died when I was nine, and I became independent.

On the second floor of what had been A. B. Davis High School, and was now a middle school, I imagined the place where biology teacher Joseph Leone called to me, a year after I "aced" his class, to ask why I had not signed up for the SAT's. Neither of my parents had gone to college, and my mother had not completed secondary school. With Joe's help, I applied and was accepted to college, and then graduated from Bucknell with a Bachelor of Arts in English and from Cornell with my Ph.D.

My greatest school memories are of my tenth grade research paper, "A Stone's Throw from the Days of Christ," about the Dead Sea Scrolls; "Pop" Phillip's Latin classes, a subject which I continued for eight more semesters in college; and Mr. Searle's introduction to Hi-Y, where I learned leadership skills.

On the bus tour, we drove down the middle of the old shopping area on the south side of town, where in junior high I had been called the "Mayor of Fourth Avenue" because I seemed to know all the shop keepers. Earlier, we had passed Memorial Field and I recalled Miss Bourne; earning nickels retrieving errant tennis balls at the courts; and baseball.

I played both Little League (Pirates) and Pony League baseball in Mount Vernon as a right-handed first baseman, with Gil Hodges of the Brooklyn Dodgers as my model. It was only later that I came to realize the importance of baseball as a metaphor for American life.

The start of each baseball season revives memories of childhood pick-up games when as young kids we would choose sides, set the rules, and arbitrate disputes. We learned teamwork and leadership, honed our skills and abilities, and developed a set of values. We learned that the sides should be equal, that everyone should play, that we could resolve our disputes without outside interference or advice, and that having fun was the goal.

For those of us who are or were adult volunteers or spectators for youth sports, the start of the season also reminds us of how parental involvement and the corporate organization of children's games have stolen some of that joy. Travel teams, all-star status, and league standings are a far cry from neighborhood fun. As a parent with children in T-Ball, I tried to restrain these efforts. As a college president, I enjoy our teams and urge them to emphasize the joy of play.

The start of the season also reminds us again that baseball, with its sibling softball, is America's sport, a metaphor for a frontier nation exploring new vistas. In this American myth, the young leave home on their own, using their talents and determination to find their way through the wilderness, overcoming obstacles, fiercely trying to stay safe, occasionally taking a respite to find a new way to proceed home with whatever bounty has been earned. The lone hitter becomes the lone runner, darting and weaving to return safely.

This is in contrast to football, where large men in protective gear, guided by electronic communications and group tactics, try to prevail in a contest without parallel for women and where penalties for unnecessary roughness are common.

In literature, it is said that we can never return home again, but in baseball, and softball, the hometown myth is preserved as a symbol of hope, derring-do, and the pursuit of safe passage to all that is good. Going home is the goal and we salute the victory.

In the years since I left Mount Vernon and graduated from college, I have had a rich and varied life, serving as a college president for the past 27 years. I continue to write, both scholarly articles and general essays as well as poetry; have been active in photography, with several exhibits of my work; and have a regular TV show which has won three Telly's, the cable version of the Emmy, two for discussions of ethics and sports, including, of course, baseball.

It was great to see people from my past, remember days of my youth, and see "home" again.

Henry Sherman

Do you believe in chance, destiny, or fate? Is luck your silent partner? Submerging my brand new Tom Godfrey Rawlings first baseman's glove in neat's-foot oil the night before, I was all juiced up for the first practice at Baker Field.

Mounting my premium package Schwinn, equipped with rear view mirror, horn, headlight and basket, I began the journey through the historic streets of Mount Vernon. I had no idea what awaited me on this day. Mr. McKee, the acidic, gruff history teacher had once pointed out a street that had my last name, sparking my interest in the Civil War (Lincoln, Sheridan, Sherman).

Starting at Pennsylvania, along with Commonwealth, chosen for that state's Civil War significance, I turned left onto Sheridan, an avenue I had biked on often, and frequently mused what it was like being a horse soldier in the general's cavalry, under the bridge, past Sherman Avenue, and then a sharp right onto Stuyvesant and into the back entrance of Baker Field.

Being overweight and on the slow side, I played first base, as it didn't require much movement. I missed several ground balls, struck out repetitively and had multiple throwing errors. My gloved palm stung and throbbed like a jellyfish bite as I caught bullets from the rifle armed infielders. My baseball days were numbered.

After the practice a handful of our team headed back for the bike rack, where Claude, a slick, sleek 24 hour man (I'll explain shortly) greeted us. "Anyone interested in handing out flyers for the circus being held in a neighboring town?" Claude had no takers, and suddenly I was the only one there, as everyone scattered. "Here son, distribute these to all your neighbors, show up tomorrow night at this address and I'll take you behind the scenes at the big top."

His thick southern accent, inflections, pronunciation and rate, rhythm of his speech drew me in. Claude was a 24 hour man for Hoxie Brothers Traveling Circus. 24 hour men arrive the day before the circus to arrange for local advertising, in addition to locating a place to kick dirt (put up a tent).

I made it to the circus near Concordia College, via the F bus, where Claude ushered me to the children's show, which is circus lingo for the freak exhibit. I was instantly surrounded by a band of dwarfs. Their big heads, bowlegs, potbellies, short extremities, swaybacks and waddling gaits were the sparkplugs for an instant love affair. I spent the next five days hypnotized by their actions. Did you know that dwarfs upper extremities are so short that they can't put on socks or complete other functions of daily living without an assistive device?

Miss Birdsell, the heavily perfumed, pasty, rotund school librarian, rounded up every book in the city on dwarfism. "Henry, here's a book on Tom Thumb." "Miss Birdsell, Tom Thumb was a midget, not a dwarf. " I had launched my medical career. The dwarfs were my introduction to medicine, but more importantly, they showed me how people suffer and live with disabilities.

On the last day of the circus, descending from the F bus at the corner of Columbus and Lincoln, I wondered how the dwarfs would navigate the last step.

Little League provided me with a pathway to my future. Not only did I enjoy the baseball experience, but I frequently look back on that chance meeting.

John Weis

In the early 1950's baseball was king on Lafayette Avenue and nowhere more so than at 646 Lafayette, home of the Weis family. Father, mother, sisters and grandparents all bled Yankee Blue. So, it was baseball that dominated my early life, first on radio, then on television and sometimes at "The Big Ballpark", the reference made famous by Red Barber that soft spoken southerner who somehow had embraced New York.

I went to my first Yankee Game in 1949 where I saw Joe D, Vic Raschi and Yogi Berra dismantle the Philadelphia Athletics, the same Athletics who were later transformed into a team of non starters in Kansas City but eventually found success and some fame in Oakland as the shortened "A's". It was an interesting time, as many east coast cities found they could no longer support more than one team; when the Giants and Dodgers left for the sunny climes of California and the Braves somehow thought they would find a home in Milwaukee. But, the Yankees remained.

When I was young every summer my family would go to a lake in Vermont, New Hampshire or Cape Cod where the Bosox ruled. My strongest memory from these vacations was listening to a static enhanced broadcast from Fenway of that hated (even then) team from Beantown.

And so it was with this background that I began my baseball journey. Before Little League there was the camaraderie that I had with my father.

"Hey Dad… how about a catch?" And out to the side yard we'd go; night after night. Our driveway had two slivers of concrete surrounding a grassy median where I fashioned a pitching hole for leverage. From age 7 to 12 my dad had the patience to "play catch"; teaching me how to throw a curve, knuckleball, change of pace and the drop. When we weren't playing catch in the yard I'd force him down the street to the open field at the Wartburg Home where he'd pitch fastballs while I tried to hit them. Sometime neighborhood kids would join us, but most nights it was just me and my dad.

Tryouts for Little League were at Hutchinson Field and on that Saturday in 1952 it snowed. Not the kind that stuck to the ground, just the type that made you bitterly cold inside and made your hands feel like frozen bricks. Hutchinson was bigger than any place I'd played and I was nervous during the whole tryout. I don't know whether they selected anyone who tried out but I was elated when I found out I was picked by the Eagles (later Embassy TV). I played for them from 1952 to 1956. When we had our first team practice I was amazed at how much bigger the older players were. They were also very good. I particularly remember our catcher Donny Cook, mainly because he was an excellent player but he also went to my Grammar School at Saint Catherine's. Even though he was in the 7th grade and I was in the 4th grade he spoke to me often at school which was pretty well unheard of.

One Thursday afternoon the team held a practice at Memorial Field. My father was the only person in our family who drove a car so my grandfather (aged 82 at the time) walked me from home across Lincoln Avenue, through Wilson Woods and along the Hutchinson River Parkway. Each time we crossed a street he would take my hand, the one without my Duke Snider Glove, and walked me across the street. He then walked me back home again. Later my grandfather came to many games but I remember this one walk together above all other things.

During my first year I played right field and second base. I was an OK fielder and a slightly better hitter. Our first game was at Hutchinson against the Orioles. I don't remember their pitchers name but he was much faster than anyone I'd seen in practice. It was another cold day, the kind that made your hands sting when you hit the ball. But on that day there weren't many Eagles whose hands were stinging as their pitcher was striking out most of us. When I came to bat late in the game, I figured that the only way I could get on base was to bunt. I did and got my first base hit in organized baseball.

Most games during my first two years were played at Longfellow School. They had two fields, one with concrete stands along the first base line and another behind the school. No one liked playing on the second field. The infield was all dirt with pebbles everywhere and the outfield was weeds that was practically never mowed. The best part of playing at Longfellow was the ice cream truck that showed up around the 4th inning.

In my last two years all games were at Baker Field which was closer to home and is where I began my yearly duel with Larry Townsend who pitched for the Orioles. Sometimes I'd strike out a dozen or more and so would Larry. Sometimes he'd win, sometimes I would… one hitters, two hitters, no hitters. Larry's battery mate was David Smith a great catcher and hitter as well. Sometimes my catcher was Billy O'Hara, my best friend from school. Billy was very funny but was a great ballplayer as well. He also played third and short and was a gifted fielder for his age. Billy was a trash talker and he was especially trashy when Larry and David were at the plate. He'd talk to them as I released the ball. It drove them crazy.

Paul Wiener

Is there such a thing as a bad memory of your Little League days? At this stage of life, wouldn't such a memory be a good one anyway? I have such good ones. I remember the tryouts;

they were such a big deal.

A beautiful spring weekend, a day long anticipated, worried over. I went with two neighborhood friends. I thought I did well. They didn't make it, but I didn't feel sorry for them. I remember very well getting the phone call from Mr. Tripodi, the coach/manager of the Pirates, a team with a winning reputation. It was dinner time. Answer the phone! I was – still am – crazy about baseball, even though my dad couldn't stand team sports, never followed them, and I'd never gone to a pro game, though Yankee Stadium was, nearly unbeknownst to me, only nine miles away.

But Mr. Tripodi didn't ask for me. He asked for Mike Hirsch to tell him he'd made the team. What the....? Oh my god no..... Luckily, it was a simple mistake. Mike was next on his phone list. I had made it too! I couldn't eat after that.

Everybody knew tons of batting averages, the Yanks, the Dodgers, the Giants. It was the Age of Mantle. Now you could have one of your own batting average. Now you could be defined, and judged, by your own batting average. But that's not why my three years from 1954 thru 1956 on the Pirates make such intense memories. Nor is it my memory of putting on those thick ivory-colored woolen shirts and pants, and the undershirt, and the long thick ribbed socks, and the proud cleats, in 90-degree summer heat – and not minding.

Not the leathery smells, or finding a bat the right length. Or walking half a mile down Sandford Boulevard – just me and the summer sun – to Hutchinson Field, or up it a mile to Brush Park to play a game. Or what seemed like crowds watching every at bat, and the angry or excited or wishful sounds the parents made that I never dreamed I'd be making one day.

Or the Sunday picnics, or the many pizzas, burgers or ice cream sodas at the Bee Hive that Mr. Trip treated the team to after almost every game. (Who paid for that?) Or the World Series my team won (was it twice?). Or the teams parading down Gramatan Avenue. Or my dad practicing catch with me; for a non-sportsman he was good – thank god.

Or the big league feeling of getting a hit (but never a home run!) – that crack and the backfire of the bat taking possession of your hand and shoulder and pride. Or making a diving catch in centerfield, or enviously watching a teammate hit those home runs consistently, even though he was smaller than me. Or being just a little bit afraid of being hit by a pitch (the real reason, I now believe, that I never hit a home run).

Two other memories stand out a little more prominently. In one, a game has just ended, against the Indians. We won. A school acquaintance of mine on the other team, Mark Weinstein, was dejected, getting his things together to leave. "Nice game!" I call out sarcastically. I guess I didn't really like Mark, didn't know why. He was a good ballplayer, a smart, good-looking kid I'd always felt competitive with.

I was a wisenheimer with a sense of humor; he was a wisenheimer without one. He looked at me for a second before he jumped on me. We rolled around in the orange dust for a few minutes, growling and grunting, but almost immediately the grownups pulled us apart. Unless they're exhibiting it, grownups can't stand the sight of bad sportsmanship, especially in kids.

But it had felt good to get angry, for Mark and for me. You were supposed to feel like winners or losers, weren't you? The feelings and the flare up passed quickly and never affected future play. But these many years later, it's still a reminder of how the nasty world of adult-sponsored aggressive competition among children became a learning experience. You don't usually choose what you learn at that age. The competitive was a world I at once felt alien to, challenged by, yet perversely comfortable in – and wasn't ultimately suited to. Nowadays learning those things can start at three years of age.

The second memory has me standing far out in my centerfield position. It's the World Series, my second one. I can't remember the field, but it wasn't on my side of town. Maybe it's the bottom of the fifth inning. The coach is gesturing me to go farther back; a big hitter is coming to bat.

The bases are loaded (I remember they were; but they would have been, wouldn't they, even if my memory is faulty). We all knew even the best hitters got it right only three or four times out of ten. The guy at the plate hits the first pitch, a hard drive that comes out far and low and drops straight toward me, where I stand ready for it, waiting.... nervously. A grounder. Are you supposed to wait for outfield grounders? My glove is down....and the ball goes right through my legs. Could Bill Buckner have been watching (but wasn't he born in California, and wouldn't he have been only six years old?). As soon as it happened, I knew it had to happen.

At least a hundred people were in the stands and had all seen my effortless error. My incompetence. I had to run after the ball and throw it in as hard as I could – just as the batter was rounding third. The fans all saw my coach bowing down to me from the stands in mock appreciation. Thank you, thank you, you little.... I didn't blame him. I felt I deserved to be humiliated; his actions were hardly as awful as what I felt myself.

Up to that moment, it was probably the day in my life I most felt like a jerk, a loser, a major disappointment, feelings that had often simmered beneath the surface of my happy childhood for no apparent reason, perhaps waiting for their moment, feelings that could and would bide their sweet time until years or decades later when they'd find another moment to loosen my grip on complacency and self-satisfaction.

Needless to say, I never held it against the Little League, coach Tripodi, baseball, team sports, my limited athletic abilities or my oversensitive nature that I was forced to live out this experience. For every kid that knows triumph and victory – and I'd been there, done that the year before, even the week before – there's got to be one, and many more than one, who knows misery, failure and humiliation. And who grows beyond it. Would I? Did I? The best of us outgrow the wins and losses that games offer children, who hunger for and wistfully remember them, never dreaming they'll have indescribable consequences or carve dark victimless notches in the handles of our character.

Made in the USA
Charleston, SC
14 December 2013